STATECRAFT AND SALVATION
Wilsonian Liberal Internationalism as Secularized Eschatology

Milan Babík

BAYLOR UNIVERSITY PRESS

"There are in history not only 'flowers of evil' but also evils which are the fruit of too much good will and of a mistaken Christianity that confounds the fundamental distinction between redemptive events and profane happenings."

—Karl Löwith, *Meaning in History* (1949)

To the memory of my grandfather

Ervín Bruzda (1920–2011)

Cover Design by John Barnett, 4 Eyes Design
Cover images ©Shutterstock/Sascha Burkard, Stephen Coburn, and Charles Knox

Credits: Chapter 2 makes partial use of Milan Babík, "Beyond Totalitarianism: (Re)Introducing Secularization Theory to Liberal Narratives of Progress," *Politics, Religion and Ideology* 13, no. 3 (2012): 289–306, and chapter 6 draws on Milan Babík, "George D. Herron and the Eschatological Foundations of Woodrow Wilson's Foreign Policy, 1917–1919," *Diplomatic History* 35, no. 5 (2011): 837–57. Permission to reprint portions of these essays is hereby acknowledged with gratitude.

This paperback edition was first published in November 2020 under ISBN 978-1-60258-744-1.

Library of Congress Cataloging-in-Publication Data

Babík, Milan, 1979–
  Statecraft and salvation : Wilsonian liberal internationalism as secularized eschatology / Milan Babík.
    277 pages cm
  Includes bibliographical references and index. ISBN 978-1-60258-743-4 (hardback : alk. paper)
  1. United States—Foreign relations—Philosophy. 2. United States—Foreign relations—20th century. 3. Wilson, Woodrow, 1856–1924—Influence. 4. Wilson, Woodrow, 1856–1924—Political and social views. 5. Internationalism—Moral and ethical aspects. 6. International relations—Moral and ethical aspects. 7. Eschatology—Political aspects—United States. 8. World politics—1900–1945. I. Title.
  JZ1480.B32 2013
  327.101—dc23
                    2012043660

CONTENTS

PREFACE

I was overcome with despair when in early August 2012, shortly after receiving one of my drafts, my editor responded, "Greetings from the beach! I am on vacation but reading it here and will comment shortly." My first attempt at an academic treatise, I gathered, had been demoted to beach reading—the league occupied by *Bridget Jones's Diary* and other masterpieces of light comedy. My editor was skimming through it for laughs during breaks from frolicking in foamy ocean water, piña colada in hand.

Fortunately, my self-confidence recovered soon enough to spare me renewed doubts that I was no good at scholarship and that I should have, after all, pursued the much more hands-on career of an artificial insemination assistant in livestock agriculture, as my wise and well-traveled brother had once suggested. Over breakfast the next morning, jubilation promptly replaced the dark terror of the previous day. Boosted by espresso shots, I grew certain that my editor was reading my manuscript on the beach precisely because the manuscript was *that* good: an unsuspected masterpiece, an instant game changer, a defining moment in the history of Western civilization, a gateway to my immortality. Not *Bridget Jones's Diary*, but St. Augustine's *Confessions*, still widely read sixteen centuries after his death, was the proper analogy for what I was about to publish.

And so it was not until day three that I finally came to my senses and realized what should have been apparent right away: that I had neither a dud nor a gem of a manuscript, but rather the most dedicated editor out there. Carey Newman, director of Baylor University Press, thus deserves my warmest gratitude, and not just for taking my scribbles on his vacation along with his snorkel and swim trunks. His incisive feedback and suggestions for further reading enabled me to improve the manuscript dramatically, and the vivid prose he used to convey them constituted an educational experience in its own right. Members of his editorial and production team, including Jordan Rowan Fannin and Jenny Hunt, were just as impressive, showering me with undivided personal attention—as if I were the only author on their list. I am incredibly lucky to have stumbled upon them all.

Well before they helped me bring the ship to harbor on bookstore and library shelves, however, many others taught me how to build and sail it in the first place. The first nebulous ideas that would later coalesce in this book reach all the way back to my M.Sc. in International Relations at the London School of Economics & Political Science, specifically to the day (about three weeks after September 11, 2001) I accidentally walked into Professor Christopher Coker's course on strategic aspects of international affairs. Of all the important moments in my university education, this one was by far the most transformative, and Chris—with his emphasis on literature, philosophy, history, and culture as key to understanding modern violence, war, and statecraft—had provoked it. His extraordinarily chaotic and inspiring lectures, the closest thing to jazz in IR programs anywhere, were ably seconded by Chris Brown, Mark Hoffman, and the late Fred Halliday, my other instructors at LSE. I thank all four of them.

When I moved to Oxford and began drafting my doctoral dissertation, from which this book is carved, Professor Jennifer Welsh felt so strongly about the project that she agreed to supervise it despite being overloaded with too many other advisees and, on top of it, finding herself in between two difficult pregnancies. Karma Nabulsi and Sudhir Hazareesingh, her colleagues in the Department of Politics and International Relations, watched over me as well, reading successive drafts and treating me to many perceptive comments, cups of coffee, and pleasant conversations at their home. Meanwhile, the Dulverton Trust cheerfully covered everything with a massively generous, all-inclusive scholarship award. Every now and then the English weather forced me to flee, but on those occasions my parents and grandparents readily provided me with a warm refuge in my native Šumperk, Czech Republic, as did my parents-in-law,

Paul and Linette Gamache, in Maine, for which I remain in debt to them all. Reading passages from this book will always take me back to my trusty Kona Paddy Wagon bicycle on the country roads between Oxford and Brize Norton, to the bakelite desk in my grandfather's small study, and to the tall pine tree, no longer standing today, in Paul and Linette's backyard: things and places that surrounded me while I was submerged in thoughts and trying to articulate them.

The stagnant academic job market I entered after completing my doctorate in September 2009, exactly one year after the fall of Lehman Brothers, nearly made the entire effort pointless: it almost strangled my professional career right at the outset and, along with it, buried any prospects of ever seeing the dissertation published. Artificial insemination increasingly seemed like the better career trajectory. Luckily, Professor Joe Reisert intervened and kept my hopes alive by offering me at least a temporary teaching appointment in his capacity as chair of the Government Department at Colby College (Waterville, Maine). His name therefore deserves to be added to the list of people I wish to thank, as do the names of Lynn Staley of the Faculty Research Council at Colgate University (Hamilton, New York), who facilitated the final stages of the manuscript preparation process with a generous publication grant, and Carolyn Weaver, who composed the index.

I considered dedicating this book to my wife, Jane, and our children, Kylián and Matyáš. Born in quick succession just as I was putting final touches on the dissertation, the boys spent most of their initial days and months lying in straw baskets next to my desk and observing me peck away on the keyboard, the one tossing and fussing, the other relaxed and quiet. Friends often asked with bewilderment how I could possibly work on a doctoral thesis while staying at home with two infants. The answer is simple: I could do it precisely because I had Kylián and Matyáš next to me. Whenever the manuscript overwhelmed me, a brief glance at them was all I needed to understand again that, compared to the problem of how to raise them without letting my clumsy parenting cause them any harm, the dissertation was entirely straightforward. Besides, the discoveries the boys were making and allowing me to witness by their side—about the flavor of mashed banana in the breakfast bowl, about the blinding warmth of sunshine suddenly coming into the crib—were far more profound and compelling than any of the discoveries I had made during the time spent reading, thinking, and writing about Wilson, religion, and American liberalism.

In the end, however, my thoughts came to rest on my grandfather Ervín Bruzda, who had been my single biggest fan since the time I was little until his death in March 2011. His life began shortly after the Great War, spanned the entire twentieth century, and faithfully reflected its endless violence and absurdity: he was conscripted into the German Wehrmacht, survived the ill-fated expedition to Stalingrad during World War II, and returned to Czechoslovakia only to observe, in August 1968, Stalingrad come after him as the Red Army invaded our country and a mechanized brigade set up barracks literally next to our house. Never one to give up, Grandpa thus spent the next two decades fighting the Soviets all over again, this time with assorted produce from our garden and, after I turned five, with me as his tactical forward operations unit. In retrospect, it was while watching him lob heads of rotten lettuce at our Soviet "liberators" across the tall concrete wall with barbed wire on top, his face aflame with rage, that my critical engagement with political religions and utopian visions commenced.

It is to his memory that I dedicate this book.

THE TWO UTOPIANISMS
Wilsonian Liberal Internationalism
vs. Secularized Eschatology

When the Czech ex-president, playwright, human rights activist, and former dissident Václav Havel died peacefully at his country cottage in Hrádeček in northeastern Bohemia on Sunday morning, December 18, 2011, the news spread fast. Within hours, his haggard face stared from the front page of every major media portal, and the Czech people and government found themselves inundated with condolences from leaders in every corner of Europe and beyond. The following Monday the European Union and NATO lowered their flags to half-staff, and on Wednesday the Czech Republic shrouded itself in three days of official mourning, culminating in a majestic funeral mass in Prague's St. Vitus Cathedral attended by, among others, Bill and Hillary Clinton, Nicolas Sarkozy, and David Cameron. Ten thousand people braved the cold and joined the funeral procession, in whose course the coffin bearing Havel's body traversed the Charles Bridge and ascended to the Prague Castle. It travelled on the same horse-drawn hearse that in 1937 carried to rest Tomáš Garrigue Masaryk, the founding president of the first independent Czechoslovak republic after World War I. The symbolism commemorated Havel's leading role in resurrecting the democratic spirit of that republic after decades of Soviet oppression during the Cold War: in 1989, he was the key figure in Czechoslovakia's Velvet Revolution against communist dictatorship.

The remarkable outpouring of sympathy reflected Havel's status as a widely revered defender of freedom, but if many people in his native country and around the world celebrated him for his commitment to liberal principles, he, in turn, carried deep admiration for another supporter of democracy: the American president Thomas Woodrow Wilson (1856–1924). On no other occasion did this become clearer than on October 5, 2011, Havel's seventy-fifth birthday. Visibly sick, frail, and nearing the end of his life, he had by then retreated from the public stage and, a few exceptions aside, was no longer accepting visitors even in private. That day, however, TV cameras spotted Havel sitting in the front row during a special outdoor ceremony in Prague: the unveiling of Woodrow Wilson's statue. At a time when many notable domestic and international politicians, intellectuals, and artists were vying for one last chance to see Havel and wish him well to what everybody sensed was his final birthday, he turned them all down and instead paid a visit to the twenty-eighth president of the United States.

This anecdote is not exceptional, but illustrative: ninety years after his death, Woodrow Wilson continues to be admired not just among Czechs, but also in many other places across Europe. The origins of his lasting legacy there, which dwarfs that of any other American statesman save perhaps for Franklin D. Roosevelt, go back to the Great War, in whose immediate aftermath Wilson's liberal internationalist principles laid the foundations for Europe's new political organization. His ability to shape the postwar order was in no small measure due to his position as commander-in-chief of the U.S. armed forces, whose entry into the conflict decided the Allied victory. He failed to secure the ratification of the Versailles Treaty by the U.S. Senate, a series of strokes in late 1919 disabled him for the remainder of his presidency, and he died a broken man in February 1924, but many of his ideals survived nonetheless. For better or worse, they set the parameters for the conduct of international politics in Europe throughout the interwar period—whether in the shape of peace movements, the League of Nations, or newly self-determined sovereign states such as Czechoslovakia. For these and other reasons, Wilson remains fondly remembered in Europe. The various public symbols, ranging from the Palais Wilson (current headquarters of the United Nations High Commissioner for Human Rights in Geneva) to the Avenue du Président Wilson in Paris and the Wilson Train Station in Prague, attest to this affection.

In marked contrast to all such adoration, the following study exudes a much cooler, less enthusiastic attitude toward Wilson's principles and legacy. It excavates the neglected religious-eschatological presuppositions of his liberal internationalism through a critical rereading of his ideas and practice in light of the so-called secularization theory, and it draws attention to the largely unacknowledged illiberal and totalizing implications of these presuppositions. The springboard for this project is a gap that exists at the crossroads of two areas of intellectual inquiry, international relations (IR) and intellectual history, concerning the category of utopianism. Each of these fields has conceptualized utopianism separately, in relative isolation from one another, and the differences are revealing.

In IR the category was delineated primarily by the British diplomat, journalist, historian, and classical realist scholar E. H. Carr (1892–1982) with reference to Wilson's program to create permanent peace in Europe after World War I: a set of ideas that was institutionalized in the Treaty of Versailles and the League of Nations and whose utopian character, according to Carr and other realists after him, paradoxically paved the road to World War II. By contrast, a number of intellectual historians such as Karl Löwith (1897–1973) and Eric Voegelin (1901–1985), all active in the same period as Carr, framed utopianism in terms of Judeo-Christian historical consciousness. From their perspective, utopianism means secularized eschatology, excavates the hidden religious foundations of modern philosophies of progress, and uses them to illuminate the deep psychological sources of popular appeal of nineteenth- and twentieth-century visions of future perfection: visions that demanded mass discipline and obedience and sanctioned systematic violence, oppression, destruction, and war.

Synthesizing the two definitions of utopianism by showing that Wilson's liberal idea of progress to durable peace in Europe rested on eschatological presuppositions is the main goal of this study. The following pages reveal that Wilson's international political utopianism derived in significant measure from his religious utopianism: his scripturally inspired belief that history was a redemptive process, with America as the providentially appointed savior of humanity. In this vein, one of the main sources of the narrow particularism that, according to Carr's critical analysis, constituted the real backbone of Wilson's allegedly universal program was patriotic American Protestant eschatology. Wilson's liberal internationalist statecraft thus stood on deeply dogmatic foundations and expressed an illiberal attempt to homogenize the plural world beyond the nation's borders: transform foreign countries and the international order as a whole in America's image, deemed the image of

Christ. Insofar as contemporary American foreign policy has continued to adhere to Wilson's principles, the same verdict applies to it as well.

Utopianism in International Relations
Wilsonian Liberal Internationalism

In IR, the beginnings of utopianism as a theoretical concept are closely connected to the beginnings of the discipline as an autonomous subject in the immediate aftermath of World War I. The catastrophic events of 1914–1918 prompted an intensive search among Western liberals for ways to prevent future conflict, and the category of utopianism was formulated in critical response to this effort: at an early stage in the development of IR theory often described as the "first great debate." The text that focused this debate, *The Twenty Years' Crisis* by E. H. Carr, is also the text that introduced the notion of utopianism into the disciplinary vocabulary.[1] Although utopianism saw some use already before the publication of Carr's book, mainly as a conservative label for progressivists, it is doubtful whether it would have achieved its popularity among subsequent generations of IR scholars without Carr's influence.[2]

Carr began by laying out his epistemological assumptions, the chief of which is that "purpose, whether we are conscious of it or not, is a condition of thought; and thinking for thinking's sake is as abnormal and barren as the miser's accumulation of money for its own sake."[3] Theory is inherently goal-driven for Carr, which is historically reflected in the fact that sciences both physical and social always came into existence in response to some pressing external stimulus. According to Carr, the urgency of this stimulus is then directly responsible for the utopian

---

[1] The first edition came out on the eve of World War II in 1939. The edition used here is E. H. Carr, *The Twenty Years' Crisis, 1919–1939: An Introduction to the Study of International Relations*, 2nd ed. (New York: Harper & Row, 1964 [1949]). As even revisionist historians of academic IR agree, "Carr, perhaps more than anyone else, is generally . . . responsible for creating the image of the interwar discourse of international relations as . . . utopian in character." Brian C. Schmidt, *The Political Discourse of Anarchy: A Disciplinary History of International Relations* (Albany: State University of New York Press, 1998), 219.

[2] Those who continue to use the concept today usually mention Carr in the same breath. See, e.g., Robert Jackson and Georg Sørensen, *Introduction to International Relations: Theories and Approaches*, 2nd ed. (Oxford: Oxford University Press, 2003), 41–42; Chris Brown, *Sovereignty, Rights, and Justice: International Political Theory Today* (Cambridge: Polity, 2002), 68; and Kimberly Hutchings, *International Political Theory: Rethinking Ethics in a Global Era* (London: SAGE, 1999), 15–16.

[3] Carr, *Twenty Years' Crisis*, 3.

character of all initial theorizing. In this phase, aspiration overshadows analysis, and the end-goal the route leading to it: "The investigators will . . . devote themselves whole-heartedly to the elaboration of visionary projects for the attainment of the ends which they have in view."[4] With respect to IR in its formative years spanning 1919 and 1939, Carr stated that

> [the science of international politics] took its rise from a great and disastrous war; and the overwhelming purpose which dominated and inspired the pioneers of the new science was to obviate a recurrence of this disease of the international body politic. The passionate desire to prevent war determined the whole initial course . . . of the study. Like other infant sciences, the science of international politics has been markedly and frankly utopian.[5]

Carr identified the utopianism of interwar IR specifically with the liberal assumption of a fundamental harmony of interests among nations, progress to which was to be achieved through national self-determination, democratization of autocratic regimes, *laissez-faire* international trade, and above all through international law and the principle of collective security.[6] Enshrined in the Covenant of the League of Nations, this principle would make the world safe for democracy by doing away with the old balance-of-power system, which was inimical to peace in leaving each state to fend for itself through power politics. In the reformed system, the sovereignty of each country would be publicly guaranteed by the collective will of the League of Nations, serving as a deterrent to aggression and making power politics unnecessary and obsolete as an instrument of foreign policy.

By the time Carr completed his study in 1939, of course, the failure of this program had become patent. The rise of Hitler and warmongering in Nazi Germany undermined the assumption that people everywhere desired peace; Italy's 1935 invasion of Ethiopia discredited the belief that the League would check aggression; and instead of free trade, protectionism was raging all across Europe. Theory was contradicted by reality, and another war loomed on the horizon. Accounting for the ways in which liberal internationalism ultimately generated an outcome almost exactly opposite to the one it had sought constituted Carr's main motivation for writing *The Twenty Years' Crisis*.

---

[4] Carr, *Twenty Years' Crisis*, 5.

[5] Carr, *Twenty Years' Crisis*, 8.

[6] Chris Brown, *Understanding International Relations*, 2nd ed. (Basingstoke: Palgrave, 2001), 23.

His explanation cuts to the very heart of liberal internationalism, targeting the assumption of the harmony of interests. "Carr's central point is that . . . the harmony of interests glosses over the real conflict that is to be found in international relations, which is between the 'haves' and the 'have-nots.'"[7] In a world of material scarcity and unlimited human desires, conflict over resources is inevitable, and any attempt to obscure this fact by preaching a harmony of interests must be understood in the context of the essential dynamic of struggle: as an ideology constructed by the dominant to maintain their position. In Carr's words,

> If theories are revealed as a reflexion of practice and principles of political needs, this discovery will apply to the fundamental theories and principles of the utopian creed, and not the least to the harmony of interests which is its essential postulate. . . . [T]he utopian, when he preaches the doctrine of the harmony of interests, is . . . clothing his own interest in the guise of a universal interest for the purpose of imposing it on the rest of the world.[8]

The critique is quasi-Marxist in character, as Carr would acknowledge decades later when he retrospectively described *The Twenty Years' Crisis* as "strongly impregnated with Marxist ways of thinking" and commented that he "did a lot of reading and thinking on Marxist lines" while writing the book.[9] Within the liberal state, according to the Marxist view, the basic conflict takes place between the bourgeois "haves" and proletarian "have-nots." The state itself is an epiphenomenon of the economic struggle and acts as a parasite exploiting the society below; it represents an instrument of class rule in the hands of the bourgeoisie, which uses it to secure a favorable *status quo*. Carr extends this argument to the international realm. Just as the liberal state is a tool used by the dominant class to promote its interests domestically, so the League of Nations, the flagship institution of liberal internationalism, is a tool used by the Great War victors to maintain a favorable *status quo* in the international arena. Drawing on "Marxism as a method of revealing the hidden springs of thought and action, and debunking the logical and moralistic façade generally erected around them,"[10] Carr thus declares that international law and morality serve the national interests of the powerful:

[7] Brown, *Understanding International Relations*, 28.

[8] Carr, *Twenty Years' Crisis*, 75.

[9] E. H. Carr, "An Autobiography," in *E. H. Carr: A Critical Appraisal*, ed. Michael Cox (New York: Palgrave, 2004), xx.

[10] Carr, "An Autobiography," xviii. Carr absorbed this method primarily through Karl Mannheim's critical analysis of sociohistorical foundations of thought in *Ideology and Utopia* (1936). It was above all Mannheim's sociology of knowledge that shaped

Politically, the alleged community of interest in the maintenance of peace . . . is capitalized . . . by a dominant nation or group of nations. Just as the ruling class in a community prays for domestic peace, which guarantees its own security and predominance, and denounces class-war, which might threaten them, so international peace becomes a special vested interest of predominant Powers.[11]

It is by uncovering this hidden agenda that Carr deals liberal internationalism the most significant blow: "The exposure of the real basis of [its] professedly abstract principles is the most damning and most convincing part of the realist indictment of utopianism."[12]

Over time, Carr's critique gave rise to his lasting disciplinary reputation as a scholar who single-handedly relegated utopianism to the waste bin of IR theory and inaugurated the age of realism.[13] The main thrust of *The Twenty Years' Crisis* seems to vindicate this view. The book, Carr informed his readers, was "written with the deliberate aim of counteracting the glaring and dangerous defect of nearly all [interwar] thinking about international politics in English-speaking countries . . . the almost total neglect of the factor of power."[14] On closer inspection, however, discrediting utopianism once and for all was not Carr's intention.[15] "Sound political thought and sound political life," he insisted, "will be found only where both [utopia and reality] have their place."[16] In fact, the body of Carr's thought displays many utopian elements. "His musings on the

---

Carr's notion that international political ideas always reflect the goals and situation of its proponents—the principle guiding his realist critique of liberal utopianism. Mannheim, as Carr understood him, "believed that the essence of reality is dynamic, and that to seek any static point within it from which to deliver 'timeless' judgments is a fundamental error. The individual's apprehension of this ever-changing reality is necessarily partial and relative. He can see it only from the perspective of time and place in which he finds himself." E. H. Carr, "Karl Mannheim," in *From Napoleon to Stalin, and Other Essays* (Basingstoke: Macmillan, 1980), 180. For a detailed discussion of Mannheim's influence on Carr, see Charles Jones, *E. H. Carr and International Relations: A Duty to Lie* (Cambridge: Cambridge University Press, 1998), chap. 6.

[11] Carr, *Twenty Years' Crisis*, 82. Similarly, with respect to economic doctrines, "*laissez-faire*, in international relations as in those [domestic ones] between capital and labor, is the paradise of the economically strong" (60).

[12] Carr, *Twenty Years' Crisis*, 87.

[13] Witness John Mearsheimer's matter-of-fact statement that "Carr is a realist" and *The Twenty Years' Crisis* "a classic realist tract." "E. H. Carr vs. Idealism: The Battle Rages On," *International Relations* 19, no. 2 (2005): 139–40. See also Hedley Bull, "*The Twenty Years' Crisis* Thirty Years On," *International Journal* 24, no. 4 (1969): 625–38.

[14] Carr, *Twenty Years' Crisis*, vii.

[15] Schmidt, *Discourse of Anarchy*, 219–22.

[16] Carr, *Twenty Years' Crisis*, 10.

distant future were much more speculative than his reflections on the past. . . . [T]he charge Carr directed at the interwar idealists . . . could be turned against him: His view of the future relied more on aspiration than analysis."[17] His contention that theoretical knowledge is inherently purpose-driven, relative to context and interests, animates less the realist and neorealist schools of international relations than critical IR theory.[18] Therefore, Carr's realist reputation is highly ambiguous. It may be better to regard him as "a progenitor of critical or post-positivist approaches to international relations"[19] or, more accurately and less simplistically still, as a "sort-of-Realist/Functionalist/Keynesian/Marxist-influenced/proto-IR-Critical Theorist."[20]

In light of this controversy, the foregoing passages should be taken to imply neither that Carr was a clear-cut realist nor that in focusing the "first great debate" he also decided it. Rather, the sole aim is to flesh out the peculiar definition of utopianism developed in the academic field of international relations, and the contours of this definition are now sufficiently clear: Carr introduced the concept to refer to a number of related elements, and the connotations have been reinforced by successive generations of IR scholars working under his direct or indirect influence.

[17] Paul Howe, "The Utopian Realism of E. H. Carr," *Review of International Studies* 20 (1994): 295.

[18] Compare Carr's views on the purpose-driven character of all theoretical thought with Robert W. Cox's seminal article introducing critical IR theory: "Theory is always for someone and for some purpose. . . . There is . . . no such thing as theory in itself. . . . When any theory so presents itself, it is the more important to examine it as ideology, and to lay bare its concealed perspective." Cox, "Social Forces, States and World Orders: Beyond International Relations Theory," *Millennium: Journal of International Studies* 10, no. 2 (1982): 128. Hans Morgenthau was certainly quite disturbed by Carr's relativism. Commonly lumped together with Carr as the founding father of classical realism in IR, he nonetheless dismissed him as lacking any "transcendent point of view from which to survey the political scene . . . an observer unfortified by a transcendent standard of ethics." Morgenthau, "The Political Science of E. H. Carr," *World Politics* 1 (1948): 134.

[19] Seán Molloy, "Dialectics and Transformation: Exploring the International Theory of E. H. Carr," *International Journal of Politics, Culture, and Society* 17, no. 2 (2003): 280.

[20] Peter Wilson, "Radicalism for a Conservative Purpose: The Peculiar Realism of E. H. Carr," *Millennium: Journal of International Studies* 30, no. 1 (2001): 130. See also Andrew Linklater, "The Transformation of Political Community: E. H. Carr, Critical Theory and International Relations," *Review of International Studies* 23, no. 3 (1997): 321–38; Charles Jones, "E. H. Carr: Ambivalent Realist," in *Post-Realism: The Rhetorical Turn in International Relations*, ed. Francis A. Beer and Robert Hariman (East Lansing: Michigan State University Press, 1997); and Seán Molloy, *The Hidden History of Realism: A Genealogy of Power Politics* (New York: Palgrave Macmillan, 2006).

First, Carr used utopianism to signify liberal thinking about international politics in England and America in 1919–1939, and this association of utopianism with Anglophone liberal internationalism remains intact in contemporary IR theory. A recent textbook characterizes the early study of IR explicitly as "utopian liberalism,"[21] while another study treats "utopianism" and "liberalism" as overlapping headings.[22] It is worth noting that Carr was not alone in branding interwar liberals as utopians, even if he may have applied the label more scathingly than other critics. Hans Morgenthau, the other heavyweight of classical realism, emphasized the connection throughout his influential writings as well.[23] "Carr used 'utopianism' and Morgenthau used 'liberalism.' . . . Although [these] terms seem quite different, both [men] were, in fact, referring to the sort of liberal idealism and scientific humanism often associated with political scientists in the tradition of Woodrow Wilson."[24]

Second, and more specifically, Carr used utopianism to signify the assumption of a fundamental harmony of interests among nations. This assumption was central to interwar liberal internationalism; it represents "[one of the] predominant characteristic[s] of utopian thought."[25] Morgenthau likewise saw this feature as an essential element of utopianism, which he described as a school of modern political thought embracing, among other things, the "belief that a rational and moral political order, derived from universally valid abstract principles, can be achieved here and now."[26] The association of utopianism with the notion of a harmony of interests is also apparent from attempts by contemporary liberals to distance themselves from interwar liberal internationalism and to reformulate their theories of international politics in a nonutopian form appropriate to empirical social science. For these liberals, purging utopianism means "reject[ing] the notion that an *automatic* harmony of interests exists among individuals and groups in society."[27]

---

[21] Jackson and Sørensen, *International Relations*, 35–40.

[22] Hutchings, *International Political Theory*, 7.

[23] See Morgenthau, *Politics among Nations: The Struggle for Power and Peace*, 6th ed. (New York: Knopf, 1985 [1948]), and idem, *Scientific Man versus Power Politics* (Chicago: University of Chicago Press, 1946).

[24] Samuel Barkin, "Realist Constructivism," in *Perspectives on World Politics*, ed. Richard Little and Michael Smith, 3rd ed. (New York: Routledge, 2006), 417–18.

[25] Ian Clark, "World Order Reform and Utopian Thought: A Contemporary Watershed?" *Review of Politics* 41, no. 1 (1979): 100.

[26] Morgenthau, *Politics among Nations*, 3.

[27] Andrew Moravcsik, "Taking Preferences Seriously: A Liberal Theory of International Politics," *International Organization* 51, no. 4 (1997): 517.

Third, utopianism connotes a decidedly modern, rationalist perspective on world affairs. In attacking utopianism, Carr was referring to "the science of international politics," and similarly Morgenthau used the term to signify a rationalistic intellectual tradition. It was in reason, education, and enlightenment that utopians saw the main pathway to durable peace; war and conflict were deemed to be consequences of a widespread failure to use reason. As Morgenthau put it, utopianism "blames the failure of the social order to measure up to the rational standards on the lack of knowledge and understanding."[28] Spreading scientific knowledge to replace irrational atavistic myths, prejudices, and superstitions was certain to yield a bright, prosperous, and concordant future. Utopianism in this vein expressed "pervasive rationalism . . . [and] the actualization of man's potential for rationality,"[29] which would run its full course at the point of achieving a "rational and intelligently designed international organization"[30] abolishing war as a feature of human affairs. Concerning the intellectual lineage of this project, Kant and late eighteenth-century Enlightenment thought about human perfectibility are the "most obvious origins [of liberal utopianism] as a perspective on international politics."[31]

To these three interrelated characteristics it is possible to add several others, such as that utopianism represents a critical category rather than a term of self-description: it is a label used by opponents, not proponents. One could also elaborate the definition of utopianism by way of enumerating and discussing the proponents. The list might include figures such as Norman Angell, Robert Cecil, Hersch Lauterpacht, and Alfred Zimmern, and its top would be occupied by Woodrow Wilson, who tends to be associated with liberal internationalism, post–World War I reconstruction, and the League of Nations more consistently than any other figure—to the point of personifying the utopian project.[32] As Morgenthau put it, "Wilson is the most eloquent prophet of the [liberal internationalist] creed."[33]

---

[28] Morgenthau, *Politics among Nations*, 3.

[29] Clark, "World Order Reform," 99.

[30] Jackson and Sørensen, *International Relations*, 38.

[31] Hutchings, *International Political Theory*, 7.

[32] Wilson is thus mentioned, sometimes exclusively, in connection with utopianism in Hans Rommen, "Realism and Utopianism in World Affairs," *The Review of Politics* 6, no. 2 (1944): 194; F. Parkinson, *The Philosophy of International Relations: A Study in the History of Thought* (London: SAGE, 1977), 156; James E. Dougherty and Robert L. Pfaltzgraff, Jr., *Contending Theories of International Relations: A Comprehensive Survey*, 5th ed. (New York: Addison Wesley Longman, 2001), 14; or Jackson and Sørensen, *International Relations*, 37–38.

[33] Morgenthau, *Scientific Man*, 63.

Yet instead of trying to grasp all minutiae of the IR definition of utopianism, it is better to conclude its overview by zeroing in on one final prominent component: the idea of progress. This was arguably the hallmark feature of interwar liberal internationalism: "The distinctive characteristic of [the post–1918 generation of utopians] was their belief in progress: the belief, in particular, that the system of international relations that had given rise to the First World War was capable of being transformed."[34] The idea of progress was implied in the core assumption of a fundamental harmony of interests, which represented the future endpoint of progress and endowed it with the same kind of alleged natural inevitability. As stepping-stones leading to the envisioned harmony, the various liberal internationalist reform proposals (democratization, national self-determination, *laissez-faire* market exchange, collective security under the League of Nations, education and enlightenment) were progressive reform proposals. In the utopian perspective, they represented a foolproof recipe to propel humanity from its long history of war, injustice, and oppression to a fundamentally new order characterized by universal peace, liberty, justice, and prosperity.

Utopianism in Intellectual History
Secularized Eschatology

If World War I represented a watershed event for students of international politics, mobilizing them to look for schemes that would guarantee future permanent peace, its impact among intellectual historians was no less dramatic. The four years of mindless mechanized slaughter introduced into European consciousness a profound sense of discontinuity and disorientation: long-held beliefs, ideas, and modes of thinking that seemed natural just a while ago were discredited and lost forever. The Viennese writer Stefan Zweig captured this discontinuity with the simple statement that "Between our today [and] our yesterday . . . all bridges have been severed. . . . We have ploughed through the catalogue of all thinkable catastrophes from one end to the other."[35] At the heart of the discredited intellectual and cultural heritage lay the assumption that history was an inherently civilizing process, one of the foundational assumptions of

[34] Hedley Bull, "The Theory of International Politics 1919–1969," in *The Aberystwyth Papers: International Politics, 1919–1969*, ed. Brian Porter (London: Oxford University Press, 1972), 34. See also Clark, "World Order Reform," 98.

[35] Zweig, *Die Welt von gestern: Erinnerungen eines Europäers* (Hamburg: Fischer Verlag, 1982), 9–10.

modern European philosophy and nineteenth-century thought in particular. The Great War negated the idea of progress, stripped it of its natural status, revealed its artificiality, and opened it to critical analysis.

Where did the idea of progress come from? Why was it so pervasive? What needs and yearnings did it respond to and fulfill? From the late 1920s onward, a number of intellectual historians scrutinized its characteristics, functions, and history. Their efforts, often mutually informed, yielded a very different definition of utopianism from that simultaneously coalescing among students of international affairs. This alternative definition is based on secularization theory and draws attention to the subtle and unspoken ways in which the notion of progress arose out of, and retained in its hidden presuppositions, the Judeo-Christian myth of salvation. From the perspective of intellectual history, utopianism thus connotes the idea of progress as secularized eschatology, with the modern categories of historical discourse (such as reason, progress, and ideal society) as veiled vestiges of their theological antecedents (faith, divine providence, and Kingdom of God).

Among earliest English-speaking historians to investigate the origins of the idea of progress was the British scholar J. B. Bury. Writing in the early 1930s, Bury set progress in sharp contrast with the biblical conception of history, whose abdication, he argued, was a precondition for the appearance of progressivist philosophies: "[I]t was not till men felt independent of Providence that they could organize a theory of Progress. . . . So long as the doctrine of Providence was . . . in the ascendant, a doctrine of Progress could not arise. And the doctrine of Providence, as it was developed in Augustine's *City of God*, controlled the thought of the Middle Ages."[36] For Bury the first philosopher to have escaped the sway of the Bible was René Descartes, the true father of the idea of progress. Bury thus stated that "The idea took definite shape in France . . . [and] has been connected with the growth of modern science [and] with the growth of rationalism."[37] These aspects of the idea of progress served Bury to further emphasize its fundamental novelty and autonomy from the preceding (theological) conception of history. He did not deny that the new scientific interpretation of history often displayed striking parallels with the old religious one, but he nonetheless refrained from any claims that the one derived from the other. Such an idea ran counter to Bury's overall

---

[36] Bury, *The Idea of Progress: An Inquiry into Its Origin and Growth* (New York: Macmillan, 1932), 21–22, 73.

[37] Bury, *The Idea of Progress*, 348.

thesis: that the two conceptions of history were fundamentally incongruous and that their succession is properly described as replacement, not as continuity in disguise.

Bury therefore did not narrate the history of progress in terms of secularization of biblical eschatology, but that was precisely the conclusion that soon began cropping up in the works of a number of scholars in his wake. An illustrative example is Ernest Lee Tuveson, who focused on the idea of progress in his capacity as one of the pioneers of intellectual history as an academic field in the United States. Tuveson had read Bury's study but found his analysis unconvincing. A careful survey of scientists and philosophers from Newton via Burnet to Darwin led Tuveson to an alternative interpretation of the history of modern Western historical consciousness and the idea of progress as its centerpiece: "Gradually the role of Providence was transferred to 'natural laws.' . . . Providence was disguised rather than eliminated."[38] Tuveson thus argued the following:

> It is not inaccurate to speak of "progress" as a "faith," for it signified confidence in a new kind of Providence—the historical process. . . . This confidence . . . resulted in part from the transformation of a religious idea—the great millennial expectation. . . . [T]he New Jerusalem [reappeared] in a utopia of mechanist philosophers; the heavenly city of the eighteenth-century philosophers and of the nineteenth-century optimists retained many features of the New Jerusalem.[39]

Where Bury saw analogy but nothing more, Tuveson saw genealogy: progress did not merely replace divine providence, but emanated from it as its updated, rationalized expression.

Tuveson represented merely the tip of an iceberg: during the same period, an entire legion of American and above all European intellectual historians performed similar analyses and reached similar conclusions, many of them far more nuanced and theoretically sophisticated.[40] However, this is not the place to examine each and every one of them in detail;

[38] Tuveson, *Millennium and Utopia: A Study in the Background of the Idea of Progress* (Berkeley: University of California Press, 1949), xi–xii.

[39] Tuveson, *Millennium and Utopia*, xi–xii.

[40] Notable examples include Carl L. Becker, *The Heavenly City of the Eighteenth-Century Philosophers* (New Haven, Conn.: Yale University Press, 1932); Nicolas Berdyaev, *The Meaning of History*, trans. George Reavey (London: Geoffrey Bles, 1936); Karl Löwith, *Meaning in History: The Theological Implications of the Philosophy of History* (Chicago: University of Chicago Press, 1949); Reinhold Niebuhr, *Faith and History: A Comparison of Christian and Modern Views of History* (London: Nisbet, 1949); and Eric Voegelin, *Die politischen Religionen* (Vienna: Bermann-Fischer, 1938).

a detailed review of secularization theory, including a critical assessment of whether it represents a valid tool of historical interpretation and a convincing account of the lineage of the idea of progress, follows in pages ahead. At this stage it is more pressing to notice where, in the diagnosis of which twentieth-century Western social phenomena, intellectual historians utilizing secularization theory today do—and do not—employ its optic. The key discovery is that, although originally formulated as an analytically wide theory covering the modern idea of progress in general, secularization theory has been applied only to some of the idea's expressions: specifically, to its illiberal and totalitarian varieties.[41]

This restriction of scope is not entirely without precedent. After all, what drove much of the initial effort in the first half of the twentieth century to investigate the origins, characteristics, and functions of the idea of progress was precisely the wish to make sense of the apparent popular and intellectual support for politics of control, exclusion, terror, and war in totalitarian regimes: Nazi Germany and Bolshevik Russia. Where did the enthusiasm for these violent movements come from? According to both the original proponents of secularization and their successors among more recent generations of intellectual historians, in large part the answer lies in the character of the Nazi and Bolshevik ideologies as secularized eschatologies or *ersatz* religions that successfully filled a spiritual void left by the demise of authentic Christianity. Their appeal stemmed from the looming threat of nihilism in post-Christian Europe—from the yearning for redemption and greater meaning in the context of the devaluation of values after World War I.[42] The Nazi and Soviet regimes responded to this yearning with grand futuristic visions of, respectively, the Third Reich and Third International, visions that, according to secularization theory, functioned as surrogates for the biblical Kingdom of God. These utopias played the main role in legitimating the regimes' total control over society and draconian policies involving, among other things, racial and class-based cleansing and aggressive territorial expansionism.

Nonetheless, liberalism deserves to be analyzed through the optic of secularization theory as well, as should be obvious especially to the IR theorist—who associates progress and utopianism precisely with interwar

---

[41] On the current secularization-totalitarianism nexus and its arbitrariness, see Milan Babík, "Beyond Totalitarianism: (Re)Introducing Secularization Theory to Liberal Narratives of Progress," *Politics, Religion & Ideology* 13, no. 3 (2012): 289–309.

[42] For a detailed analysis of this dynamic, see Stefan Elbe, "European Nihilism and Annihilation in the Twentieth Century," *Totalitarian Movements and Political Religions* 1, no. 3 (2000): 43–72.

liberal internationalism, and not at all with Nazism or Bolshevism. Insofar as secularization theory traces the origins and functions of the modern idea of progress, liberal internationalism should, as far as IR scholars see it, be the point of departure rather than a site of neglect. One can only speculate as to why IR has not exported this insight to intellectual history and filled the gap. The missed opportunity to contribute to secularization theory may be due to prevailing methodological biases within IR, thanks to which most of its scholars are not even aware of intellectual history, let alone its conceptual toolkit. "A dominant attitude, partly against history, partly just indifferent to it, became part of IR's tradition."[43] This neglect applies with twice the force to the history of ideas about history. In the sense that secularization theory starts with the idea of progress as a pervasive feature of modern historical consciousness and proceeds to an exploration of its hidden presuppositions and deep origins, it involves metahistory: history of (progressive conceptions of) history—more than enough to go unnoticed by IR.

Be that as it may, setting the definition of utopianism formulated within intellectual history side by side with the one developed by IR scholars reveals an interesting discrepancy across the disciplinary divide. This discrepancy surfaces in two mirror omissions. On the one hand, IR scholars have discussed "their" utopianism (Wilson's liberal internationalist idea of progress after World War I) oblivious to its definition in intellectual history, showing no knowledge of the optic of secularized eschatology. This omission concerns the interpretive apparatus of IR and is evident from the opening survey of elements making up the IR definition of utopianism. On the other hand, intellectual historians have deployed "their" utopianism (the optic of secularized eschatology) oblivious to its definition in IR, neglecting the idea of progress espoused by Wilson and other interwar liberal internationalists. This omission concerns the scope of secularization theory and appears in the tendency to associate secularized eschatology predominantly with illiberal and totalitarian ideologies: especially Nazism and Bolshevism. Taken together, these two omissions trigger an intriguing question: what happens when IR utopianism is approached through the lens of utopianism as the term is understood among intellectual historians? Is it possible to interpret the liberal internationalist idea of progress as secularized eschatology?

---

[43] Barry Buzan and Richard Little, "Why International Relations Has Failed as an Intellectual Project and What to Do about It," *Millennium: Journal of International Studies* 30, no. 1 (2001): 25.

A Cross-Disciplinary Synthesis
Liberal Internationalism as Secularized Eschatology

The answer is yes: a careful examination of Woodrow Wilson international political thought in its proper context—that is, the context of the broader American liberal tradition—indicates that it represented a secularized expression of Protestant eschatological convictions about the shape of history and America's position in it. Whether progress, harmony of interests, liberty, reason, or education, to list some of the main elements of the IR definition of utopianism, Wilson comprehended all of them in religious terms. His foreign policy ideology reveals, among other things, that he regarded universal history as a progressively unfolding struggle between Christ and Satan; the United States as God's designated vanguard in this struggle; World War I as the apocalyptic climax of the struggle; and his statecraft as the divinely ordained pathway to the Millennium of freedom, peace, justice, and material plenty. Politics, domestic and international, was fundamentally a spiritual and eschatological mission for Wilson, a matter of translating religion into practice in order to unite American citizens and subsequently the world in the spirit of Christ, thereby achieving perfect harmony. In this vein, in Wilson's mind the utopia of collective security and the League of Nations was simultaneously utopian in the sense that it signified the fulfillment of the biblically prophesied Kingdom of God on earth, *in hoc sæculo*.

Both IR and intellectual history have much to gain from the synthesis of their respective conceptions of utopianism. For intellectual history, the main benefit consists of filling a gap in secularization theory whose proponents have, until now, tended to focus predominantly on interwar totalitarian and illiberal progressivisms, neglecting the liberal idea of progress. For IR, fleshing out the religious-eschatological dimension of Wilson's diplomacy nuances and enriches Carr's analysis of liberal internationalism with an important insight. In *The Twenty Years' Crisis* Carr repeatedly emphasized the partial and biased character of Wilson's allegedly universal principles of international morality; relativizing these principles was one of Carr's main achievements. However, in suggesting where these narrow principles came from, precisely from what cultural source, Carr seems to have skipped a step in his quasi-Marxist critique. Narrating liberal internationalism as a direct expression of the underlying material conflict between the international "haves" and "have-nots," he failed to give proper due to the mediating role of religion as a vehicle for sanctifying the values, purposes, and interests of the "haves" in the international arena. Secularization theory restores the missing religious element. With respect to Wilson's liberal internationalism, it suggests that the most immediate "real basis of its professedly abstract principles,"[44] to use Carr's words, was late nineteenth-century American Protestant eschatology.[45]

The reasons for constraining the focus to Wilson are twofold. The first set is methodological. In his ideas and practice Wilson combined more elements of IR utopianism than any other liberal internationalist of his generation. In addition, he appears to have been the main target of Carr's analysis in *The Twenty Years' Crisis*—and to this extent represents the scholar-statesman most representative of IR utopianism in the eyes of the critic who is widely held responsible for the category's disciplinary definition. Wilson's status as the face of utopianism has been as lasting as Carr's influence on this definition. A third methodological consideration is that focusing on a single figure avoids the danger of constructing a school of utopianism where there might have been none—a danger unheeded by Carr, exploited by many IR scholars (realists) in his wake, and loathed by current historians of interwar international thought, who strive to undo it.[46]

The second set of reasons for singling out Wilson has to do with his lasting legacy: profound in international politics, more powerful still in American foreign policy. "Wilsonianism should be seen not as a transient phenomenon . . . but as a potent definer of contemporary history."[47] The ideals under which Wilson committed the United States to the Great War, such as universal morality, progress, and America's special mission to civilize the world, defined much of subsequent twentieth-century American diplomacy and statecraft, giving rise to what has been called

---

[44] Cf. Carr, *Twenty Years' Crisis*, 87.

[45] Whether the *ultimate* basis was American national interest in wealth and power, as a Marxist critique would assert, is an issue beyond the present scope of this work. In recovering the religious dimension of Wilson's politics, this study merely implies that if American national interest indeed was the ultimate basis, then Wilson first sacralized it into a religious narrative casting the United States as the world redeemer, and this narrative was subsequently secularized to yield the political doctrine of liberal internationalism.

[46] The latter include David Long and Peter Wilson, eds., *Thinkers of the Twenty Years' Crisis: Inter-War Idealism Reassessed* (Oxford: Clarendon, 1995).

[47] Akira Iriye, *The Cambridge History of American Foreign Relations*, vol. 3, *The Globalizing of America, 1913–1945* (Cambridge: Cambridge University Press, 1993), 45, 71–72.

the "Wilsonian Century" and culture of "Wilsonianism."[48] Even someone as unsympathetic to Wilsonianism as Henry Kissinger agreed that "for three generations critics have savaged Wilson's analysis and conclusions . . . [but] Wilson's principles have remained the bedrock of American foreign-policy thinking."[49]

The ongoing appeal of Wilson's tenets surfaced especially after the end of the Cold War and the fall of the Soviet Union. The conviction that history is a teleological process, that its final meaning is political and economic liberalism, and that the United States, having decoded this meaning, represents the force of progress, peace, prosperity, and freedom in the world has animated especially neoconservative intellectuals and practitioners.[50] However, the allegiance to liberal internationalism cuts across party lines, uniting neoconservatives with liberals, Republicans with Democrats. Both "the first two post–Cold War presidents, George Bush and Bill Clinton, articulated visions of the new era that may be characterized as broadly Wilsonian in rhetoric and aspiration."[51]

The lasting influence of Wilson's ideas extends the relevance of this study well beyond his interwar context. By virtue of his legacy, excavating the buried eschatological foundations of his liberal internationalism also carries implications for contemporary international politics and especially American foreign policy, where Wilson's presence remains most pronounced. Secularization theory is essentially an instrument of critical hermeneutics intended to "bring to the self-understanding of the present . . . a whole dimension of hidden meaning."[52] To focus on Wilson is to perform this function not only on his ideas and practice, but also simultaneously on recent American foreign-policy thinking, bringing to light its narrow, provincial, and essentially dogmatic underpinnings. The opportunity to engage critically with American liberal internationalism today may be the ultimate reason for aiming the optic of secularization

---

[48] The terms come, respectively, from Frank Ninkovich, *The Wilsonian Century: U.S. Foreign Policy since 1900* (Chicago: University of Chicago Press, 1999), 5–6, and Lloyd E. Ambrosius, *Wilsonianism: Woodrow Wilson and His Legacy in American Foreign Relations* (New York: Palgrave Macmillan, 2002), 7.

[49] Kissinger, *Diplomacy* (New York: Simon & Schuster, 1994), 52.

[50] The classic statement of this position is Francis Fukuyama, "The End of History?" *The National Interest* 16 (1989): 3–18, and the expanded version in idem, *The End of History and the Last Man* (London: Hamish Hamilton, 1992).

[51] John G. Ruggie, *Winning the Peace: America and World Order in the New Era* (New York: Columbia University Press, 1995), 2.

[52] Hans-Georg Gadamer, review of *Die Legitimität der Neuzeit*, by Hans Blumenberg, *Philosophische Rundschau* 15 (1968): 201.

theory on Wilson rather than on other interwar liberal utopians such as Norman Angell or Lord Cecil.

Outline

It would be tempting to turn directly to Wilson and subject his international political thought to secularization analysis right away, showing that his liberal philosophy of domestic and international political progress was informed by religious-eschatological convictions. Thanks to the efforts of Arthur S. Link, a Princeton scholar who dedicated his entire professional life to collecting and editing Wilson's writings, the twenty-eighth president of the United States may be the most thoroughly documented modern statesman; the mammoth *Papers of Woodrow Wilson* project counts sixty-nine volumes and includes material ranging from Wilson's presidential speeches to an itemized list of things he had bought with his pocket money when a freshman in college.[53] The *Papers* contain not only an extensive record of Wilson's public and private utterances, but also a wealth of independent corroborating evidence from newspaper reports, Wilson's family, friends, colleagues, staff members, domestic and foreign politicians, and others who had come in contact with him. In terms of primary sources, no obstacle stands in the way of undertaking the secularization analysis of Wilson's IR utopianism straightaway.

However, not every intellectual historian accepts secularization theory as a valid tool of historical interpretation. On the contrary, it is shrouded in controversy, and so the story must begin elsewhere: with a critical discussion of the secularization optic. This is the purpose of the first two chapters. Chapter 1 zeroes in on the core thesis of secularization theory and subjects it to close scrutiny: the thesis that the modern idea of history as progress rests on hidden biblical presuppositions and represents a secularized extension of the eschatological myth of salvation driven by divine providence. The most rigorous discussion of this thesis has occurred in German-speaking circles: within the so-called Löwith-Blumenberg debate. Chapter 1 therefore traces and evaluates this debate in detail, including a close reading of Karl Löwith's *Meaning in History* (1949) and Hans Blumenberg's reply in *The Legitimacy of the Modern Age* (1976), respectively the main statement of and the main attack on the secularization thesis. It concludes that the notion of secularization remains a valid tool of historical understanding, that Blumenberg's

---

[53] See Arthur S. Link et al., eds., *The Papers of Woodrow Wilson*, 69 vols. (Princeton, N.J.: Princeton University Press, 1966–1994).

differences with Löwith are not as significant as may meet the eye, and that based on the terms of their debate alone Wilson's idea of progress represents an especially suitable candidate for secularization analysis.

Chapter 2 concerns the current scope of secularization theory. It begins by noticing and illustrating the widespread fixation of secularization theory on totalitarian ideologies of progress and utopia, asks whether this fixation precludes exporting secularization theory to liberal progressivisms, and answers in the negative. In addition, the chapter identifies and removes a second obstacle to applying the secularization optic to Wilson's liberal internationalism: the claim that this optic is inconsistent with Christian ideologies of progress and suitable only for non- or antireligious ones. The chapter rejects this claim by pointing out that in the context of secularization theory the term "secularization" does not necessarily mean "de-Christianization," but rather the process of bending biblical eschatology *ad sæculum*: investing the myth of salvation with temporal-historical meaning. Chapter 2 thus reaffirms the suitability of Wilson's Protestant-inspired liberal philosophy of progress for secularization analysis.

With a critical review of the interpretive apparatus complete, the foray into the unexplored territory at the crossroads of IR and intellectual history may begin, commencing the main task: a synthesis of the two definitions of utopianism by recovering the eschatological foundations of Wilson's liberal idea of progress. While this synthesis will be performed primarily by working with the texts in the *Papers of Woodrow Wilson*, it would be a grave mistake to neglect their historical and ideological setting; context is equally important in its capacity as "an ultimate framework for helping to decide what conventionally recognizable meanings, in a society of *that* kind [nineteenth-century United States], it might in principle have been possible for someone [Wilson] to have intended to communicate."[54] Writing an intellectual history of Wilson's idea of progress necessarily involves delving into the history of American religious and political thought in order to delineate the range of referents that "America," "liberty," "progress," "history," "providence," "God," and other terms used by Wilson could reasonably have signified in his mind and in the minds of his audiences. The need to pay attention to the history of the United States and American liberalism is all the greater because Wilson was a professional historian and constitutional scholar who often

---

[54] Quentin Skinner, "Meaning and Understanding in the History of Ideas," *History and Theory* 8, no. 1 (1969): 49.

referred to the national past. Together with Wilson's Protestant religion, his understanding of his country's historical experience represents one of the main intellectual foundations for his liberal internationalism and as such an important approach to its meaning.[55]

In light of these considerations, chapters 3 and 4 discuss the origins and development of American liberalism to demonstrate the pervasive influence of Protestant eschatology down to Wilson's time. Mainstream representations of American political history tend to deny that religion possessed any political role after the American Revolution, which would mean that Wilson's eschatological liberalism was either an idiosyncrasy or merely a linguistic cover for what was really a nonreligious doctrine. Drawing on nineteenth-century observers such as Alexis de Tocqueville and on recent revisionist historiography of American church and society, however, chapters 3 and 4 show that Protestant millennialism shaped not only colonial government, as is widely accepted, but also the American Revolution and nineteenth-century American political thought, giving rise to a sort of liberal-republican millennialism. The Bible and the myth of salvation served as the ultimate moral guide for policy even after the constitutional separation of church and state. For example, chapter 4 points out that the nineteenth-century idea of national progress and expansion stood on the belief in America's "manifest destiny" as God's appointed redeemer of the world. From this perspective Wilson's domestic and international politics of salvation was no idiosyncrasy. It had precedents as old as the first Puritan sermons about America's sacred purpose in history.

Chapters 5 and 6 move from Wilson's context to the man himself and perform the key rereading of his political ideas as secularized eschatology. Chapter 5 documents the central role of religious faith in Wilson's views on knowledge, education, politics, history, liberty, and American democracy. It demonstrates that the Bible represented his cognitive access key to all secular reality and structured his actions within it. Much like his foreign policy, Wilson's domestic policies are frequently considered in isolation from his Protestant upbringing and eschatological convictions, but this is not how Wilson comprehended them. For him, they were practical expressions of his spiritual project to dissolve all national tensions and transform the United States into a harmonious Kingdom of God on earth. Chapter 6 then reveals that Wilson's foreign policy encapsulated

---

[55] Lloyd E. Ambrosius, *Wilsonian Statecraft: Theory and Practice of Liberal Internationalism during World War I* (Wilmington, Del.: SR Books, 1991), 21.

the same eschatological mission writ large: a mission to transform the world, under American leadership, from conflict and crisis into a global harmony of interests. The chapter gives clear evidence that in entering World War I and pushing for the League of Nations Wilson saw himself as fulfilling the biblical prophecy of universal salvation. His IR utopianism was an outward (political) manifestation of his spiritual utopianism and cannot be divorced from his Protestant eschatological convictions.

The conclusion casts a second look at the definition of utopianism in the writings of the original realist critics of interwar liberal internationalism. It makes the surprising discovery that, unlike many contemporary IR specialists, these critics possessed a broad multidisciplinary perspective including a keen interest in intellectual history, which enabled them to grasp the religious foundations of the liberal idea of progress. This is evident not only from Carr's writings, but also and especially from those of Reinhold Niebuhr. Celebrated in IR for his vociferous Christian realist opposition to interwar utopianism, this prominent American theologian was simultaneously—outside those of his texts appropriated by IR—a leading secularization theorist. Merging the two definitions of utopianism from IR and intellectual history thus may be regarded as a recovery procedure: one restoring the richer and more synthetic definition that existed earlier on but was lost in the subsequent process of disciplinary specialization, with IR and intellectual history each retaining only a fragment of the concept's original content. The conclusion then moves on to outline the main benefits of the synthesis, above all a better understanding of the illiberal and totalizing tendencies of Wilsonian liberal internationalism flowing from its heretofore obscured eschatological core. Final thoughts reflect critically on the suitability of liberal internationalism *qua* secularized eschatology as a guide for future American foreign policy.

CHAPTER ONE

FROM PROVIDENCE TO PROGRESS
Secularization Theory

Among the legion of scholars who have written about President Woodrow Wilson, many noticed his deep eschatological convictions, and many others cast his international political thought as a form of utopianism. The former group includes Wilson's main twentieth-century biographer, Arthur S. Link, and the latter, E. H. Carr, whose realist critique of Wilsonian liberal internationalism in the wake of World War I was outlined earlier. Few if any, however, have done both things at once: interpreted Wilson's political utopianism as a secularized expression of his eschatological consciousness. This interpretation, along with its various implications, is the principal focus of this study.

Unfortunately, as a framework for this interpretation the concept of secularization is neither self-evident nor uncontroversial. On the contrary, different thinkers have understood secularization in different ways, and even where several theorists share the same definition of the concept, more often than not serious disagreements exist among them. Compounding the difficulties is the fact that the shift from religious to modern modes of thought can be narrated using other frameworks entirely; secularization is not the only option available. Alternative accounts have been formulated and are readily at hand.

Therefore, it is appropriate to begin by delving into secularization theory in depth in order to specify the meaning of the concept as it is used here, differentiate it from other possible definitions, identify its strengths and weaknesses, and assess its analytical scope and applicability. These are the most immediate goals to accomplish. Emphatically, they do not include defending the concept of secularization chosen to serve as the principal optic for the subsequent analysis of Wilson—the secularization thesis formulated by the German philosopher Karl Löwith—from all its criticisms, nor do they necessarily seek to elevate this particular concept of secularization above all the other accounts. It suffices to demonstrate that Löwith's thesis is well established and that numerous reasons exist to direct it at a heretofore neglected target: Wilson's progressive diplomacy in the broader context of American liberal internationalism.

Secularization as a Contested Concept

Although the term "secularization" enjoys extensive popular usage, or perhaps precisely for that reason, its definition is ambiguous and contested: it is a generic concept encompassing a wide range of meanings. If these share anything in common, it is only the broad understanding of secularization as a shift from the religious worldview to the modern one.

In sociological literature, the term frequently connotes the decline of religion in the public sphere as one of the distinguishing features of the modern era. This conception of secularization pervades the work of, for example, Peter L. Berger and Thomas Luckmann, who have described the process as "the progressive autonomization of societal sectors from the domination of religious meanings and institutions."[1] Cast in terms of the separation of church and state performed by the U.S. Constitution and Bill of Rights, this definition of secularization is a staple of mainstream American political and religious historiography. A recent contribution to this scholarship thus uses the rubric "secularization" to signify "the loss of *visible* religiosity, especially in regard to *public* religiosity, which often is termed or seen as religious deinstitutionalization."[2]

Since this definition of secularization does not address the question of private religiosity, however, it does not necessarily mean complete godlessness. This brings up a second, more radical definition: secularization as the extinguishing of all religious faith, including and especially

---

[1] Peter L. Berger and Thomas Luckmann, *The Social Construction of Reality: A Treatise in the Sociology of Knowledge* (Garden City, N.Y.: Doubleday, 1966), 74.

[2] Charles Mathewes and Christopher McKnight Nichols, eds., *Prophesies of Godlessness: Predictions of America's Imminent Secularization from the Puritans to the Present Day* (Oxford: Oxford University Press, 2008), 10; emphasis original.

within the individual soul. This definition has its classic expression in Nietzsche's pronouncement that "God is dead."[3] On this reading, the disappearance of public piety is merely symptomatic of a more fundamental process: the loss of private belief.

A third definition of secularization was recently formulated by Charles Taylor in his magisterial account of the emergence of Western modernity.[4] This definition notes the resilience of traditional religiosity down to the present day and concerns itself not so much with decline in faith as with changes in its background or pre-ontology: "the whole context of understanding in which our moral, spiritual or religious experience and search takes place."[5] From this perspective, secularization signifies primarily the onset of critical reflexivity: a gradual relativization of the initially axiomatic faith in God. In tracing the origins of the secular age, Taylor tells a story about "how . . . we move[d] from a condition where, in Christendom, people lived naïvely within a theistic construal, to one in which . . . everyone's construal shows up as such; and in which, moreover, unbelief has become for many the major default option."[6]

Even a cursory exploration of secularization as a tool of historical understanding thus reveals significant diversity: some scholars use it to map changes in social structure and public institutions, while others concern themselves almost exclusively with ideas and private spirituality—without necessarily agreeing on the nature or consequences of their transformation. In addition to these differences, it is worth noting that the origins of the modern era have also been interpreted in other ways not involving the concept of secularization at all, at least not explicitly. As a framework for historical analysis, that is, secularization has no monopoly over explanations of modernity.

The influential works of Max Horkheimer, Theodor Adorno, Herbert Marcuse, and other founding members of the Frankfurt Institute for Social Research offer an illustrative example. According to these scholars, the origins of European modernity stem from the Enlightenment as a project of rational critique and demythologization. This project, which "has always aimed at liberating men from fear and establishing their

---

[3] Friedrich Nietzsche, *The Gay Science*, ed. Walter Kaufmann (New York: Vintage, 1974), §125.

[4] Charles Taylor, *A Secular Age* (Cambridge, Mass.: Belknap, 2007).

[5] Taylor, *A Secular Age*, 3.

[6] Taylor, *A Secular Age*, 14.

sovereignty,"[7] introduced the possibility of human emancipation from both natural and artificial constraints, above all from social oppression and injustice based upon religious superstition. In the process of its unfolding, however, rational thought ceased to be emancipatory and turned reactionary, affirmative of the status quo: "Progress becomes regression . . . and enlightenment reverts into mythology."[8] Instrumentalized and reified, reason lost its critical dimension and dialectically morphed into a means of total bureaucratic control: "Knowledge originally developed to *fight* the established order," as Marcuse put it, "is now applied in its *service*."[9] From the perspective of the Frankfurt School, modernity thus failed to live up to its promise. Simultaneously with releasing human beings from prior self-imposed obstacles to the full realization of their potential, it disciplined them to voluntarily embrace new, ever more total forms of oppression and exploitation.[10]

This narrative of modernity is fascinating in its own right, but in the present context its most striking feature is that it leaves "secularization" almost entirely out of its conceptual vocabulary: one would look in vain for this term in Horkheimer's or Adorno's studies. This raises the intriguing question of whether and how, if at all, the Frankfurt School account of the pathogenesis of the modern age connects to the different conceptions of secularization outlined earlier, and whether and how these conceptions connect to each other. A comparative analysis would no doubt reveal significant divergences as well as important overlaps, such as in Nietzsche's emphasis, also shared by the Frankfurt School, on the decay of traditional religious belief as a constitutive moment in the genesis of the modern era.

Such an analysis, however, goes well beyond the scope of this book, whose principal aim is something else: to interpret Wilsonian liberal

---

[7] Max Horkheimer and Theodor W. Adorno, *Dialectics of Enlightenment*, trans. John Cumming (New York: Herder & Herder, 1972), 3.

[8] Horkheimer and Adorno, *Dialectics of Enlightenment*, xv–xvi.

[9] Herbert Marcuse, *Negations: Essays in Critical Theory*, trans. Jeremy J. Shapiro (Boston: Beacon, 1968), 33. Max Horkheimer similarly observed that the traditional "scholar and his science are incorporated into the apparatus of society; his achievements are a factor in the conservation and continuous renewal of the existing state of affairs." See Horkheimer, *Critical Theory*, trans. Matthew J. O'Connell et al. (New York: Herder & Herder, 1972), 196; emphasis original.

[10] The best concise introduction to the Frankfurt School, including its account of the origins of modernity, remains Robert J. Antonio, "The Origins, Development, and Contemporary Status of Critical Theory," *Sociological Quarterly* 24, no. 3 (1983): 325–51.

internationalism through the lens of yet another conception of secularization distinct (though not necessarily completely separate) from the ones identified earlier. This is the conception of secularization developed by intellectual historians such as Karl Löwith to comprehend the complex transition from biblical historical consciousness to modern historical consciousness. In laying it out, the forthcoming passages focus specifically on the thesis that modern philosophies of history, dominated by categories of reason, progress, and future ideal society, are secularized vestiges of Judeo-Christian eschatology, dominated by categories of faith, divine providence, and heaven.

Secularization in Nineteenth- and Twentieth-Century Social and Historical Theory

More or less explicit variants of this thesis are not difficult to find in nineteenth- and early twentieth-century philosophy and historical theory. Working from different perspectives, several eminent thinkers, some already mentioned, came to feel that modern historical consciousness somehow conserved and perpetuated religious modes of thinking about history, and that allegedly scientific philosophies of progress were in fact disguised extensions of biblical providentialism.

Among the first of these scholars was Nietzsche. Born in the middle of a century characterized by a widespread belief in scientific progress, Nietzsche resisted this belief and analyzed it from a critical distance. In the words of Stefan Elbe, "Nietzsche was amongst the earliest to problematize the collapse of an overarching and teleological idea of Europe within the secular configuration of European modernity."[11] He not only proclaimed the "Death of God," but also noticed that it caused growing concerns among Europeans about the purpose of events and actions. These concerns struck Nietzsche as deeply revealing. The widespread perception of history's apparent meaninglessness as a problem, and the corresponding demand for an overarching goal, confirmed to him that eschatological consciousness had survived into the scientific era. "The nihilistic question 'for what?'" Nietzsche had commented, "is rooted in the old habit of supposing that the goal must be put up, given, demanded *from outside*—by some *superhuman authority*. Having unlearned faith in that, one still follows the old habit and seeks another *authority* that

---

[11] Stefan Elbe, *Europe: A Nietzschean Perspective* (London: Routledge, 2003), 12.

can *speak unconditionally* and *command* goals and tasks."[12] Although in the scientific age Europeans no longer deemed the idea of God credible, according to Nietzsche they did not manage to liberate themselves from all biblical dogmas. Among other things, they remained hostage to the presupposition that history possessed deeper meaning and coherence as a linear process moving irreversibly forward to a final goal. The only difference was that now they no longer imagined the driving force as lying outside the world, but rather as residing within the laws of nature.

Nietzsche thus realized that modern philosophies of progress inherited, rather than rejected, the eschatological blueprint furnished by the Bible two thousand years ago. Modern historical consciousness was scientific only on the surface. Underneath the surface it remained religious through and through, as Nietzsche did not hesitate to point out: "What, there are no longer any living mythologies? What, the religions are dying out? Just behold the power of the religion of history."[13] Modern reason did indeed destroy most of the Judeo-Christian views, but not the vision of salvation and the attendant eschatological consciousness devaluing the present for the sake of the ideal future. The ethics of asceticism and self-sacrifice on behalf of better tomorrows stayed in place. "Science today," Nietzsche declared in this vein, "is not the opposite of the ascetic ideal but rather the latter's own *most recent and noble manifestation*. . . . Unconditional, honest atheism . . . is . . . *not* opposed to the ascetic ideal as it appears to be; instead, it is only one of the ideal's last phases of development."[14]

Not long after Nietzsche's suggestion that modern historical consciousness and philosophies of history contained unacknowledged religious elements, the German jurist and legal scholar Carl Schmitt made a similar claim when tracing the origins of constitutional law as the backbone of the modern state. In his *Political Theology* (1922), Schmitt argued that all essential concepts of the modern state (such as sovereignty, *raison d'état*, or the friend-enemy distinction) were products of systematic structural derivation from their theological precedents—in

[12] Friedrich Nietzsche, *The Will to Power*, trans. Walter Kaufmann and R. J. Hollingdale (New York: Random House, 1968), §20; emphasis original.

[13] Friedrich Nietzsche, "On the Uses and Disadvantages of History for Life," in *Untimely Meditations*, ed. Daniel Breazele, trans. R. J. Hollingdale (Cambridge: Cambridge University Press, 2000), §8.

[14] Friedrich Nietzsche, "Second Essay: What Do Ascetic Ideals Mean?" in *On the Genealogy of Morality*, ed. Keith Ansell-Pearson, trans. Carol Diethe (Cambridge: Cambridge University Press, 1994), §23, §27; emphasis original.

other words, that they were secularized theological concepts.[15] Thus for Schmitt the juridical and political modernity inaugurated by the Peace of Westphalia was more apparent than real. If the purpose of the Peace was to terminate religious war, for instance, this goal was achieved merely through reterritorializing the conflict along different borders: from those demarcating a religious denomination to those demarcating the modern state and, later still, society.[16] In this vein the Peace of Westphalia did not end religious violence at all, but merely postponed it, as became all too evident to Schmitt during World War I. Much like the Thirty Years War, the Great War too was essentially a conflict among religious communities espousing opposed theological doctrines of salvation—only now these manifested themselves in the form of, respectively, secular states and modern political ideologies of progress.

In the work of Eric Voegelin, the Viennese contemporary of Schmitt, the religious foundations of these ideologies received special attention. Voegelin employed the notion of secularization to explain the origins, symbolism, and practice of what he called "the gnostic mass movements" of early twentieth-century Europe: doctrines such as Nazism, fascism, communism, Marxism, positivism, psychoanalysis, and all variants of progressivism. What unified these heterogeneous narratives, according to Voegelin, was their shared immanentization of Christian eschatology and their resultant claim to special knowledge (*gnosis*) about the correct path of history to redemption: while radical differences existed among their respective contents, in the structure of their *gnosis* the doctrines broadly resembled each other. All expressed dissatisfaction with the present state of affairs, located the root of the inadequacy in improper organization of existence, declared salvation humanly achievable, and sought a thorough reorganization of sociohistorical reality. The often draconian measures adopted to achieve this were justified by the promise of future utopia. According to Voegelin, this promise stemmed from the Christian *eschaton* and its role as *sanctificatio* with respect to suffering. In this vein,

---

[15] Carl Schmitt, *Politische Theologie: Vier Kapitel zur Lehre von der Souveränität*, 2nd ed. (Munich: Duncker & Humboldt, 1934 [1922]).

[16] As one scholar described Schmitt's view of the process, "the dynamic of modernity [is sketched out] as a process of reshuffling. The disposition to flee the political through neutrality-seeking and depoliticization [*Neutralisierungen und Entpolitisierungen*] only transferred the political to another site." Reinhard Mehring, "Karl Löwith, Carl Schmitt, Jacob Taubes und das 'Ende der Geschichte,'" *Zeitschrift für Religions- und Geistesgeschichte* 48, no. 3 (1996): 233.

Voegelin concluded that "The gnostic movements derive their ideas of perfection from Christianity.[17]

Notably, Voegelin was clear that in the course of this derivation authentic Christianity became perverted beyond all recognition. The gnostic effort to immanentize the *civitas Dei* in the vision of a perfect future society struck him as fundamentally irreligious. As he commented, echoing St. Augustine, the authentic Christian idea of perfection was not historical, but strictly moral and transcendental, "represent[ing] the insight that human nature does not find fulfillment in this world, but only in the *visio beatifica*, in supernatural perfection through grace in death."[18] Voegelin thus located the second key origin of modern utopianism in the teachings of the medieval Calabrian mystic and Cistercian abbot Joachim of Floris (c. 1132–1202), who began portraying the otherworldly *civitas Dei* of St. Augustine in increasingly historical, secular terms. Insofar as Joachim's historical exegesis initiated the breakdown of the Augustinian distinction between the biblical myth and temporal history, it was the Calabrian monk who paved the road leading to modern heresies—what Voegelin called "ersatz religions."[19]

Yet another important figure in early twentieth-century secularization theory was Jacob Taubes. In *Abendländische Eschatologie* (1947), based on his dissertation at the University of Zürich, Taubes stated that all philosophies portraying history as a unified and orderly process necessarily involved biblical assumptions, above all the assumption of a final goal: the *eschaton*. In his words, "Order and measure [*Maß und Stand*] are obtainable in the question about the nature of history only when one asks from the perspective of the *eschaton*. For in the *eschaton* history rises above its borders and becomes visible to itself."[20] For Taubes the

---

[17] Eric Voegelin, "Ersatz Religion: The Gnostic Mass Movements of Our Time," in *Science, Politics and Gnosticism: Two Essays* (Chicago: Henry Regnery, 1968), 89.

[18] Voegelin, "Ersatz Religion," 88. See also Voegelin, *The New Science of Politics* (Chicago: University of Chicago Press, 1952).

[19] See also Norman Cohn's thesis in *The Pursuit of the Millennium: Revolutionary Millenarians and Mystical Anarchists of the Middle Ages* (London: Paladin, 1970), 287–88, that the Communist and Nazi visions of apocalypse are "a secularized version of a fantasy that is many centuries old. . . . However modern their terminology, however realistic their tactics, in their basic attitudes Communism and Nazism follow an ancient tradition—and are baffling to the rest of us because of those very features that would have seemed so familiar to a chiliastic prophet of the Middle Ages."

[20] Jacob Taubes, *Abendländische Eschatologie* (Würzburg: Königshausen & Neumann, 2001 [1947]), 3.

coherence of history was artificial, a product of specifically Judeo-Christian convictions about the nature of the temporal process.

In an interesting twist, Taubes applied this insight not only to modern philosophies of history, but also to the process of secularization itself. After all, secularization too constitutes an ordered history: a coherent narrative about the evolution of Western historical interpretation. To this extent Taubes held that secularization, as a linear story recounting the succession of Western eschatologies from Jewish messianism via Augustinian transcendentalism to modern philosophies of progress, rested on religious foundations. This movement was itself eschatological for Taubes and represented a kind of meta-eschatology or "Occidental Eschatology," the title of his book. Insofar as its axiological origin was the revolution of ancient Jews against Rome, "Occident" was for Taubes a term of war.[21]

Lest it be thought that secularization theory was exclusive to German-speaking scholarship, the recognition that modern theories of progress reincarnated biblical eschatology also sprung up in other intellectual milieus. In Europe, it occurred to, for example, the great Russian philosopher and theologian Nicolas Berdyaev and the Czech phenomenologist Jan Patočka, founder of *Cercle philosophique de Prague*. Patočka's reading of nineteenth-century philosophies of history prompted him to note the striking degree to which their teleological and deterministic character echoed the biblical idea of providence:

> Everywhere in these philosophies . . . there is involved . . . a superhuman process whose "purpose" is dictated by powers higher and more powerful than the finite human individuality; they involve [either] a manifestation of the spirit, a divine idea which "comes to itself" in history . . . [or] a material process to which the individual can but subordinate himself, which he willy-nilly obeys.[22]

Similarly, Berdyaev's analysis of the modern ways of finding meaning in history led him to assert that "the ancient belief in the realization . . . of the Kingdom of God, the reign of perfection, truth and justice . . . becomes secularized in the doctrine of progress."[23] Biblical presuppositions were so essential to modern historical consciousness according to Berdyaev that it could not exist without them. It was "Christianity [that] introduced

---

[21] Mehring, "Karl Löwith, Carl Schmitt," 241.

[22] Jan Patočka, "O filosofii dějin," in *Sebrané spisy Jana Patočky*, vol. 1, *Péče o duši I* (Prague: Oikoymenh, 1996), 111.

[23] Nicolas Berdyaev, *The Meaning of History*, trans. George Reavey (London: Geoffrey Bles, 1936), 186. See also his excellent discussion of secularization on pp. 187–92.

historical dynamism," he stated, "and thus made possible a philosophy of history."[24] The modern striving to rationalize the Judeo-Christian myth of salvation into narratives of inevitable progress struck Berdyaev, much like his Austrian contemporary Voegelin, as perverse and farcical.

Interestingly, concurrently with Europeans such as Schmitt, Voegelin, or Patočka, suspicions that the modern idea of progress was rooted in biblical eschatology began cropping up also in the United States. Here the effort to interpret modern progressivism as secularized salvationism was spearheaded by Carl L. Becker, whose career as a professional historian incidentally overlapped with that of Woodrow Wilson.[25] However, unlike the future president, who was deeply committed to progress as an essential logic of history, as subsequent parts of this book reveal, Becker belonged to a younger generation of "new historians" espousing a far more critical-reflexive epistemology, one bordering on relativism in Becker's case.[26] His diagnosis of the religious moorings of the idea of progress represented part of his broader effort to destabilize and deconstruct preconceived notions about the meaning of history. In a series of lectures focusing on the eighteenth-century transition from medieval modes of thought to modern rationalism in France, Becker argued provocatively that

> the *Philosophes* were nearer the Middle Ages, less emancipated from the perceptions of medieval Christian thought, than they quite realized or we have commonly supposed. . . . The underlying preconceptions of eighteenth-century thought were still . . . essentially the same as those of the thirteenth century. . . . [T]he *Philosophes* demolished the Heavenly City of St. Augustine only to rebuild it with more up-to-date materials. . . . Having denatured God, [they] deified nature.[27]

[24] Berdyaev, *The Meaning of History*, 33.

[25] Their paths almost intersected when Wilson, while still a professor at Princeton, considered appointing Becker to the faculty and solicited a letter of reference from Frederick Jackson Turner, Wilson's close friend and Becker's graduate supervisor at the University of Wisconsin. See Wilson to Turner (March 10, 1900), and Turner to Wilson (March 12, 1900), in *The Papers of Woodrow Wilson*, ed. Arthur S. Link et al. (Princeton, N.J.: Princeton University Press, 1966–1994), 9:498–99, 506–7.

[26] See especially his American Historical Association (AHA) Presidential Address, "Everyman His Own Historian," *American Historical Review* 37, no. 2 (1932): 221–36.

[27] Carl L. Becker, *The Heavenly City of the Eighteenth-Century Philosophers* (New Haven, Conn.: Yale University Press, 1932), 29–31, 63.

On the one hand, Becker contended, scientific atheism discredited the Bible and undermined the prophesied Second Coming of Christ, but on the other hand the uncritical faith in the capacities of human reason led modern philosophy to draw up new visions of perfection, reproducing many biblical concepts in a secular form. In Becker's words, "The picture of salvation in the Heavenly City . . . [was translated into the image] of a 'future state' . . . or a more generalized earthly and social *félicité* or *perfectibilité du genre humain.*"[28] He noted that even after God's departure the universe was "still believed . . . to be a beautifully articulated machine designed by the Supreme Being according to a rational plan."[29] The continuing infatuation with the hidden realm of perfection indicated to Becker that eighteenth-century rationalism remained in the grip of hidden Judeo-Christian assumptions. Modern philosophy dismissed the otherworldly utopia of Christianity as religious superstition, but not without secularizing it at the same time: reinstating it on worldly foundations as an earthly paradise achievable through rational-scientific progress.

From Becker one could go on to Ernest Lee Tuveson, discussed earlier, and a number of other scholars; this overview of secularization theory is by no means exhaustive and could be extended further.[30] Rather than continue along this path, however, it is time to focus on the German philosopher Karl Löwith (1897–1973), whose *Meaning in History* (1949) represents the classic statement of the secularization thesis and the principal analytical framework for the purposes of this book.[31] One reason for narrowing the discussion in this manner is to avoid constructing a school of secularization theorists where there might have been none, although a study dedicated exclusively to the various figures would likely reveal a significant measure of shared language and ideas.[32] The main reason for

---

[28] Becker, *The Heavenly City*, 48–49.

[29] Becker, *The Heavenly City*, 31.

[30] Additional important works include Henri de Lubac, *The Drama of Atheist Humanism*, trans. Edith M. Riley (New York: New American Library, 1950); Rudolf Bultmann, *History and Eschatology* (Edinburgh: Edinburgh University Press, 1957); Oscar Cullmann, *Heil als Geschichte*, trans. Sidney G. Sowers (New York: Harper & Row, 1967); and Hans Jonas, *The Gnostic Religion: The Message of the Alien God and the Beginnings of Christianity* (Boston: Beacon, 1958).

[31] Karl Löwith, *Meaning in History: The Theological Implications of the Philosophy of History* (Chicago: University of Chicago Press, 1949).

[32] For instance, Tuveson was familiar with Becker's *Heavenly City* and referred to it in his work; Löwith's *Meaning in History* repeatedly cites Taubes and Berdyaev;

concentrating on Löwith, however, is that it was primarily to him that Hans Blumenberg subsequently addressed his critique of secularization as a valid tool of historical understanding. What may be called the Löwith-Blumenberg debate is not the only forum in which secularization has been subjected to critical scrutiny.[33] However, no other exchange on the concept of secularization was nearly as direct, protracted, and theoretically rigorous. Consequently it deserves to be laid out in detail.

Karl Löwith and the Theological Foundations of Modern Historical Consciousness

The first edition of Löwith's *Meaning in History* came out in 1949. Löwith, who commenced his scholarly career in the 1920s with a dissertation on Nietzsche under the supervision of Martin Heidegger, wrote the study during his American exile from Nazism and published it shortly before his return to Germany.[34] Notably, the subtitle of the first (American) edition, "The Theological Implications of the Philosophy of History," contained a slight but important imprecision, as became evident when the German edition appeared a few years later. Whether the imprecision was due to Löwith's limited feel for English or some other factor is not clear, but in the subsequent German edition, translated by Hanno Kesting under Löwith's close scrutiny, the word "implications" was replaced with

---

and Patočka, *Kacířské eseje o filosofii dějin* (Prague: Academia, 1990 [1975]), 79, prizes Löwith's argument about the Judeo-Christian foundations of modern historical consciousness as an exceptionally powerful insight into the origins of European nihilism.

[33] It would be possible to choose a different avenue to present and assess the concept, such as Peter Gay's general argument that the eschatological-utopian elements of the Enlightenment have been overemphasized—an argument formulated in part by responding to the claims made by Becker in the 1930s. See Peter Gay, "Carl Becker's Heavenly City," *Political Science Quarterly* 72, no. 2 (1957): 182–99; idem, *The Enlightenment: An Interpretation*, vol. 2, *The Science of Freedom* (New York: Norton, 1996 [1969]); and idem, *The Party of Humanity: Essays in the French Enlightenment* (New York: Norton, 1959 [1954]).

[34] For Löwith's doctoral thesis, see his "Auslegung von Nietzsches Selbst-Interpretation und von Nietzsches Interpretationen" (D.Phil. diss., University of Munich, 1923). According to Enrico Donaggio, "Zwischen Nietzsche und Heidegger: Karl Löwiths anthropologische Philosophie des faktischen Lebens," *Deutsche Zeitschrift für Philosophie* 48, no. 1 (2000): 37–48, Nietzsche and Heidegger were Löwith's two principal inspirations during his intellectual development. Both provided important stimuli (negative, in the case of Heidegger) guiding him toward the secularization thesis.

"presuppositions" (*Voraussetzungen*).[35] With this correction in place, the subtitle became an accurate summary of Löwith's thesis: that modern philosophy of history is impossible without specifically Judeo-Christian presuppositions about the nature of the historical process.

Is the meaning of history inherent in historical events themselves, and if not, where does it come from? This is the twofold question motivating Löwith's study. His answer to the first part is in the tradition of classical skepticism: "Historical processes as such do not bear the least evidence of a comprehensive and ultimate meaning."[36] They are essentially chaotic, a random amalgamation of events and occurrences. If they did manifest meaning, after all, philosophers would not search for it. Yet Löwith emphasizes that the absence of any purely empirical meaning, while a necessary precondition for the quest for meaning to begin, is not alone sufficient to initiate it. One may use Aristotle to illustrate this point: although he regarded history as an unintelligible collection of accidents, this did not compel him to ask whether they possessed any deeper significance. Instead, he simply abandoned history as uninteresting.

Consequently, what drives the search for the meaning of history, Löwith notes, is something more than the mere recognition of history as chaos. It is the perception of the chaos *as a problem* and, most fundamentally, the acquired conviction that in the background there exists a unifying principle of order. Put differently, the actual meaninglessness of history can arise only against a preestablished horizon of meaning: the Judeo-Christian *eschaton*, salvation as the end of history in the twin sense of *finis* and *telos*. In Löwith's words, "The claim that history has an ultimate meaning implies a final purpose or goal transcending the actual events."[37] His answer to the second part of his question thus may be summarized as follows: if philosophy of history refers to "a systematic interpretation of universal history in accordance with a principle by which historical events and successions are unified and directed toward an ultimate meaning,"[38] then "the very existence of a philosophy of history and its quest for a meaning is due to the history of salvation; it emerged from the faith in an ultimate purpose."[39] Modern philosophies of progress are

---

[35] Karl Löwith, *Weltgeschichte und Heilsgeschehen: Die theologischen Voraussetzungen der Geschichtsphilosophie* (Stuttgart: Kohlhammer, 1953).

[36] Löwith, *Meaning in History*, 191.

[37] Löwith, *Meaning in History*, 6.

[38] Löwith, *Meaning in History*, 1.

[39] Löwith, *Meaning in History*, 5.

rational and scientific only on the surface. Under the surface they rely on eschatological hope and expectation—precisely because their vantage point is located in the future, which is empirically unavailable.[40]

The method of *Meaning in History* is loosely genealogical. Löwith reads the history of ideas backwards, starting from nineteenth-century philosophies of history and tracing the irrational element of futuristic utopia as far into the past as possible—ultimately to the biblical narrative of salvation. The Bible, occupying the final chapter of Löwith's book, is for him the silent origin of modern progressivism. It is the Bible that, for the first time, unifies temporal events into a coherent story of advancement by interpreting them from the perspective of the prophesied moment of salvation as their purpose and conclusion. Ancient Greeks and Romans knew nothing of last days and final events, of time as a finite linear movement toward a climactic horizon. As Löwith asserts with regard to Herodotus' *History*, for example, "the temporal scheme of the narrative is not a meaningful course of universal history aiming toward a future goal, but, like all Greek conception of time, is periodic, moving within a cycle."[41] Polybius and Lucretius were no exceptions. The monumental change in the consciousness of time, from cyclical recurrence to one-way (irreversible) time, arrives only with Judeo-Christian religion and in direct consequence of its salvationist dogma. According to Löwith, "the living toward a future *eschaton* . . . is characteristic only for those who live essentially by hope and expectation—for Jews and Christians," and in this vein "future and Christianity are indeed synonymous."[42]

Preceding the chapter on the Bible in Löwith's book are chapters on Saint Augustine and his pupil Paulus Orosius. If the authors of the Bible laid out the myth of salvation, Augustine and Orosius established its relevance to universal history. Speculations that biblical concepts were more than strictly figurative—that is, that they possessed historical significance—predate Augustine and Orosius; Löwith could easily have discussed Irenæus of Lyons or Eusebius of Cæsarea instead. Yet as a

[40] As Löwith stated elsewhere, "We 'know' the future only through belief and expectation." See his *Nature, History, and Existentialism, and Other Essays in the Philosophy of History*, ed. Arnold Levison (Evanston, Ill.: Northwestern University Press, 1966), 132.

[41] Löwith, *Meaning in History*, 7.

[42] Löwith, *Meaning in History*, 84. The point that the Judeo-Christian myth of salvation is directly responsible for transforming the cyclical consciousness of time into a progressive historical consciousness, and in this sense represents the latter's origin, has also been made by other secularization theorists discussed earlier, such as Patočka (*Kacířské eseje*, 77–80) and Berdyaev (*Meaning of History*, 33–35).

theologian of history, Augustine towers high above any of his precursors, contemporaries, and successors at least up to Thomas Aquinas. Augustine's monumental *City of God* (*De civitate Dei contra paganos*, written 413–426) set the paradigm for all subsequent Christian historical thinking. In Löwith's words, "Augustine's *City of God* is the pattern of every conceivable view of history that can rightly be called 'Christian.'"[43] In this pattern the biblical *civitas Dei*, the Kingdom of God prophesied to come at the end of time, represents the hidden meaning of every temporal event, including those that have yet to occur.

Löwith does not forget to stress, however, that Augustine refrained from predicting when the *civitas Dei* would arrive or, for that matter, *that* it would arrive. In Augustine's perspective, Löwith points out, "the City of God is not an ideal which could become real in history."[44] Redemption is for the great Doctor of the Latin Church exclusively an existential issue and a spiritual experience. Its possibility as a historical event is severely circumscribed. In Augustine's reading, eschatology (the biblical discourse about salvation) thus endows secular history with coherence and meaning, but the two do not intersect.

The crucial figure behind the closing of the Augustinian gap between the biblical story of salvation and the history of the human *sæculum* is for Löwith Joachim of Floris. In Joachim's "theological historism," as Löwith refers to the Cistercian monk's mode of biblical interpretation, the Bible becomes a road map of history and exegesis becomes cryptanalysis. With the proper key, which Joachim alleged to have received during his mystical union with God at Pentecost, the figurative categories of the Bible can be decoded to disclose the providential path of history to the Millennium. Whereas for Augustine the world moves toward salvation only subjectively, when pondered within the confines of the religious soul, for Joachim the movement is objective, taking place in the material order of existence. Biblical providence is immanent in the *sæculum* and unfolds as historical progress. In Löwith's words, "The real significance of the sacraments is not, as with Augustine, the signification of a transcendent reality but the indication of a potentiality which becomes realized within the framework of history."[45] The *civitas Dei* no longer lies beyond history for Joachim, but is nascent within history, which accommodates it and serves as a medium for its disclosure: "in his understanding," Löwith

[43] Löwith, *Meaning in History*, 166.
[44] Löwith, *Meaning in History*, 166.
[45] Löwith, *Meaning in History*, 151.

sums it up, "actual history . . . was nothing else than sacred history in terms of secular history."[46]

Thanks to Joachim's historical exegesis, Augustine's otherworldly *civitas Dei* thus began metamorphosing into an achievable ideal society, divine providence into secular progress, and religious faith into knowledge of the future. Löwith would no doubt have endorsed Voegelin's observation that "half-baked" secularization of eschatology commenced already in the Middle Ages: within Christianity itself and well before the birth of the modern age.[47] The mode of religious expectation changed accordingly: from Augustinian pessimism and resignation based on the awareness that history is a never-ending *series calamitatis*, to optimism and transformative revolutionary action undertaken by medieval sects such as the Franciscan Spirituals or the Adamites, Joachim's self-professed disciples, on behalf of the impending Millennium. To the extent that in Protestantism and Reformation the latter posture became a major force shaping Western modernity, Löwith referred to Joachim's *unio mystica* at Pentecost, which spurred Joachim to formulate his historical eschatology, as "a decisive moment in the history of the Church."[48] It set in motion a process whereby the myth of salvation gradually assumed a secular dimension and ultimately, centuries later, yielded modern narratives of progress: "it was the attempt of Joachim and the influence of Joachism which opened the way to these future perversions."[49] Next to the Bible, Joachim thus represents for Löwith the second principal source of nineteenth- and twentieth-century utopianisms.

Prior to Joachim, Löwith discusses a number of other great European thinkers, each more recent as one moves toward the beginning of the book: Bossuet, Vico, Voltaire, the French positivists (including Comte), Hegel, and Marx. However, the point that Löwith demonstrates time and again remains the same: that the various philosophies of history rest on authentically Christian assumptions about the nature of the historical process. The only difference is the extent of these assumptions. Some of the figures presuppose not only that history is progress to an ideal future, but also that this ideal future is the biblical Kingdom of God on earth and the progressive movement is divine providence. These openly Christian

---

[46] Löwith, *Meaning in History*, 147.

[47] See Voegelin's letter to Leo Strauss in *Faith and Political Philosophy: The Correspondence between Leo Strauss and Eric Voegelin, 1934–1964*, trans. and ed. Peter Emberley and Barry Cooper (Columbia: University of Missouri Press, 2004), 73.

[48] Löwith, *Meaning in History*, 146.

[49] Löwith, *Meaning in History*, 159.

thinkers include Bossuet and Hegel, who regarded world history as the progress of Spirit, Spirit as the Divine Idea, and his own philosophy as "the true *Theodicœa*, the justification of God in History."[50] Others retained only the first assumption, history as progress, and rejected the rest: their philosophies of history are Christian only structurally and hermeneutically, whereas the conscious message is non-Christian or anti-Christian. Marx epitomizes this latter group of thinkers. His commitment to utopia and history as a teleological process is patent, but the process as well as the *eschaton* are expressly irreligious: a materialist dialectic culminating in a universal community of atheists.

Insofar as all the philosophies of history are contaminated by Christian eschatology to some degree, however, Löwith concludes that "philosophy of history originates with the Hebrew and Christian faith in a fulfillment and . . . ends with the secularization of its eschatological pattern."[51] This process does not necessarily mean total de-Christianization, but primarily the bending of transcendental (Augustinian) eschatology *ad sæculum*: investing the allegorical, figurative categories of the biblical story of salvation with temporal, historical significance. Whether secularization is partial or total, whether it merely introduces the Augustinian *civitas Dei* in history (Joachim, Hegel) or goes further and also de-Christianizes eschatology, replacing the *civitas Dei* with an irreligious utopia (Voltaire, Marx), is of secondary importance: the resulting idea of progress may, but does not have to, profess atheism.[52] Both religious and irreligious narratives of progress are secularized salvationism for Löwith. In this vein, be it Christian overtly or covertly, "Western historical

---

[50] Georg W. F. Hegel, *The Philosophy of History*, trans. J. Sibree (Amherst, N.Y.: Prometheus Books, 1991 [1900]), 457. In Löwith's words (*Meaning in History*, 59), Hegel "translated the eyes of faith into the eyes of reason and the theology of history as established by Augustine into a philosophy of history which is neither sacred nor profane. It is a curious mix of both, degrading sacred history to the level of secular history and exalting the latter to the level of the first." Hegel thus effectively repeated the move performed by Joachim six centuries earlier: merged eschatology with temporal history. For a detailed analysis of Hegel's secularized theology of history, see Löwith, "Hegel and the Christian Religion," in idem, *Nature, History, and Existentialism*.

[51] Löwith, *Meaning in History*, 2.

[52] This is evident especially from Löwith's rendition of Joachim, Hegel, and the tradition of Protestant millennialists prepared by the former and epitomized by the latter, all of whom secularize biblical eschatology while remaining consciously and openly Christian.

consciousness is eschatological from Isaiah to Marx, from Augustine to Hegel, from Joachim to Schelling."[53]

Western historiography escapes the orbit of secularization only at the point of abandoning the various theological presuppositions about the nature of the historical process, such as the notion of a future end of history on the horizon of hope and expectation. Among the figures discussed in *Meaning in History*, only the nineteenth-century Swiss historian Jacob Burckhardt had accomplished this feat. This is why Löwith begins the volume with Burckhardt, who had carved out enough critical distance from the Bible to break its spell over his mind. Burckhardt did not concern himself with constructing an overarching philosophy of history: "Philosophy of history [was] to him a contradiction in terms, inasmuch as history co-ordinates observations, while philosophy subordinates them to a principle."[54] Having recognized the illusory nature of all narratives of progress, Burckhardt contended that nothing more could be said about history other than that it displayed continuity. In the absence of any solid principles endowing events in the world with unity and deeper meaning, he understood his task chiefly in terms of cultivating a "historical sense," which would allow him to impose on the chaos of events at least a temporary form—that of his own perspective.[55] To this extent it is possible to say that secularization has run its course with the appearance of what has been termed "impressionistic historiography."[56]

Secularization Theory
Vulnerable Areas

It is not difficult to identify areas of potential weakness in Löwith's argument: like any thesis, the secularization thesis is open to various

---

[53] Löwith, *Nature, History, and Existentialism*, 23. A useful summary of Löwith's overall argument is W. Emmerich, "Heilsgeschehen und Geschichte—nach Karl Löwith," *Sinn und Form* 46, no. 6 (1994): 894–915.

[54] Löwith, *Meaning in History*, 21. See also Löwith, *Jacob Burckhardt: Der Mensch inmitten der Geschichte* (Stuttgart: Kohlhammer, 1966).

[55] According to the contemporary American historical and literary theorist Hayden White, whose reading of Burckhardt displays striking similarities with Löwith's, "[Burckhardt's] intention was not to tell the *whole* truth about (history) but *one* truth. . . . He had abandoned the dream about telling the truth about the past . . . because he had long since abandoned the belief that history had any inherent meaning or significance." See White, *Tropics of Discourse: Essays in Cultural Criticism* (Baltimore, Md.: Johns Hopkins University Press, 1978), 44.

[56] White, *Tropics of Discourse*.

challenges. To begin with, one can question Löwith's selection of thinkers: why does he analyze the ones he does and not others? This is perhaps an easy criticism to make, but all figures covered in *Meaning in History* come from the continental European—especially French and German—tradition. Including key representatives of English-speaking philosophy, such as Locke or Hobbes, and demonstrating that they too espoused an idea of progress rooted in eschatological assumptions would have put Löwith's argument on firmer ground, albeit without altering its general Eurocentric bias.

Setting aside the issue of selection, one can also dispute how Löwith portrays each thinker chosen. With respect to Marx, for instance, Löwith's rendition of the teleological and deterministic character of historical materialism flies in the face of a sizeable portion of contemporary scholarship on Marxist thought, where these aspects are hotly debated.[57] At the very least, Löwith fails to notice the distinction, often made today, between scientific (orthodox) Marxism, committed to the notion of historical inevitability, and critical (western) Marxism, embracing a much more voluntaristic framework recognizing the role of spontaneity.[58] His treatment thus may be too simplistic, exuding the generally hostile attitude toward Marxism typical of the Cold War era.

A weightier, more serious challenge concerns the status of the Bible as the global origin of the linear-teleological conception of time. The assertion by Löwith and other secularization theorists that modern progress is a vestige of Judeo-Christian eschatology contains the narrower and often unarticulated claim that the genealogy of the idea of progress cannot be traced deeper than the Bible or to sources in other cultures and civilizations. To this extent, the success of secularization theory as a valid tool of historical interpretation depends on showing not only the logic of continuity between modern and biblical ideas about history, but also, and first, the *dis*continuity between biblical ideas on the one hand and pre- or nonbiblical ideas on the other. Neglecting this task leaves secularization theory vulnerable to, for instance, the criticism that Judaism and Christianity, much like modernity later on, appropriated an earlier tradition of historical thought, and that consequently the real

---

[57] See especially Raymond Williams, "Base and Superstructure in Marxist Cultural Theory," in *Problems in Materialism and Culture: Selected Essays* (London: NLB, 1989).

[58] For the distinction, see Antonio, "Critical Theory," 327–28, and Alvin W. Gouldner, *The Two Marxisms* (New York: Seabury Press, 1980), 45–51.

foundations of the modern idea of progress are not biblical, but ancient Greek or even older.[59]

In response to this challenge, however, it must be said that while Tuveson or Becker indeed ignored the issue, many other secularization theorists paid close attention to underscoring the authenticity of Judeo-Christian eschatology as a fresh start in thinking about time and history. As the preceding discussion of *Meaning in History* hints, Löwith in particular went to great lengths demonstrating the radical novelty of biblical consciousness against the background of its most immediate and influential predecessor: the classical Greek and Roman mindset. Manifest in Pythagorean, Stoic, and Platonic philosophy as much as in ancient historiography ranging from Herodotus and Thucydides to Polybius and Lucretius, this mindset regarded the immutable as far superior to that which varies. "The unchanging and everlasting, which surfaces year after year in the revolution of celestial bodies," Löwith observed in this vein, "embodied for the Greek mind a deeper truth and a higher interest than radical historical change."[60] Time was conceptualized accordingly: as the moving image of unmoving eternity, which it imitates by revolving in a cycle.[61] This cyclical consciousness ruled out the possibility of progress except on a fleeting, temporary basis: in due course, any improvement was bound to suffer a reversal. Charles Cochrane, whose seminal study *Christianity and Classical Culture* informs Löwith's analysis in *Meaning in History*, thus famously characterized the Greek and Roman perspective on time as a "self-defeating . . . process . . . like the oscillation of a pendulum."[62] What finally broke the cycle of eternal recurrence and

---

[59] According to Norman Cohn, "How Time Acquired a Consummation," in *Apocalypse Theory and the Ends of the World*, ed. Malcolm Bull (Oxford: Blackwell, 1995), 21, the discovery of one-way time and linear historical consciousness predates the Bible and occurred in ancient Iran under the prophet Zoroaster (c. 1400–1000 B.C.): "the first person to break out of [the] static view of the world and to tell of a coming consummation."

[60] Karl Löwith, "Christentum und Geschichte," *Numen* 2, no. 1 (1955): 152. See also idem, *Nature, History, and Existentialism*, 23; Charles-Henri Puech, "Gnosis and Time," in *Man and Time*, ed. Henry Corbin (New York: Routledge and Kegan Paul, 1957), 40–41; and J. B. Bury, *The Idea of Progress: An Inquiry into Its Origin and Growth* (New York: Macmillan, 1932), 10–11.

[61] Plato, *Timaeus*, trans. Benjamin Jowett (Indianapolis: Bobbs-Merrill, 1949), 37d. Cf. Puech, "Gnosis and Time," 40–41. Insofar as this conception implicitly denied that anything new ever happens in the world, Patočka ("Filosofie dějin," in *Péče o duši I*, 344) stated that classical thought "was non-historical in its basic metaphysical conceptions."

[62] Charles Norris Cochrane, *Christianity and Classical Culture: A Study of Thought and Action from Augustus to Augustine* (London: Oxford University Press, 1944), 468–69.

occasioned the rise of a new, linear consciousness of time was the Bible, specifically its insistence on the appearance of Jesus Christ as a singular event that took place once and once only.[63]

Löwith's sensitivity to these differences and his general attention to the classical mindset are no accident: a deep admirer of Greek philosophy, he was on one occasion described as a Stoic *"sceptico sereno"*[64] seeking to free Western modernity from eschatological consciousness and, as Jürgen Habermas has put it, "forge the path back to the ancient view of the world."[65] Even if Löwith and other proponents of the secularization thesis neglected to demonstrate the dramatic departure of Judeo-Christian eschatology from prior conceptions of time, however, it would not necessarily pose a problem for them. This is because the Bible's status as an authentic origin of linear historical consciousness has been defended in a variety of other fields such as anthropology and religious studies. The paradigmatic position of the Bible and Augustine's interpretation of its eschatological myth has been affirmed by, for example, Jaroslav Pelikan: "For the use of the idea of design in history," this preeminent historian of Christian doctrine avowed, "Western thought is fundamentally indebted to Augustine's *City of God*. . . . Augustine made the question of the pattern and meaning of history part of the agenda of Western modernity."[66] The influential Romanian anthropologist Mircea Eliade reached a similar conclusion, despite writing from a different disciplinary perspective.

---

[63] Based on this dogmatic postulate, and despite absorbing and openly praising a great deal of Platonic philosophy, Augustine flatly rejected Plato's definition of time: "Heaven forbid . . . that we should believe [the cyclical theory of world history]. 'For Christ died once for all our sins', and 'in rising from the dead he is never to die again.' . . . Let us keep to our straight way, which is Christ . . . and turn our minds from the absurd futility of [the] circular route of the impious." See Saint Augustine, *Concerning the City of God against the Pagans*, trans. Henry Bettenson (London: Penguin, 2003), 8.3–10.

[64] Dieter Heinrich, "Sceptico Sereno," in *Natur und Geschichte: Karl Löwith zum 70. Geburtstag*, ed. Hermann Braun and Manfred Riedel (Stuttgart: Kohlhammer, 1967). See also Matthias Bormuth, "Meaning in History—A Comparison between the Works of Karl Löwith and Erich Auerbach," *Religions* 3, no. 2 (2012): 156.

[65] Jürgen Habermas, "Karl Löwith: Stoic Retreat from Historical Consciousness," in *Philosophical-Political Profiles* (Cambridge, Mass.: MIT Press, 1983), 82.

[66] Jaroslav Pelikan, *The Mystery of Continuity: Time and History, Memory and Eternity in the Thought of Saint Augustine* (Charlottesville: University Press of Virginia, 1986), 140. According to Erich Dinkler, the revolutionary moment occurred already in Book XI of Augustine's *Confessions*, which is where "the Greek cyclical notion of time and history is definitively replaced with the linear, purpose-oriented, expectant notion of the Judeo-Christian perspective, laying the basis for the Christian conception of history." See Dinkler, "Augustins Geschichtsauffassung," *Schweizer Monatshefte* 34 (1954/55): 518.

His famous comparative analysis of ritual and symbolic responses to the transcultural problem of random evil—what Eliade called "terror of history"—led him to argue that it was the Bible and the Hebrew prophets who first "placed a value on history, succeeded in transcending the traditional vision of the circle, and discovered one-way time."[67] In its underlying assumption about Judeo-Christian eschatology as the origin of linear historical consciousness, the secularization thesis thus receives considerable support from this scholarship.

The same holds about other elements of the secularization thesis, which likewise dovetail with well-established, independently formulated positions in cognate fields. An example is the distinction between Augustine's transcendental reading of the myth of salvation on the one hand and Joachim's historical interpretation on the other, with the latter regarded as a major step in the metamorphosis of biblical eschatology into secular progress. This distinction features prominently in both Löwith's and Voegelin's accounts, but it is far from unique to them; scores of theologians and religious scholars have made it as well. Rosemary Radford Ruether, for instance, has observed with respect to Augustine's exegesis that "there is really no redeeming development in history *as* history" and that "no messianic reign of God [is] to be expected within history. . . . Messianic hope is split from social possibilities."[68] Others have argued similarly that for Augustine "there is no true 'progress' to be found in the course of human history"; that "there can be no talk of any . . . progressive victory of the *civitas Dei* over the *civitas terrena*"; that "no human action is capable of transforming the exile [of temporal history] into the [heavenly] home"; and that Augustine therefore "maintained a strict agnosticism toward all attempts to determine the time of the end."[69] In contrast, discussions of Joachim's exegesis stress that

[67] Mircea Eliade, *The Myth of the Eternal Return, Or, Cosmos and History*, trans. Willard R. Trask (Princeton, N.J.: Princeton University Press, 1991 [1949]), 104.

[68] Rosemary Radford Ruether, "Augustine and Christian Political Theology," *Interpretation* 29, no. 3 (1975): 262.

[69] These statements come, respectively, from Theodor E. Mommsen, "St. Augustine and the Christian Idea of Progress: The Background of the City of God," *Journal of the History of Ideas* 12, no. 3 (1951): 374; Christof Müller, *Geschichtsbewusstsein bei Augustinus: Onthologische, anthropologische und universalgeschichtlich/heilsgeschichtliche Elemente einer augustinischen "Geschichtstheorie"* (Würzburg: Augustinus-Verlag, 1993), 316; Ernst Schmidt, *Zeit und Geschichte bei Augustin* (Heidelberg: Carl Winter Universitätsverlag, 1985), 108–9; and Bernard McGinn, "The End of the World and the Beginning of Christendom," in *Apocalypse Theory*, ed. Bull, 62.

"Joachim expects . . . a new order of existence within history"[70] and that the future that will redeem humankind is "a historical future for [him], a future which can be physically experienced and temporally calculated."[71] Without this redefinition of the *eschaton* in historical terms, Judeo-Christian consciousness would have remained Augustinian and "Janus-faced," combining inward hope in salvation with outward pessimism about any prospects for gradual improvement in worldly affairs.[72] Consequently Jürgen Moltmann, the world's leading Protestant liberation theologian today, proclaimed that "ever since the Middle Ages, there is hardly anyone who has influenced European movements for liberty in church, state and culture more profoundly than [Joachim]."[73] This assessment parallels Löwith's and Voegelin's evaluation of the Cistercian abbot as a key figure in the genealogy of the modern idea of secular progress.[74]

In light of consonances such as these, it is not surprising that Löwith's book quickly garnered widespread recognition, enough of it to prompt worries that secularization theory was becoming the new orthodoxy about the origins of Western modernity. The popularity of Löwith's thesis was at least partially due to the timing of its publication. The complex yet lucidly written study culminated two decades of theorizing in which leading intellectuals such as Becker, Berdyaev, and Voegelin addressed the same subject with similar thoughts as they sought to explicate the sources of popular support for modern ideologies of salvation and utopia such as Nazism and Bolshevism. As a result of all these efforts, by the late 1950s the notion that the Enlightenment was in many respects a ruse, and that modern rationalism merely secularized medieval Christian theology, had become almost matter-of-fact among intellectual historians. Reinhart Koselleck appealed to this common notion when he proclaimed that "We know the process of secularization, which transposed eschatology into

---

[70] A. J. Conyers, "The Revival of Joachite Apocalyptic Speculation in Contemporary Theology," *Perspectives in Religious Studies* 12, no. 3 (1985): 202.

[71] Jürgen Moltmann, "Christian Hope: Messianic or Transcendent? A Theological Discussion with Joachim of Fiore and Thomas Aquinas," *Horizons* 12, no. 2 (1985): 331.

[72] Henri Irénée Marrou, "Das Janusantlitz der historischen Zeit bei Augustin," in *Zum Augustin-Gespräch der Gegenwart*, ed. C. Andresen (Darmstadt: Wissenschaftliche Buchgesellschaft, 1975), 1:358.

[73] Jürgen Moltmann, *The Trinity and the Kingdom* (San Francisco: Harper & Row, 1981), 203.

[74] The only difference is that whereas Moltmann emphasized exclusively Joachim's liberal legacy, Löwith and Voegelin were more sensitive to his role in also preparing illiberal and totalitarian variants of progress.

a history of progress."[75] Not everybody was as receptive, however. The opposition was spearheaded by Hans Blumenberg (1920–1996), whose attack on secularization theory remains unmatched in terms of both its breadth and depth.

Hans Blumenberg's Critique of the Secularization Thesis

Blumenberg is one of the heavyweights of twentieth-century continental social and historical theory; he has been described as an author whose "works . . . are comparable, for both path-breaking originality and widely recognized importance, only to the works of Jürgen Habermas."[76] His initial challenge to Löwith's thesis took place at the Seventh German Philosophy Congress held in 1962 under the theme "Progress," where Blumenberg rejected secularization as an adequate account of the genesis of the modern idea of progress and proposed a different narrative. His revision sought to demonstrate that the idea of progress was no vestige of Christian eschatology but a genuine break with the past, meaning that Western modernity was legitimate: equal to its self-description as *Neuzeit* ("new-time"). According to Blumenberg, the appearance of vestigiality and illegitimacy, the *leitmotif* uniting the writings of the secularization theorists, was due to an unfortunate but by no means inevitable historical development: degeneration of the original modern notion of progress, which was quite limited in its aspirations, into overambitious doctrines of universal salvation.

By 1966 Blumenberg had expanded this argument into a full-fledged study of the origins of Western modernity *in toto*, no longer restricting himself to the subject of progress, and he published the study under the title *The Legitimacy of the Modern Age.*[77] Scrupulously researched, highly imaginative, and both much less lucid and four times longer than Löwith's *Meaning in History*, the book was heavily reviewed by leading

[75] Reinhart Koselleck, *Critique and Crisis: Enlightenment and the Pathogenesis of Modern Society* (Cambridge, Mass.: MIT Press, 1988 [1959]), 10–11. "In the course of unfolding the Cartesian *cogito ergo sum* as the self-guarantee of a man who has dropped out of the religious bonds," Koselleck continued, "eschatology recoils into Utopianism."

[76] Robert M. Wallace, "Introduction to Blumenberg," *New German Critique* 32 (1984): 93.

[77] Blumenberg, *Die Legitimität der Neuzeit* (Frankfurt am Main: Suhrkamp, 1966). Between 1973 and 1976 Blumenberg expanded and reworked the study further. The edition used here is Hans Blumenberg, *The Legitimacy of the Modern Age*, trans. Robert M. Wallace (Cambridge, Mass.: MIT Press, 1983), the only English translation of the second and definitive German edition.

philosophers everywhere. Some of them found it thoroughly unconvincing. Hans-Georg Gadamer, for instance, reacted to Blumenberg's critique of secularization with frank puzzlement: "I am unable to follow . . . It seems to me . . . that the concept performs a legitimate hermeneutic function."[78] Others, however, were much more generous in their judgment, on one occasion even proclaiming Blumenberg's work "a death blow to the [secularization] thesis."[79]

Blumenberg's study consists of four parts; it is in the opening one, "Secularization: Critique of a Category of Historical Wrong," that he mounts his challenge to secularization theory. The preliminary tasks include specifying the meaning of the secularization thesis in historical theory and identifying its principal proponent. Secularization is for Blumenberg "[the] thesis that modern historical consciousness is derived from the secularization of the Christian idea of the 'salvation story' [Heilsgeschichte],"[80] and he associates it principally, though not exclusively, with Karl Löwith. Other names on the list include Koselleck and Schmitt. Blumenberg enters into several disagreements at once, but their crux is the same. As Alasdair MacIntyre has commented, in all of them Blumenberg advances the "unrestrictedly general claim that so radical are the differences between concepts specific to modernity and all theological concepts that the former cannot be understood as transformed versions of the latter."[81]

The ensuing critique consists of three criteria with which Blumenberg sets out to test the validity of the secularization thesis: "identifiability" (of the content of modern historical consciousness with the original Christian), "authentic ownership" (of the original content by Christianity), and "unilateral removal" (of the original Christian content by an agent outside it).[82] A study dedicated solely to secularization theory would have to scrutinize each in turn, but in the present context it is permissible to focus only on the first one, since this criterion is key in terms of both Blumenberg's emphasis and Löwith's subsequent response: identifiability as the criterion concerning the logic of continuity between Christian eschatology and

---

[78] Hans-Georg Gadamer, review of *Die Legitimität der Neuzeit*, by Hans Blumenberg, *Philosophische Rundschau* 15 (1968): 201.

[79] Martin Jay, *Fin-de-Siècle Socialism and Other Essays* (New York: Routledge, 1988), 159.

[80] Blumenberg, *Legitimacy*, 27.

[81] Alasdair MacIntyre, review of *The Legitimacy of the Modern Age*, by Hans Blumenberg, *American Journal of Sociology* 90, no. 4 (1985): 924.

[82] Blumenberg, *Legitimacy*, 24.

modern progressivism.[83] Blumenberg's thinking behind the criterion is as follows: unless Christian eschatology and modern progressivism share an identifiable substance of ideas, where Christian eschatology represents its original form and modern progress its new or secularized form, the secularization thesis fails precisely because there is nothing to have been secularized—no identifiable body of thought to have undergone the alleged transformation from the Christian epoch to the modern one. In such circumstances, modern philosophy of history may resemble biblical eschatology, but resemblance is where their relationship ends. There is no substantive bridge across the epochal divide and hence no genealogical connection between the two formations of thought.

To show that exactly this is the case, Blumenberg argues that the ideas surrounding modern progress are diametrically different from those associated with biblical eschatology. One example is the concrete shape of the end of history: "It is . . . a manifest difference," according to Blumenberg, "that an eschatology speaks of an event breaking into history, an event that transcends and is heterogeneous to it, while the idea of progress extrapolates from a structure present in every moment to a future that is immanent in history."[84] Whereas in Christian theologies of history the world terminates with a miraculous incursion from outside the temporal sequence, modern philosophies of history cast the consummation as inherent in the world and achievable from within. Moreover, the differences do not end here, in the definition of the *eschaton* as transcendent and beyond time in the one case and immanent and within time in the other. The postures toward the *eschaton* also diverge. Progress, Blumenberg contends, signifies "hopes for the greater security of man in the world," while "eschatology . . . was more nearly an aggregate of terror and dread."[85] Whereas Christian believers pondered the last things and final events trembling with fear, the founders of the modern age looked to the future with a measure of confidence stemming from the practical improvements that could

---

[83] In an essay summarizing the issues at stake between Löwith and Blumenberg, Robert Wallace similarly evaluated the first criterion as "central to Blumenberg's critique of Löwith" and gave it exclusive attention. See Wallace, "Progress, Secularization and Modernity: The Löwith–Blumenberg Debate," *New German Critique* 22 (1981): 69. Löwith recognized "the identity of expropriated and alienated substance in its historical metamorphoses . . . [as] the first and most important criterion for the legitimacy of any talk about secularization." Löwith, review of *Die Legitimität der Neuzeit*, by Hans Blumenberg, *Philosophische Rundschau* 15 (1968): 196.

[84] Blumenberg, *Legitimacy*, 30.

[85] Blumenberg, *Legitimacy*, 31.

be achieved through reason and science. Taken together, these disparities lead Blumenberg to conclude that the Christian and modern epochs do not share a common substance of ideas about history and that, consequently, progress cannot be secularized providence: "Regarding the dependence of the idea of progress on Christian eschatology, there are differences that . . . block any transposition of the one into the other."[86]

If modern progress does not derive from medieval eschatology, where does it come from? Proposing an alternative lineage of the idea, Blumenberg associates its origins with three phenomena: late-medieval theological nominalism, human "self-assertion" (*Selbstbehauptung*), and astronomy. Theological nominalism was embodied especially in the teachings of William of Ockham (c. 1287–1347) and generated a crisis of religious confidence by pushing the notion of God's transcendence and omnipotence beyond the limits of human intelligibility. Doctrinal needs, making God increasingly a matter of abstract logical proofs, inadvertently depersonalized him, severed the bond between him and the flocks of human believers, and left the latter feeling estranged, arbitrary, and irrelevant. This sparked the second phenomenon, human self-assertion: a project to carve out a niche in the world despite and regardless of God. "Deprived by God's hiddenness of metaphysical guarantees for the world," Blumenberg describes this development, "man constructs for himself a counterworld of elementary rationality and manipulability. . . . Because theology meant to defend God's absolute interest, it allowed and caused man's interest in himself and his concern for himself to become absolute."[87] The main representative of this new posture was Francis Bacon (1561–1626), whose pragmatic philosophy expressed, as Richard Rorty described it in his review of *The Legitimacy of the Modern Age*, "the attitude that says 'Who cares how things look to God? Let us find out how they can be made to work for us.'"[88] Finally, in the science

[86] Blumenberg, *Legitimacy*, 30.

[87] Blumenberg, *Legitimacy*, 173, 197. As Walter Sparn has commented, "[Blumenberg] explains . . . the [epochal] transition, wrongly described as 'secularization', in terms of unavoidable self-assertion of the human being against a theology that had become absolutist, disconnected from human concerns." "Hans Blumenbergs Herausforderung der Theologie," *Theologische Rundschau* 49, no. 2 (1984): 177. For a lucid summary of Blumenberg's explanation of the dynamic between theological nominalism and self-assertion, see also Bernard Yack, "Myth and Modernity: Hans Blumenberg's Reconstruction of Modern Theory," *Political Theory* 15, no. 2 (1987): 253–56.

[88] Cited in Laurence Dickey, "Blumenberg and Secularization: 'Self-Assertion' and the Problem of Self-Realizing Teleology in History," *New German Critique* 41 (1987): 152.

of astronomy, human self-assertion attained the concrete contours of the idea of progress. Copernican, Keplerian, and Galilean discoveries, along with their first successful practical applications in sea navigation and elsewhere, slowly solidified into the belief that humans might improve their lot in the world by bringing the processes of nature under their control. Blumenberg denotes this product of modern self-assertion as the idea of "possible progress," and he regards it as the source of the legitimacy of the modern age.

It needs to be re-emphasized that for Blumenberg "possible progress" differs vastly from any eschatological schemes of history. It too displayed a degree of transcendence, but according to Blumenberg this transcendence had nothing to do with religious assumptions or faith in dogma. Rather, it reflected the practical method underlying "possible progress": slow accretion and transmission of data that, in order to become perceptible, required observations exceeding individual lifetimes of those who performed them.[89] "Possible progress" was thus transcendent only in a very limited sense: only by virtue of representing, in Blumenberg's words, "a process that generates knowledge in a trans-subjective manner" and involves "the unity of methodologically regulated theory as a coherent entity developing independently of individuals and generations."[90] Unlike eschatology, "possible progress" did not allege to be universal in scope, nor did it profess certainty about any kind of future salvation. Instead, its scope was local, and its hopes for improvement were held in check by critical reason. Its yardstick for self-evaluation was not absolute knowledge about the overall plan of history, but practical success in discovering how the world can be made more secure for the human being.

Blumenberg could have ended his engagement with secularization theory here; he has rejected Löwith's thesis about the genesis of progress, and he has proposed a substitute lineage. What prevents him from resting his case, however, is the sheer weight of empirical evidence against his position: the great bulk of eighteenth- and nineteenth-century philosophy of history does in fact resemble biblical eschatology and not the concept of "possible progress." Recognizing this evidence, Blumenberg thus takes his argument a step further and gives it a subtle twist: he concedes

---

[89] As Blumenberg explained elsewhere, "From the standpoint of natural optics . . . what happens in the sky is nothing; only very long time frames allow us to assume value changes. . . . These time frames bear no relation to the human life span." "On a Lineage of the Idea of Progress," *Social Research* 41, no. 1 (1974): 8.

[90] Blumenberg, *Legitimacy*, 31, 33.

to Löwith that the universal metanarratives created by high moderns such as Comte, Hegel, or Marx are more or less thinly disguised salvationisms, and that what resides underneath their self-avowed rationality is dogma. However, Blumenberg differentiates these *de facto* theologies of history from his notion of "possible progress" and categorizes them separately under the rubric "necessary progress." This allows him to give his polemic against Löwith a new direction. From this point on, Blumenberg's critique becomes about writing a different history for the same outcome: explaining how and why the same result, "necessary progress," came about through a process different from that suggested by Löwith.

Instead of secularization, Blumenberg conceptualizes the history of the idea of "necessary progress" as something else: "functional reoccupation." As the term already hints, this alternative account rests on a particular theory of knowledge, in which Blumenberg distinguishes functional knowledge (variously termed as "functions," "questions," or "answer positions") from substantive knowledge ("substance," "content," "answers"). Christian eschatology was an aggregate of both. Functional knowledge was present in the form of the question "What is the meaning of history?" and the space or answer position created by this question was occupied with the corresponding content or answer: the *civitas Dei*. In other words, functional knowledge was present as the habitual presupposition that history had an end, and substantive knowledge as the idea that this end was the *civitas Dei*.

Blumenberg's central point in his revision of the transition from Christian eschatology to the idea of "necessary progress" is then as follows: "The continuity of history across the epochal threshold lies not in the permanence of . . . substances," as the secularization thesis alleges, but rather in "a functional reoccupation that creates the appearance of a substantial [*sic*] identity lasting through the process of secularization."[91] Modern philosophers successfully rejected the substantive idea that the *civitas Dei* was the end of history, but not the less obvious functional presupposition that history had an end to begin with. The belief in the transcendent *civitas Dei* fell victim to critical reason, but the belief in an *eschaton* (as a structural feature of historical narratives) escaped unharmed. It remained vacant in place and, according to Blumenberg, was swiftly reoccupied with a new answer: immanent social utopia as the content of modern philosophies of progress. In this sense, "the identity upon which the secularization thesis rests," Blumenberg declares, "is not

[91] Blumenberg, *Legitimacy*, 48, 60, 89.

one of contents but one of functions."[92] The authentic idea of "possible progress" thus collapsed into narratives of "necessary progress" under the burden of the surviving religious presuppositions about the nature of the temporal process—too deeply entrenched in European consciousness to be eliminated. "What . . . occurred in the process that is interpreted as secularization," Blumenberg summarizes his alternative history of modern progress, "should be described not as the *transposition* of authentically theological contents into secularized alienation from their origin but rather as the *reoccupation* of [functions] that had become vacant."[93]

Setting Blumenberg's lineage of the modern idea of "necessary progress" next to Löwith's, the crux of their dispute emerges with clarity: both consider "necessary progress" to have derived from eschatology, but Blumenberg does not deem the derivation to have been automatic or inevitable. He agrees with Löwith that in eighteenth- and nineteenth-century philosophy the idea of historical progress turned religious and dogmatic, but not that this outcome was bound to happen.[94] Whereas Löwith argues that modern historical consciousness largely conserved medieval eschatology and failed to generate any novel ideas of its own, Blumenberg insists that it did conceive revolutionary thoughts—only it miscarried them soon thereafter. There existed at one point a highly original notion of method-driven "possible progress," but over the period spanning the birth of modernity and its high noon this notion went awry: degenerated into the dogma of "necessary progress," on whose behalf it suffers from the appearance of inauthenticity and illegitimacy. The miscarriage occurred because modern philosophers exerted insufficient critical effort and succumbed to the pressure of concerns enunciated in the preceding age. Instead of amputating the inherited eschatological questions, they set about reanswering them through reason, forcing authentic rationality to perform a function for which it was ill-suited: the function of faith. In the process the avenues opened up by the idea of "possible progress" became obscured.

That Western historical consciousness took a wrong turn and abandoned these avenues shortly after discovering them does not, however, make the discovery illusory for Blumenberg. In his view, the failure of the idea of "possible progress" to survive in the long run does not make the idea any less real; miscarriage does not indicate that no conception

---

[92] Blumenberg, *Legitimacy*, 64.
[93] Blumenberg, *Legitimacy*, 65; emphasis original.
[94] Wallace, "Progress, Secularization and Modernity," 73.

took place at all. The appearance of modern philosophies of "necessary progress" and salvation was a historical accident. From Blumenberg's perspective, secularization theorists such as Löwith were too indiscriminate in their analysis of early modern philosophy to have noticed the revolutionary notion of "possible progress." Recovering it from underneath the cloud of Hegelian, Marxian, or Comteian eschatologies ultimately represents the main thrust of Blumenberg's effort in *The Legitimacy of the Modern Age*.

The Religious Agenda of Modern Self-Assertion

Does Blumenberg's critique of Löwith succeed? Does it undermine the secularization thesis as a valid account of the foundations of the modern idea of progress, in which case it would make no sense to apply it to Wilson's liberal internationalism or indeed any other ideology? Three separate but related points can be made in response to this question. The first concerns Blumenberg's theory of historical knowledge, especially his distinction between function and substance; the second concerns his recognition of "residual needs" as a major factor shaping the modern agenda; and the third relates to his reading of Christian eschatology. All three suggest that Blumenberg ultimately fails to discredit Löwith's thesis.

The problem with Blumenberg's theory of historical knowledge, which represents the backbone of his alternative lineage of "necessary progress," is that the dichotomy of function (question, answer position) and substance (content, answer) may be a false one. This is because functions implicitly communicate substantive ideas. In other words, it is possible to show that theological questions about history are simultaneously theological answers to yet more fundamental questions about history. The question of *what* the meaning of history is offers an excellent example. It not only asks something, but also simultaneously claims *that* history has meaning, which is a specifically Judeo-Christian answer to the still more basic and ulterior question concerning *what*, if anything, is worth knowing about history to begin with. Judeo-Christian theology in this sense taught the believer two substantive ideas, neither of which existed in Greece. One was that the *civitas Dei* was the end of history, and the other, concealed in the first, was that history had an end in the first instance: *eschaton* as the future moment of salvation.

Crucially, it is above all the latter (structural) idea that Löwith argues has survived into the modern era, not so much the former one. He does not necessarily contend that the transcendental *civitas Dei* made it across the epochal break, only that the *eschaton* did: the habit of comprehending history in terms of an eschatological narrative structure. Whether the salvation be transcendent or immanent, both the Christian and modern historical consciousness are eschatological and future-oriented. "The essential commonality," Löwith wrote in his reply to Blumenberg, "is that both live by hope insofar as they conceive of history as proceeding toward final fulfillment [*erfüllendes Ziel*] which lies in the future."[95] To the extent that Blumenberg grants this continuity too, his functional reoccupation model effectively converges with Löwith's secularization model.[96] If functions may be said to communicate hidden content, and if, as Blumenberg admits, theological functions survive into the modern age (where they are reoccupied), there exists a substantive connection between the two epochs after all. A more holistic theory of knowledge, where the dichotomy of function and substance is abolished, turns reoccupation of theological functions into secularization of theological substance.

It is not necessary to challenge Blumenberg's theory of historical knowledge, however, in order to suggest that his critique of Löwith falters. Even if one accepts the dichotomy of function and substance, there is a second area of weakness in Blumenberg's argument. It emerges after a closer examination of his explanation as to why "possible progress" ultimately collapsed back into "necessary progress" through functional reoccupation. Blumenberg, it was noted, finds the culprit in insufficient critical effort: modern philosophers of history theorized away God, but not the silent assumption of the overall meaning of history. The transcendent *civitas Dei* was removed as superstition, but the *eschaton* that it used to inhabit remained unproblematized, vacant, and available for subsequent reoccupation with various secular *ersatz* utopias. Yet insufficient critical effort is not the end of the story: a careful reading reveals a second, supplementary explanation, which is quite different from the

[95] Löwith, review of *Die Legitimität*, 199.

[96] Robert Pippin indeed found it difficult to distinguish between them, raising the question whether Blumenberg's argument is a critique at all: "the disanalogies between the eschatological and modern progressive views should cause no great concern to Löwith. He is not claiming that the modern notion of progress is Christian eschatology, but just that . . . [it cannot dispense] with a Christian *assumption* that human history as a whole must have some redeeming point to it. . . . Blumenberg agrees with a good deal of what Löwith and others claim. For all his criticism, he agrees that the modern view of progress . . . is a remnant of sorts of the premodern tradition. . . . A reader might wonder what could possibly be at stake in 'secularization' versus 're-occupation' models . . . if so much of the territory modernity 're-occupies' is, it is admitted, not its own." "Blumenberg and the Modernity Problem," *Review of Metaphysics* 40 (1987): 541–42.

first one. In an odd sentence that does not tie in with the surrounding text, Blumenberg adds: "I have represented [reoccupation] too one-sidedly as being due to a lack of critical intensity and have not referred often enough to the importance . . . of 'residual needs.'"[97] What he seems to be saying here is that the theological question of the meaning of history survived not only because of lazy minds and inadequate critique, but also because it was not really criticizable at the time. Its arbitrariness may be obvious today, but at the birth of the modern age, in the immediate after-math of the Christian tradition, this question was commonsense to such an extent that it did not even offer itself as a question. The question about the end of history was, as it were, unquestionable. It was so matter-of-fact that it was invisible and beyond inquiry: a deeply entrenched cognitive habit. Two millennia of Judeo-Christian theology had worked their effect, instilling artificial knowledge as natural.

Blumenberg's recognition of the deterministic weight of "residual needs" represents perhaps the single most damaging blow to his defense of the legitimacy of the modern age. This defense, it was seen, relies fundamentally on his ability to narrate the birth of the modern epoch in terms of the revolutionary idea of "possible progress" spawned during human self-assertion against God, but now Blumenberg effectively admits that, from the beginning, self-assertion had been contaminated and shaped by the surviving religious agenda—and that it could not have happened otherwise. It was impossible for even the most inquisitive and critical minds at the dawn of modernity to escape the residual biblical question about the end of history. From day one, "possible progress" had been formulated on the basis of eschatological assumptions about the structure of the historical process, which is to say that progress never was regarded merely as possible, but always as inevitable.

Expanding this argument, one can make the case that modern human self-assertion represented not a revolutionary turn away from God in protest to his unintelligibility, as Blumenberg suggests, but rather a conservative effort to find new, better proofs of God's existence *in this world*: rational-scientific proofs. What lends this case plausibility is, among other things, the fact that early modern science and philosophy are saturated with theological language and imagery persisting well into the late eighteenth century. This holds not only for figures such as Lessing, whom Blumenberg regards as bearing the main share of responsibility for inflating "possible progress" to theological proportions, but also for

---

[97] Blumenberg, *Legitimacy*, 65.

Francis Bacon, for Blumenberg the personification of authentic modern self-assertion. Even Bacon, reacting to the great scientific advancements in sea navigation and other areas of human activity that occurred during his lifetime, based his expectations of future scientific progress on a providential warrant: advancement of learning would occur "For so the prophet Daniel speaking of the latter times foretelleth."[98] Copernicus and Newton were no different: neither of them divorced their revolutionary intellectual undertakings from conservative concerns with providential design. Quite to the contrary: Newton penned not only *Opticks* and the famous *Principia Mathematica*, but also numerous theological manuscripts, including a 1733 treatise on the prophecies of Daniel and the Apocalypse of St. John.[99]

Blumenberg is aware of the theological imagery, but according to him the sacral expressions merely reflect linguistic deficiency at the beginning of the modern era. Bacon, Copernicus, and other founders of modernity simply lacked adequate vocabulary to express their revolutionary ideas, and so they made "recourse to the traditional stock of means of [theological] expression in constructing a secular terminology."[100] Blumenberg warns that this constancy of language should not be misinterpreted. The theological vocabulary was not intended to preserve theological ideas, but rather acted as a kind of Trojan horse in whose guise the new thinking could penetrate the old consciousness. Laurence Dickey calls it the "cover thesis": "[Blumenberg] seems to regard the recourse some moderns made to the vocabulary of theology as 'a cover' to 'mask' or 'hide' the radicalism of new modes of thought, value and behavior from their traditionally minded audiences."[101] If Bacon tied his idea of progress to biblical prophecies, he did not do it because of any lingering eschatological convictions. Rather, he was exploiting a rhetorical device in order to make the accumulation of scientific discoveries look legitimate.

In sharp contrast to Blumenberg's "cover thesis," however, one may rejoin that the theological vocabulary had a much different function: the founders of modernity used it sincerely and without any deeper agenda because they understood their self-assertion in religious terms, as a dialogue with God through a new medium, that of science and philosophy.

---

[98] Francis Bacon, *The Advancement of Learning* (Oxford: Clarendon, 1974), 78.

[99] See *Sir Isaac Newton's Daniel and the Apocalypse*, ed. William Whitla (London: Murray, 1922). That Newton turned to eschatology in search of the purpose of his celestial mechanics did not escape Löwith (*Meaning in History*, 237).

[100] Blumenberg, *Legitimacy*, 78.

[101] Dickey, "Blumenberg and Secularization," 161.

At best, Blumenberg preempts this issue; at worst, he actively miscon-
strues the constancy of religious expressions. For him the sacral language acted as a vehicle of revolution: helping authentic modern ideas
to infiltrate and conquer the residual Christian framework. He neglects
that the theological vocabulary could just as well have functioned as a
vehicle of conservation, and that it may be read as an accurate index
attesting to the fixation of the idea of progress to residual eschatological
assumptions.

This brings up the third problematic area of *The Legitimacy of the
Modern Age*, which concerns Blumenberg's reading of Christian eschatology: he represents it as exclusively transcendental (Augustinian) and
ignores its separate historical branch. Not a single mention is made in
the book of Joachim of Floris—an omission too conspicuous to go unnoticed in the extensively researched volume. The reason for the exclusion
is that in Joachim's historical theology, and in Protestant millennialism for which Joachim prepared the ground, the attachment of secular
progress to the biblical blueprint is patent: Joachim derived the idea of
historical progress from the Bible, and the various empirical "signs of
times" in turn confirmed to him the veracity of scriptural prophecies. In
the period surrounding the birth of modern science and philosophy, this
nexus of progress and providence remained intact and indeed became
tighter. The new scientific ideas combined with preexisting theological
concerns to such an extent that "to many seventeenth-century thinkers,
[science and theology] merged into one idiom, part of a veritable secular
theology."[102] Protestantism represented a major force behind this development. By questioning the necessity of the mediating priestly hierarchy,
it democratized religion and opened the sphere of doctrinal concerns to
laypersons—including and above all scientists, who promptly picked up
the question about the meaning of history and set about answering it
with rational methods.[103] In this vein, "the seventeenth-century founders of modern science and philosophy had theological commitments

---

[102] Amos Funkenstein, *Theology and Scientific Imagination from the Middle Ages to
the Seventeenth Century* (Princeton, N.J.: Princeton University Press, 1986), ix.

[103] "Theology," Funkenstein adds (*Theology and Scientific Imagination*, 3–5),
"became 'secularized' in many parts of Europe in the . . . sense of . . . appropriated by
laymen," and "also in the sense that it was oriented toward the world, *ad sæculum*. . . .
[Protestantism] encouraged the sacralization of the world, even of 'everyday life.' Human
labor *in hoc sæculo* was not perceived anymore as a mere preparation for the future life; it
acquired its own religious value in that, if well done, it increases God's honor."

which shaped their whole enterprise."[104] The surviving religious agenda of seeking universal, timeless, and objective knowledge, what Toulmin calls the "Quest for Certainty," oriented the lines of scientific inquiry from the outset.

Acknowledging Joachim's historical exegesis and the idea of secular progress formulated under his influence by the ensuing tradition of Protestant millennialism would force Blumenberg to confront the unhappy recognition that modern self-assertion was frequently intended to conserve and augment theology, not to undermine it. Early modern scientists and philosophers did not adhere to religious expressions cunningly and as a cover, as Blumenberg would have it, but often honestly. Newton did not write a treatise on biblical prophecies in order to sell his physics to an audience still under the spell of the Scriptures, but because he comprehended his scientific activity in spiritual terms: as decoding God's mind and the course of divine providence.[105] In this vein, it is dubious whether the founders of modernity conceived any idea of "possible progress" divorced from biblical presuppositions, as Blumenberg alleges, and if they did not, the secular theologies of "necessary progress" cannot be said to have come about through the corruption of "possible progress." Modern philosophy did not miscarry when it inflated the idea of progress to eschatological proportions. It was born that way.

Secularization as a Valid Tool
of Historical Interpretation

Secularization theory remains a hotly contested area among intellectual historians, but within the confines of the debate between Karl Löwith and Hans Blumenberg the critique advanced by the latter seems to fall short of discrediting the claims advanced by the former. To this extent, Löwith's thesis that modern philosophies of progress stand on eschatological presuppositions remains a compelling optic for analyzing modern historical consciousness. Blumenberg's alternative reoccupation thesis essentially agrees that biblical assumptions, called "functions" in Blumenberg's

---

[104] Stephen Toulmin, *Cosmopolis: The Hidden Agenda of Modernity* (Chicago: University of Chicago Press, 1990), 37.

[105] Cf. Toulmin's comment (*Cosmopolis*, 105, 110) that Newton's scientific ideas "were shaped by a concern for intellectual coherence with a respectable picture of God's material creation, as obeying Divine laws. . . . The 'laws of nature' were a material expression of God's Will and Wisdom for the world: in revealing the laws by which nature operates, scientists saw themselves as doing God's work—even reading His mind."

narrative, survived into the modern era and shaped its ideas about history in decisive ways.

However, this is not the only conclusion worth making here. In the process of examining the Löwith-Blumenberg debate, two additional points have become apparent. The first is that rather than to lump all modern philosophies of progress under the same heading of secularized eschatology—a situation that currently places religious narratives (such as Hegel's) side by side with irreligious ones (such as Marxism)—it may be fitting to fine-tune the concept by introducing a distinction. Instead of secularization plain and simple, it may be more appropriate to break the category down into a couple of more discrete subcategories: partial or first-degree secularization and complete or second-degree secularization. The former would encompass those modern philosophies of progress that preserve the Christian conception of history in their form and function as well as, still, in their conscious content. In other words, it would encompass religious progressivisms that secularize the biblical story of salvation only in the limited sense of immanentizing the transcendent (Augustinian) *civitas Dei* within the historical world as a goal of moral, political, and technological striving. The latter subcategory, complete secularization, would then refer to progressivisms that allege to have abandoned the Bible and no longer consciously retain any religious content. The Christian idea of history remains present in these only in the subterranean and hermeneutical sense—that is, only in their structural and functional aspects—while their surface message is non- or anti-Christian. Such philosophies of progress not only immanentize the otherworldly *civitas Dei*, but in addition sever it from its biblical origin and present the end of history as a scientific utopia that is unrelated to religion or indeed, as in Marxism, presupposes the disappearance of religion.

The second point is that products of partial or first-degree secularization—that is, modern philosophies of progress that remain consciously Christian in their content—are especially safe from Blumenberg's critique. This is because they meet Blumenberg's own test of secularization, a test based heavily on the requirement that modern progressivism must be shown to possess the same substance of ideas about history as Christian eschatology. It is not even necessary to challenge the framework of Blumenberg's critique to defend their status as secularized eschatology. They succeed within his terms—which is why Blumenberg silently leaves them out of his book.[106] In this vein, one is on particularly solid

---

[106] As Martin Jay has observed, Blumenberg's claim that medieval eschatology and

ground when applying the concept of secularized eschatology to modern doctrines of progress and utopia formulated on the basis and in the language of Protestant millennialism.

The significance of this point emerges when one turns attention to what lies ahead. From New England Puritanism in the seventeenth century to Woodrow Wilson's Social Gospel at the beginning of the twentieth, the American idea of progress to peace, liberty, and prosperity flowed precisely out of religious (predominantly Protestant) principles, as their secular or political manifestation. It will be seen that Wilson comprehended politics fundamentally in terms of faith enacted in practice, and that his idea of national and international progress grew out of his Presbyterian millennialism. The Löwith-Blumenberg debate thus not only suggests that secularization is a valid tool with which to analyze modern historical consciousness, but also hints that the explicit religious content of Wilson's idea of progress makes him eminently suitable for this kind of analysis.

---

modern progressivism share no substance of ideas "underplays the persistence of another, more optimistic Christian tradition which may well have anticipated the later doctrine of progress. . . . [T]he millenarianism associated with figures like Joachim of Fiore, a figure strangely ignored by Blumenberg, may still be accounted a substantialist rather than merely functionalist link with secular utopias of the modern age." Review of *The Legitimacy of the Modern Age*, by Hans Blumenberg, *History and Theory* 24, no. 2 (1985): 192. Cf. Dickey's conclusion ("Blumenberg and Secularization," 164) that the strength of Blumenberg's argument "lies in its capacity to persuade the readers that the Christian eschatological tradition is wholly Augustinian ('theocentric') and never synergistic and accommodationist ('egocentric')," as in Joachim's historical theology.

CHAPTER TWO

SECULARIZATION AND TOTALITARIAN MOVEMENTS

Probing the Limits of the Concept

The secularization thesis in many ways boils down to the insight that modern philosophies of progress are impossible without certain presuppositions about the nature of the historical process that originate in Judeo-Christian eschatology. Some progressivisms retain these presuppositions explicitly, remain loyal to the Bible, and secularize the myth of salvation only in the limited sense of reinterpreting the originally transcendent *civitas Dei* in historical terms: as a possibility lying within the scope of human achievement. Others go a step further, reject the Bible, and replace the *civitas Dei* with a non- or antireligious utopia. In such ideologies, of which Marxism represents a prominent example, biblical foundations are hidden and unconscious, implicit in lingering structural assumptions, such as that history is teleology. Regardless of whether modern progressivisms secularize biblical eschatology partially or completely, however, they all contain a measure of religious dogma.

This insight opens up the possibility of interpreting Wilson's liberal idea of progress as secularized eschatology, but before performing this interpretation it is worth noting that traditionally secularization theory has been used almost exclusively on totalitarian and illiberal ideologies, not liberal ones.[1] The concepts of totalitarianism and secular (political)

---

[1] This is not to deny the existence of literature on political theology as it relates to

religion share extensive bridges and tend to be regarded as two parallel categories for analyzing twentieth-century dictatorships. This fixation of secularization theory on totalitarianism, what may be called the secular-ization-totalitarianism nexus, raises the question of whether it is legiti-mate to extend secularization theory to liberal progressivisms in the first place. In addition, political religion historiography is also heavily skewed toward non- and antireligious movements and ideologies, implicitly rais-ing a second important issue: is secularization theory applicable to reli-gious ideas of progress? After all, one might ask, how could an ideology possibly be both religious and secularized at the same time?

Both of these objections are directly relevant to any attempt at a sec-ularization analysis of Wilson's progressive "New Diplomacy" and the broader tradition of American liberal-republican millennialism exempli-fied by it. Wilson was nothing if not a patriotic American liberal and a deeply devout Presbyterian in whose understanding progress, liberty, and religion were inseparable: "Let no man suppose that progress can be divorced from religion," he declared on one occasion, adding on another that he "could not imagine liberty in a world in which there was no prog-ress."[2] Therefore, it is necessary to probe the analytical limits of secular-ization theory, scrutinize these objections, and determine whether they are valid. What will emerge is that neither the secularization-totalitarianism nexus nor the fixation on irreligious ideologies is justified; ample space exists within secularization theory to accommodate other modern narra-tives of progress and perfection, including liberal and religious ones. The neglect of these narratives by current political religion historiography reflects insufficient attention to the subtleties of secularization theory: the general scope of Löwith's thesis and the fact that secularization does not necessarily mean de-Christianization.

---

the liberal nation-state. Notable recent examples include Giorgio Agamben, *The King-dom and the Glory: For a Theological Genealogy of Economy and Government*, trans. Lorenzo Chiesa and Matteo Mandarini (Stanford: Stanford University Press, 2011); Charles Taylor, *A Secular Age* (Cambridge, Mass.: Belknap, 2007); and Hent de Vries and Lawrence E. Sullivan, eds., *Political Theologies: Public Religions in a Post-Secu-lar World* (New York: Fordham University Press, 2006). However, this literature is not informed by Karl Löwith's classic statement of the secularization thesis in *Meaning in History: The Theological Implications of the Philosophy of History* (Chicago: University of Chicago Press, 1949).

[2] See, respectively, Woodrow Wilson, "Address in Denver on the Bible" (May 7, 1911), in *The Papers of Woodrow Wilson*, ed. Arthur S. Link et al. (Princeton, N.J.: Princeton University Press, 1966–1994) [henceforth *PWW*], 23:20, and Wilson, "Lecture on Democracy" (December 5, 1891), in *PWW* 7:363, 365.

Historical Origins of the
Secularization-Totalitarianism Nexus

The beginnings of secularization theory, it was seen, roughly correspond to the aftermath of World War I. Löwith, who fought in the Prussian army and sustained heavy wounds, had barely returned from his Italian captivity when he enrolled at the University of Freiburg and started formulating the root ideas for his *Meaning in History*. Berdyaev, who saw the Great War bring down the tsar in Russia, published his *Meaning of History* in 1932, and Voegelin first used the term "political religion" in an essay written in 1938.[3] By turning the fruits of modern reason, science, and technology to destructive purposes, the Great War rid modern European civilization of its innocence and naivete: it shattered the nineteenth-century belief in progress, stripped it of its previous appearance as something natural and commonsense, and prompted its critical re-examination. The attempts by Löwith, Berdyaev, Voegelin, and others to explain the origins of this belief may be understood as part of a wider European intellectual effort to come to grips with the defunct cultural heritage of the past.

Simultaneously with the philosophical inquiry into the foundations of the modern faith in progress, the Great War initiated another, different development in Europe: the rise of a new regime type, one so unprecedented that it was impossible to describe with the existing vocabulary of political theory. While traditional terminology could still accommodate Salazar's and Franco's rule in Spain, Piłsudski's government in Poland, and perhaps even Mussolini's fascism in Italy, Soviet Bolshevism and German National Socialism defied all available conceptual frameworks and rendered them obsolete. The ideologies of permanent revolution under whose banner Lenin, Stalin, and Hitler set upon the path of terror, mass violence, systematic liquidation of enemies, territorial expansion, and war engendered the frightening recognition that Europe had entered an entirely novel political era.

Scholarly and literary circles quickly spawned a multitude of concepts in an attempt to define the new phenomenon. Some of these, such as dictatorship, tyranny, and Caesarism, sought to revive and reintroduce older categories, but their semantic borders proved too restrictive. For instance, the notion of dictatorship, rooted in Roman constitutional theory, was too intertwined with notions of legality, state, and administrative rule: it tended to signify merely a passing disturbance to an established and in principle respected political order, and as such it could not

---

[3] Eric Voegelin, *Die politischen Religionen* (Vienna: Bermann-Fischer, 1938).

accommodate the temporally and spatially unlimited dynamic of revolution displayed by the new regimes.[4] Tyranny was equally inadequate. Its emphasis on subjective evil embodied in the figure of the tyrant obscured the degree to which violence had become anonymous and impersonal in the new despotisms, part and parcel of their organizational structure.

Classic concepts thus yielded to neologisms, among which "totalitarianism" soon achieved predominance. Coined in the early 1920s by clerical Italian antifascists such as Giovanni Amendola and Luigi Sturzo in reference to Mussolini's regime, the term was quickly picked up by the German thinker Waldemar Gurian, a conservative Catholic celebrated by his contemporaries for his uncompromising realism and deep contempt for all sorts of perfectionists.[5] Gurian promptly redirected the notion of totalitarianism first at Bolshevism and, after 1933, expanded it to cover Nazism as well.[6] By the late 1930s the concept had gained widespread currency, which was reinforced after World War II by a generation of major theorists such as Raymond Aron, Carl Friedrich, and Hannah Arendt. Thanks to their works, and reflecting a broader need for a popular catchphrase with which to denounce the Soviet adversary during the Cold War, totalitarianism became part of everyday vocabulary in the West.

Crucially, from the very beginning theories of totalitarianism incorporated the notion of secularized eschatology as one of the hallmark features of the new regimes. The resort to secularization analysis is apparent already in the work of Gurian, founder of totalitarianism as a theoretical approach by virtue of having systematized the first tentative references to the term. "The various forms of totalitarianism," Gurian stated with respect to Nazism and Soviet Communism, "are politico-social secularized religions, characteristic of our epoch."[7] Gurian's most notable successors after his premature death in 1954, including Aron, Friedrich, and

---

[4] Hans Maier, " 'Totalitarismus' und 'politische Religionen': Konzepte des Diktaturvergleichs," *Vierteljahrshefte für Zeitgeschichte* 43, no. 3 (1995): 390.

[5] Hannah Arendt, *Men in Dark Times* (New York: Harcourt, Brace & World, 1968), 261.

[6] See especially Gurian, *Der Bolschewismus: Einführung in Geschichte und Lehre* (Freiburg: Herder, 1931), and idem, *Der Kampf um die Kirche im Dritten Reich* (Luzern: Vita nova, 1936). Cf. Maier, " 'Totalitarismus' und 'politische Religionen,'" 391–96.

[7] Gurian, "Totalitarianism as Political Religion," in *Totalitarianism*, ed. Carl J. Friedrich (Cambridge, Mass.: Harvard University Press, 1954), 122. See also idem, "Totalitarian Religions," *Review of Politics* 14, no. 1 (1952): 3. Cf. Heinz Hürten, "Waldemar Gurian und die Entfaltung des Totalitarismusbegriffs," in *Totalitarismus und Politische Religionen: Konzepte des Diktaturvergleichs*, ed. Hans Maier and Michael Schäfer (Paderborn: Schöningh, 1996) 1:68–70.

Arendt, followed suit: all of them registered the *ersatz*-religious quality of Nazism and Bolshevism and incorporated secularization in their definitions of totalitarian dictatorship.

Aron's work illustrates the conceptual bridges between totalitarianism and secularization theory especially well. This conservative French sociologist and historian employed secularization theory as early as 1939 and considered himself the father of the term "secular religion" (in his later terminology also "temporal religion").[8] He had written several essays utilizing the concept.[9] His definition of it appeared in an article published in *La France libre* in 1944: "I propose to call 'secular religions' the doctrines that in the soul of our contemporaries take the place of a vanished faith and situate . . . humanity's salvation . . . in this world, in the distant future, in the form of a social order that has to be created."[10] This definition displays clear overlaps with the secularization theories of Löwith or Voegelin; indeed, the latter served Aron as a direct inspiration.[11] Aron saw totalitarian ideologies as surrogate religions erected on the remnants of Christianity and reorienting its eschatological hope toward worldly utopias. In *The Opium of the Intellectuals* (1957), he thus discussed Marxism, Nazism, and their theorists and practitioners using categories such as "Church," "Churchmen," and "faith."[12] The very title of Aron's classic book is a pun intended to highlight the religiosity of the Marxist ideology: Marx famously stated that traditional Christian religion is the opiate of the people, and Aron now subjected Marxism to the same criticism. Despite its surface rationality and atheism, its foundations were theological. Reproducing Löwith's thesis almost verbatim, Aron was unequivocal that "philosophies of history are secularized theologies."[13] In Marxism he saw a "religion of hyperrationalism."[14]

---

[8] Brigitte Gess, "Die Totalitarismuskonzeption von Raymond Aron und Hannah Arendt," in *Totalitarismus und Politische Religionen*, ed. Maier and Schäfer, 1:264–65.

[9] Many of them are collected under "Les Religions Séculières" in Aron, *Une histoire du vingtième siècle*, ed. Christian Bachelier (n.p.: Plon, 1996), 139–222.

[10] Aron, "L'avenir des religions séculières," in *Une histoire*, 153.

[11] Gess, "Totalitarismuskonzeption," in *Totalitarismus und Politische Religionen*, ed. Maier and Schäfer, 1:264–65.

[12] Aron, *The Opium of the Intellectuals*, trans. Terence Kilmartin (Garden City, N.Y.: Doubleday, 1957), especially chap. 9, "The Intellectuals in Search of a Religion." See also idem, *Democracy and Totalitarianism* (London: Weidenfeld & Nicolson, 1968).

[13] Aron, *Opium*, 149.

[14] Aron, "L'avenir des religions séculières," in *Une histoire*, 155. Cf. Alain Besançon's thesis about the religious foundations of the Leninist doctrine: "From Schelling, and above all from Hegel on, one can say that . . . there occurred a rationalization of Gnostic

Concurrently with Aron, the long-time Harvard professor Carl Friedrich, another leading conservative critic of totalitarianism during the Cold War, evaluated Marxism in identical terms: "One might return the argument [of Marx who spoke of religion as the 'opiate of the people'] by suggesting that through Marx history has become the opiate of the proletariat and more especially of its communist elite."[15] Soon after delivering this assessment, Friedrich enlarged its scope beyond the Marxist movement to totalitarianism *per se*, which he defined as consisting of six basic elements. Among these, Friedrich placed official ideology at the very top of the list, and it was an eschatological ideology: a grand narrative of progress "focused and projected toward a perfect final state of mankind" and containing "a chiliastic claim, based upon a radical rejection of the existing society and conquest of the world for a new one."[16] This ideology was so indispensable, according to Friedrich, that without it totalitarianism was unthinkable, and it derived from the Bible. Any narrative "which depicts history as the unfolding of a meaningful progression toward a goal that is shown to be the destiny of mankind" struck Friedrich, echoing the secularization thesis, as "most improbable except in conjunction with God. . . . The philosophy of history is a dimension of religious faith."[17]

In Friedrich's perspective, the eschatological structure of totalitarian ideologies was the main source of their popular appeal: in the context of secular European modernity, they offered new visions of salvation and utopia in place of the defunct *civitas Dei* of traditional Christianity. Friedrich captured the dialectical substitution using language reminiscent of Hans Blumenberg's "functional reoccupation" model: "When the theological explanations become untenable as a result of the decline of religious faith . . . 'secular religions' . . . fill the vacuum."[18] Friedrich placed special emphasis on the functional link between biblical eschatology and modern progress: the two fulfilled the same spiritual and psychological needs, so that "when the faith in a personal God declines, the philosophy

---

esotericism, or that modern rationalism was 'esotericized.'" *The Rise of the Gulag: Intellectual Origins of Leninism*, trans. Sarah Matthews (New York: Continuum, 1977), 42.

[15] Friedrich, "Religion and History," *Confluence: An International Forum* 4, no. 1 (1955): 114.

[16] Carl J. Friedrich and Zbigniew Brzezinski, *Totalitarian Dictatorship and Autocracy* (Cambridge, Mass.: Harvard University Press, 1956), 9, 13.

[17] Friedrich, "Religion and History," 106.

[18] Friedrich and Brzezinski, *Totalitarian Dictatorship*, 88.

of history can actually take the place of religion."[19] For Friedrich the real origin of totalitarianism, then, was modern nihilism and the desperate search for new, secular idols of worship in post-Christian Europe. Totalitarian leaders garnered legitimacy for policies of destruction, genocide, and war because their utopian ideologies responded to the deep-seated desires previously cultivated and satisfied by biblical eschatology, above all the desire for the meaning of history.

Even Hannah Arendt, perhaps the most famous of all Cold War theorists of totalitarianism, recognized the process whereby ideologies of progress and salvation replaced biblical eschatology as its modern surrogates. Her affinity with secularization theory is not immediately obvious. Indeed, Arendt exuded a markedly hostile attitude toward the concept of political or secular religion and vigorously combated any and all interpretations of Nazism and Bolshevism utilizing it.[20] One will not find in her voluminous writings any mention of secularized eschatology.[21] Arendt avoided the term because her understanding of secularization diverged from that at the heart of the secularization thesis. "Secularization as a tangible historical event," she explained her view, "means no more than separation of Church and State, of religion and politics."[22] This definition makes no assertion about the dialectical substitution of transcendent Christian eschatology with modern narratives of this-worldly perfection. "Whatever the word 'secularization' is meant to signify in current usage," Arendt stated in this respect, "it cannot be equated with worldliness; modern man . . . did not gain this world when he lost the other world."[23]

Nonetheless, moving past semantic differences to the substance of Arendt's arguments, there can be no doubt that she regarded totalitarianism as modern *ersatz* for lost Christianity. This emerges clearly from her discussion of the psychological appeal of totalitarian regimes: the key

[19] Friedrich and Brzezinski, *Totalitarian Dictatorship*, 88.

[20] This is evident from, e.g., her correspondence with the French sociologist Jules Monnerot, who supported the concept. See Peter Baehr, *Hannah Arendt, Totalitarianism, and the Social Sciences* (Stanford: Stanford University Press, 2010), 6, 13.

[21] Gess, "Totalitarismuskonzeption," in *Totalitarismus und Politische Religionen*, ed. Maier and Schäfer, 1:270.

[22] Arendt, *The Human Condition* (Chicago: University of Chicago Press, 1958), 255.

[23] Arendt, *The Human Condition*, 320. In this vein, Elizabeth Brient argued that it was not worldliness, but world*loss* (*Entweltlichung*), what Arendt meant by "secularization." "Hans Blumenberg and Hannah Arendt on the 'Unworldly Worldliness' of the Modern Age," *Journal of the History of Ideas* 61, no. 3 (2000): 515.

to their success lay precisely in their ability to fill the spiritual vacuum created by the decline of traditional religion. "[Their] language of prophetic scientificality," Arendt noted, "corresponded to the needs of the masses who had lost their home in the world and now were prepared to be reintegrated into eternal, all-dominating forces which by themselves would bear man, the swimmer on the waves of adversity, to the shores of safety."[24] Aside from restoring in atomized individuals a sense of belonging by binding them together in a new type of church organized on the basis of, respectively, class and race, Bolshevism and Nazism reassured them that behind the flux of everyday existence there was hidden order and purpose. Their allegedly scientific laws of history, what Arendt called "suprasense," replicated the role previously played by God's providence: rendering the accidental meaningful by translating all instances of random evil into ultimately positive expressions of a deeper plan of salvation.[25] To this extent Arendt, much as Friedrich, effectively portrayed totalitarian ideologies as functional replacements for Christian eschatology, repeatedly drawing attention to the religious imagery pervading the totalitarian "style."[26]

As a term of political theory, totalitarianism was thus born with the notion of secularized eschatology as part of its genetic makeup, and the nexus was cemented throughout the Cold War. From Gurian to Aron to Arendt, luminaries trying to come to grips with Nazism and Bolshevism tended to regard totalitarianism as a phenomenon reflecting and exploiting the human religious impulse in the context of a widespread crisis of traditional faith, a symptom of modernity. The drive to replace the biblical Heaven with a human-made heaven on earth struck them as theologically blasphemous, philosophically farcical, and above all—in light of the policies of mass exclusion, murder, and destruction inspired by it—as tragic.

---

[24] Arendt, *The Origins of Totalitarianism* (New York: Harcourt, Brace & World, 1966 [1951]), 350.

[25] Arendt, *The Origins of Totalitarianism*, 352, 458.

[26] That she nonetheless opposed the secularization thesis reflected her aversion to sociology in general and functionalist analysis in particular, which she deemed scandalously insensitive to idiosyncrasies differentiating concrete historical phenomena. Above all, it reflected her trenchant belief that totalitarianism was a uniquely twentieth-century phenomenon, a belief that required her to deny its continuity with anything in the past. See Baehr, *Arendt, Totalitarianism, and Social Sciences*, 19.

The Secularization-Totalitarianism Nexus
in Current Historiography

Concurrently with the evolution of theories of totalitarianism, the frequent resort to the concept of secularized eschatology generated an important byproduct: the supposition that only authoritarian movements represent the proper subject for secularization analysis. Cultivated throughout the Cold War era, this supposition has survived to the present day. Following scholarly precedents reaching all the way back to the 1930s and 1940s, current applications of secularization theory continue to restrict themselves to illiberal regimes and dictatorships, thereby reaffirming and further solidifying the preestablished conceptual bond between totalitarianism and secularization theory.

This ongoing bond is discernible already from the original name and content of the journal established in 2000 to serve as the main arena for current political religion historiography: *Totalitarian Movements and Political Religions*. The journal's title, aims, and scope have broadened since its inception and currently encompass such non-Western phenomena as Ba'athism and Islamism.[27] However, the initial focus was overwhelmingly on totalitarian and authoritarian movements in twentieth-century Europe, especially German Nazism, Italian Fascism, and Soviet Bolshevism, and these continue to make regular appearances to this day.[28] This intellectual agenda is in no small measure the legacy of Emilio Gentile, Michael Burleigh, and Roger Griffin, the journal's founding editors and frequent contributors, who were and remain primarily students of modern mass dictatorship. All three have employed the optic of political religion in the course of researching totalitarian and authoritarian politics in interwar Europe, with Gentile specializing in Italian Fascism, Burleigh in the Third Reich, and Griffin in generic fascism.[29] Much as during the Cold War, secularization theory thus continues to be confined to totalitarian

[27] The current title of the journal is *Politics, Religion & Ideology*.

[28] This is clearly apparent from the back issues. For a complete list of articles, see the journal's homepage at http://www.tandf.co.uk/journals/authors/ftmpauth.asp [accessed June 1, 2012].

[29] For main examples of their early work, see Emilio Gentile, "Fascism as Political Religion," *Journal of Contemporary History* 25, no. 2/3 (1990): 229–51; idem, *The Sacralization of Politics in Fascist Italy* (Cambridge, Mass.: Harvard University Press, 1996); Michael Burleigh, *The Third Reich: A New History* (New York: Hill & Wang, 2000); and Roger Griffin, ed., *International Fascism: Theories, Causes, and the New Consensus* (London: Oxford University Press, 1998).

and fascist studies. This has channeled its application in decisive ways, screening it off from liberal political eschatologies such as Wilsonian liberal internationalism and keeping it within the preestablished mold of the secularization-totalitarianism nexus.

Gentile offers a good example. Laying down the conceptual framework for the revival of political religion historiography in an influential essay at the center of the journal's inaugural issue, he defined totalitarianism in terms of "a *palingenetic ideology*, institutionalized in the form of a *political religion*, that aims to shape the individual and the masses through an *anthropological revolution* in order to regenerate the human being and create a *new man* . . . [and] a *new civilization* beyond the Nation-State."[30] Griffin similarly uses palingenesis and political religion as the main interpretive optics to illuminate the psychological foundations of totalitarian regimes in interwar Europe. According to him, the heuristic value of secularization theory has been tacitly recognized by other leading students of totalitarianism, including Juan Linz and Simon Tormey. In an effort to facilitate this "new consensus," as he calls it, Griffin has therefore proposed that political religion and totalitarianism be regarded as parts of a single conceptual cluster for the study of German Nazism and Italian Fascism.[31] Burleigh opened *The Third Reich*, his award-winning history of the Nazi project, with the remark that "theories of totalitarianism have rarely been incompatible with theories of political religions" and subsequently penned several essays on Nazism

---

[30] Gentile, "The Sacralization of Politics: Definitions, Interpretations and Reflections on the Question of Secular Religion and Totalitarianism," trans. Robert Mallett, *Totalitarian Movements and Political Religions* 1 [henceforth *TMPR*], no. 1 (2000): 19–21; emphasis original. See also his ensuing reaffirmation of this definition in idem, "Fascism, Totalitarianism, and Political Religion: Definitions and Critical Reflections on Criticism of an Interpretation," trans. Natalia Belozentseva, *TMPR* 5, no. 3 (2004): 326–75. Gentile eventually noted that "political religion does not refer exclusively to totalitarianism" but distanced the concept from liberal societies such as the United States nonetheless. See his "Political Religion: A Concept and Its Critics—A Critical Survey," *TMPR* 6, no. 1 (2005): 19–32.

[31] See Griffin, "The Palingenetic Political Community: Rethinking the Legitimation of Totalitarian Regimes in Inter-War Europe," *TMPR* 3, no. 3 (2002): 24–43; idem, "God's Counterfeiters? Investigating the Triad of Fascism, Totalitarianism, and (Political) Religion," *TMPR* 5, no. 3 (2004): 291–325; idem, "Cloister or Cluster? The Implications of Emilio Gentile's Ecumenical Theory of Political Religion for the Study of Extremism," *TMPR* 6, no. 1 (2005): 33–52; and idem, *Modernism and Fascism: The Sense of a Beginning under Mussolini and Hitler* (Basingstoke: Palgrave Macmillan, 2007).

as secularized eschatology.[32] His recent work includes a magisterial two-volume history of political religion from the French Revolution to the present, which maps the formation of totalitarian ideas in nineteenth-century Europe and their coalescing into Nazism, fascism, and communism a century later.[33]

The ongoing fixation of secularization theory on totalitarianism is not peculiar to *Totalitarian Movements and Political Religions*; it characterizes other important contributions to contemporary political religion historiography. For instance, already in the mid-1990s the Swiss historian Philippe Burrin described political religion as a forgotten twin to the more popular concept of totalitarianism. Tracing their separate lineages back to a shared origin, the unique form of dictatorship born in interwar Europe, he effectively welded them together as two parallel approaches to the same phenomenon.[34] A similar view informs the work of Hans Maier, currently the leading exponent of secularization theory and political religion in German-speaking circles. For Maier, totalitarianism and political religion represent a closely related pair of concepts for the comparative study of dictatorship, the former mapping the bureaucratic machinery of power, the latter illuminating the ideational sources of mass appeal and the "psychology of justification."[35] The secularization-totalitarianism nexus thus permeates contemporary political religion literature in general, which discursively produces and reproduces it through stand-alone essays, journal agendas, monographs, and extensive multivolume studies alike.[36]

Against the background of this long-standing discourse treating secularization and totalitarianism as two sides of the same coin, this study

[32] See Burleigh, "National Socialism as a Political Religion," *TMPR* 1, no. 2 (2000): 1–26, and idem, "Political Religion and Social Evil," *TMPR* 3, no. 2 (2002): 1–60. The quote is from Burleigh, *Third Reich*, 18.

[33] See Burleigh, *Earthly Powers: The Clash of Religion and Politics in Europe from the French Revolution to the Great War* (New York: HarperCollins, 2005), and idem, *Sacred Causes: The Clash of Religion and Politics from the Great War to the War on Terror* (New York: HarperCollins, 2007).

[34] Burrin, "Political Religion: The Relevance of a Concept," *History and Memory* 9, no. 1 (1997): 321–49.

[35] Maier, " 'Totalitarismus' und 'politische Religionen,' " 404–5. Maier's restriction of the concept of political religion to totalitarian and authoritarian regimes is further evident from his essay "Political Religions and Their Images: Soviet Communism, Italian Fascism, and German National Socialism," *TMPR* 7, no. 3 (2006): 267–81.

[36] A major example of the latter type of publication is Maier and Schäfer, eds., *Totalitarismus und Politische Religionen: Konzepte des Diktaturvergleichs*, 3 vols. (Paderborn: Schöningh, 1996, 1997, 2003).

appears nothing short of radical: instead of Hitler, Stalin, Mussolini, and their visions of progress and utopia, it proposes to aim the optic of secularization at Woodrow Wilson in the broader context of the American liberal tradition, arguing that their eschatological impulses flowed from the same Judeo-Christian cultural heritage as the utopian yearnings of Nazism and Marxism-Leninism. Wilson's exalted vision of progress to lasting world peace, rooted in part in the nineteenth-century doctrine of America's "manifest destiny," would seem to lend itself to secularization analysis exceptionally well: its eschatological undercurrents and inspirations flowing from Puritan millennialism are frequently in plain sight.[37] Yet one would search in vain in current political religion historiography for analyses of Wilsonianism or other liberal philosophies of progress and salvation; there are none to be found in forums and outlets such as *Totalitarian Movements and Political Religions*. These remain dedicated exclusively to illiberal narratives.

The Fixation of Secularization Theory on Irreligious Utopianisms

The belief that secularization theory is suitable strictly for totalitarian and illiberal regimes is not the only obstacle preventing analysis of liberal utopianisms such as Wilson's. There is another one: the assumption that the concept of secularized eschatology is applicable only to irreligious philosophies of progress—a criterion that leaves Wilson and American liberal internationalism out on account of their explicit religiosity. Perceptible already in the Cold War analyses by Arendt, Aron, and others discussed earlier, today this assumption is evident not only from the definition of secularization at the heart of contemporary political religion historiography, but also from some of the criticisms of this historiography. Both reveal that in recent political religions discourse, loss of traditional religion is regarded as an essential element of the process of secularization responsible for the rise of modern totalitarian ideologies.

---

[37] Literature drawing attention to these undercurrents includes Milan Babík, "George D. Herron and the Eschatological Foundations of Woodrow Wilson's Foreign Policy, 1917–1919," *Diplomatic History* 35, no. 5 (2011): 837–57; Lloyd E. Ambrosius, *Wilsonian Statecraft: Theory and Practice of Liberal Internationalism during World War I* (Wilmington, Del.: SR Books, 1991), 10–13; Malcolm D. Magee, *What the World Should Be: Woodrow Wilson and the Crafting of a Faith-Based Foreign Policy* (Waco, Tex.: Baylor University Press, 2008); and Robert M. Crunden, *Ministers of Reform: The Progressives' Achievement in American Civilization, 1889–1920* (New York: Basic Books, 1982).

The first place where this supposition surfaces to visibility is in the interpretive optic underpinning current political religion historiography, whose representatives have been self-consciously transparent about what they mean by political religion and its genealogy. Gentile has described the dynamic of secularization as follows: "Precisely because it . . . has swept away age-old collective beliefs and institutions, modernity has created crisis and disorientation—situations which have, in turn, led to the re-emergence of the religious question, even if this has led the individual to turn not to traditional religion, but to look to new religions that sacralize the human."[38] In this influential interpretation, secularization is comprehended as a dialectical development triggered by and predicated on religious decline: reason and science first have to discredit the Bible, so that subsequently the carry-over pressure of traditional biblical concerns (such as the question about the meaning of history) can engender new, ostensibly rational narratives of salvation, in whose hidden presuppositions and structural features Judeo-Christian eschatology quietly survives into the modern age.

As products of this process, political religions are therefore perceived as new wine in old bottles: identical to traditional Christianity in form and function, but alienated from it in content. "The 'religion' of [contemporary] political religion theory," in other words, is predominantly "the act of believing, not *that which is believed*."[39] Insofar as political religions postulate grand visions of future perfection and excite their worship, they continue in the mold of Judeo-Christian eschatology. Yet insofar as these visions are now defined in terms of race, class, or nation, not the biblical *civitas Dei*, which is dismissed as an atavistic myth and a roadblock to progress, political religions are radically new and revolutionary. Overall, they express neither traditional Christianity nor modern heresy, but both at once, representing a strange amalgam that is religious in origin but—and this is key—irreligious in manifestation.

Case studies of individual totalitarian movements evince this understanding of secularization well. They constitute the second area within contemporary political religion historiography where the conviction that secularization presupposes the rejection of traditional Christianity comes into view. Burleigh's widely acclaimed portrayal of German National Socialism is illustrative: "the fundamental tenets [of Christianity] were

---

[38] Gentile, "Sacralization of Politics," 30–31.

[39] Richard Steigmann-Gall, "Nazism and the Revival of Political Religion Theory," *TMPR* 5, no. 3 (2004): 380; emphasis original.

stripped out, but the remaining diffuse religious emotionality had its uses."[40] The political religion of the Third Reich categorically rejected authentic Christian religion, which it diligently "bashed over the head" with science.[41] For Burleigh, the essence of Nazi religiosity thus lies in the ideology's hypertrophied rationality and scientism: the belief that the *Rassenprinzip* is the logic of history, the conviction that racial science is the pathway to the millennial Reich, and the various rituals of national consecration based on these suppositions.[42] In this vein, Nazism simultaneously destroyed traditional religion and presented itself as its profane, irreligious reincarnation. As such, the ideology of the Third Reich must have induced "nausea in any fastidious rationalist or person of genuine religious faith."[43]

Yet this *völkisch* ideology, too religious to pass for genuine science and too worldly to pass for genuine religion, was precisely what appealed to the masses of ordinary Germans recoiling from the Nietzschean "Death of God" and yearning for something else to take the place of his Kingdom as the meaning of history. The plea issued by the French Romantic nationalist Michelet repeatedly strikes Burleigh as emblematic of the psychological interplay driving secularization and the rise of political religions: "It is from you that I shall ask for help, my noble country, you must take the place of the God who escapes us, that you may fill within us the immeasurable abyss which extinct Christianity has left there."[44] The Nazi masterminds recognized this vast spiritual abyss and quickly filled it with surrogate ideals. Their success in securing popular support for policies of exclusion, genocide, and war resulted precisely from their

---

[40] Burleigh, *Third Reich*, 256.

[41] Burleigh, *Third Reich*, 254. Burleigh supports this by citing, among other things, Hitler's words at the NSDAP Congress *Grossdeutschland* in Nuremberg in 1938: "National Socialism," the *Führer* insisted, "is a cool and highly reasoned approach to reality based upon the greatest of scientific knowledge and its spiritual expression." See Max Domarus, ed., *Hitler: Speeches and Proclamations, 1932–1945*, trans. Chris Wilcox and Mary Fran Gilbert (London: I. B. Tauris, 1992), 2:1146, speech dated September 6, 1938, cited in Burleigh, *Third Reich*, 253.

[42] For scientism as the religion of totalitarianism, see Tzvetan Todorov, "Totalitarianism: Between Religion and Science," trans. Brady Brower and Max Likin, *TMPR* 2, no. 1 (2001): 28–42.

[43] Burleigh, *Third Reich*, 264.

[44] Cited in Burleigh, "National Socialism as a Political Religion," 6, and again in idem, "Political Religion and Social Evil," 5.

ability to sacralize the *Volk*: elevate it into the position previously occupied by the biblical *civitas Dei*.[45]

The third and final area revealing the assumption that only irreligious ideologies can possibly qualify as political religions lies in some of the criticisms of current political religion historiography, notably the criticism targeting its tendency—exemplified by Burleigh's work—to represent Nazism as a non- or anti-Christian movement. This representation skirts the surprising extent to which Christianity, above all Protestantism, seems to have been central to Nazi self-understanding: many top Nazis viewed themselves as soldiers of Christ mounting a mission to revive the forgotten spirit of Luther's teachings, rescue it from the dark cloud of corrupt beliefs and institutions, and complete the project of the German Reformation. In their imagination, as Richard Steigmann-Gall has shown, "Nazism was not the result of a 'Death of God' in secularized society, but rather a radicalized . . . attempt to preserve God *against* secularized society," and its program encapsulated "a syncretic mix of the social and the economic tenets of confessional Lutheranism and the doctrine and ecclesiology of liberal Protestantism."[46] Whereas political religion historiography portrays Nazism as new wine in old bottles, apostasy custom-designed to fit the mold of vacated eschatological idioms, it may have been the old wine itself: authentic Christianity, albeit highly unorthodox and with a strong racialist twist. The idea of progress to the Third Reich was not just generic utopianism identical to biblical eschatology only in form and function; the identity extended to content.

Whether this revisionist account of Nazism as a religious movement holds any water is of secondary importance.[47] What deserves attention is

---

[45] Burleigh's interpretation of the Third Reich as a functional *ersatz* echoes not only the aforementioned interpretations by Gurian, Aron, Friedrich, and Arendt, but also other seminal readings of Nazism by historians such as George L. Mosse and Fritz Stern. Mosse suggested that "For the National Socialist [the] basic [Christian] form could not be abandoned, but should simply be filled with a different content." *The Nationalization of the Masses* (New York: Fertig, 1975), 80. Stern saw Nazism as a Germanic religion in which "The religious *tone* remained, even after the religious faith and the religious canons had disappeared." *The Politics of Cultural Despair: A Study in the Rise of the Germanic Ideology* (Berkeley: University of California Press, 1974), xxv.

[46] Steigmann-Gall, *The Holy Reich: Nazi Conceptions of Christianity, 1919–1945* (Cambridge: Cambridge University Press, 2003), 12, 262–63. See also idem, "Rethinking Nazism and Religion: How Anti-Christian Were the 'Pagans'?" *Central European History* 36, no. 1 (2003): 75–105.

[47] The main entry-point into this issue is Richard J. Evans, "Nazism, Christianity, and Political Religion: A Debate," *Journal of Contemporary History* 42, no. 1 (2007):

something else—namely, the implications perceived to have been generated by this account for the political religion approach to the Third Reich: Steigmann-Gall flatly rejected it.[48] He did this precisely on the assumption that is the central subject here: that as a category political religion applies exclusively to irreligious movements. Extracting his understanding of the concept from a survey of works by historians such as Burleigh, Steigmann-Gall noted that "political religion theory emphasizes Nazi form (the hypnotic power of a new charismatic faith) over Nazi content (the message of that religion and to whom it appealed)."[49] As such, the political religion approach to Nazism reflected the recent culturalist turn in historical scholarship: it was this turn—the expansion of history to cultural history, the broadening of the subject matter beyond texts to cultural practices—that had enabled Burleigh and others to discover formal and functional identities between Nazism and Christianity and, based on these identities, to portray Nazism as an *ersatz* religion. Yet the heightened sensitivity to Nazi aesthetics and ritual came at a cost: it took the advocates of the political religion approach away from the substance of the ideology. "The political religion thesis," insofar as Steigmann-Gall could glean it from current historiography, "presumes the attraction to Nazism was based on emotion instead of idea, on form instead of content. Whatever the Nazi 'platform' may have been is deemed irrelevant, or at best secondary."[50] This overly functionalist definition of religion was then directly responsible for the erroneous characterizations of Nazism as a surrogate faith. Had scholars such as Burleigh paid more attention to ideological content, they would have discovered that the Nazi vision of the Third Reich was not merely structurally analogous to Christian (Protestant) eschatology, but that it was Christian eschatology. Instead of political religion, Steigmann-Gall therefore proposed to call Nazism "religious politics"—certifying that the former concept, as currently configured by its proponents, is restricted to non- or anti-Christian ideologies.

For present purposes, the relevance of the claim that religious narratives of progress and utopia rule out any talk of political religion springs from the fact that traditional Christian faith was just as essential

---

5–7, and the symposium on Steigmann-Gall's *Holy Reich* in the same volume. See also Richard Steigmann-Gall, "Christianity and the Nazi Movement: A Response," *Journal of Contemporary History* 42, no. 2 (2007): 185–211.

[48] Steigmann-Gall, "Nazism and Revival of Political Religion Theory," 376–96.

[50] Steigmann-Gall, "Nazism and Revival of Political Religion Theory," 377.

[50] Steigmann-Gall, "Nazism and Revival of Political Religion Theory," 380.

to Wilson's self-understanding as, according to Steigmann-Gall, it was to the Nazi worldview. The entire history of the American idea of progress to liberty is on one level a history of groups and individuals consciously acting out their religious, predominantly Protestant, beliefs. If many Nazis comprehended their movement in terms of a sacred mission completing the German Reformation, in their turn generations of leading Americans from John Winthrop, governor of Massachusetts in the early 1600s, to Wilson, president of the United States at the dawn of the twentieth century, comprehended their actions and struggles in terms of a sacred millennial mission completing the English Reformation. The argument that the presence of religious (Protestant) content precludes reading the Nazi ideology through the lens of secularization thus inevitably poses a problem for the ensuing pages, which seek to do just that with American liberalism and Wilson.

Extending Secularization Theory to American Liberal-Republican Millennialism

That something has gone awry in the widespread perception that Christian content automatically disqualifies this or that ideology from the domain of political religion should be clearly discernible against the background of the Löwith-Blumenberg debate on secularization. This debate revealed that modern narratives of progress containing elements of Protestant millennialism are the strongest candidates for the label of secularized eschatology, not the weakest. Where the ideology in question is self-consciously Christian, its status as secularized eschatology tends to be even better-founded than in the case of only unconscious continuity on the level of hidden theological functions and preconceptions about the nature of history (although functional identity alone suffices). In other words, and referring to the more precise taxonomy of secular eschatologies developed earlier, products of partial or incomplete secularization are especially immune to Blumenberg's critique of Löwith's thesis about the theological presuppositions of modern philosophy of history. This is because they merely reinterpret the *civitas Dei* in temporal terms, remain loyal to the Bible, and hence satisfy Blumenberg's demand that modern progress and medieval eschatology share biblical content.

In light of the Löwith-Blumenberg debate, accounts rendering modern doctrines of progress as forms of Protestantism thus do not undermine the secular religion approach to them, but just the reverse: they make it more plausible. By demonstrating that the political ideology under consideration is Christian not only in function but also in content, such accounts

unwittingly meet the litmus test of secular religion proposed by secularization theory's harshest and most sophisticated critic. With respect to
Nazism, the thesis that the movement consciously regarded itself as the
political expression of the German Reformation should have propelled
Steigmann-Gall toward affirming the political religion interpretation, not
toward rejecting it.[51] That he has nonetheless declared the interpretation
inapplicable reflects insufficient familiarity with secularization theory:
his idea of political religion represents only a truncated version of the
rigorous model encapsulated within the Löwith-Blumenberg debate.

Steigmann-Gall is only partly to blame, however. Insofar as he extracts
his understanding of the secularization approach (including its fixation
on irreligious ideologies) from contemporary political religion historiography, a larger problem manifests itself here, one extending beyond him
to this historiography as a whole: a disjunction seems to exist between
Burleigh, Gentile, and other historians utilizing the concept of political
religion, on the one hand, and philosophers and social theorists who have
formulated it, on the other. The former group appears to proceed in relative oblivion to the deeper philosophical debates that have shaped the
secularization approach and warrant its status as a valid tool of historical interpretation in the first place. If the journal *Totalitarian Movements
and Political Religions* represents the flagship of contemporary political
religion historiography, references to Löwith—simultaneously one of the
greatest yet least-known twentieth-century German philosophers—are
distressingly absent.[52] This is not to say that political religion historians

---

[51] It is instructive to compare Steigmann-Gall to Claus-Ekkehard Bärsch, whose representation of leading Nazi ideologists as Christian thinkers converges with Steigmann-
Gall's almost point-to-point (including in the focus on the substance of their ideas rather
than on form and function). For Bärsch, however, the religious content of Nazism serves
to demonstrate—not undermine—the character of Nazism as a political religion. In other
words, a broadly similar description of the movement has propelled Bärsch to a position
exactly counter to the one reached by Steigmann-Gall as regards the validity of the secularization approach to Nazism. As such, Bärsch's work represents a notable exception to
the conventional wisdom that the category of political religion is inapplicable to religious
movements. See especially Bärsch, *Die politische Religion des Nationalsozialismus: Die
religiöse Dimension der NS-Ideologie in den Schriften von Dietrich Eckart, Joseph Goebbels, Alfred Rosenberg und Adolf Hitler* (Munich: Fink, 1998), and also idem, "Alfred
Rosenbergs *Mythus des 20. Jahrhunderts* als politische Religion," in *Totalitarismus und
Politische Religionen*, ed. Maier and Schäfer, 2:227–48.

[52] Preliminary signs that Löwith's rediscovery may be in the making include Vincent L. Pecora, *Secularization and Cultural Criticism: Religion, Nation, and Modernity*
(Chicago: University of Chicago Press, 2006), and Jean-Claude Monod, *La querelle de la
secularization de Hegel à Blumenberg: Theologie politique et philosophies de l'historie*

neglect theoretical issues completely; particularly Voegelin has received repeated attention.[53] Nor again is it to insist that political religion historiography become thoroughly philosophical; a certain gap between history and theory is inevitable and warranted by other benefits from the division of intellectual labor. But it is to suggest that at present this gap is too wide, especially given that political religion historiography stands to gain significantly from becoming more theoretical.

What are some of the potential gains? One is that political religion historiography would no longer need to eschew religious ideologies of progress and utopia. Historians employing the concept could expand their subject matter from *ersatz* (non- or anti-Christian) eschatologies to Christian progressivisms. From the perspective of Blumenberg's critique of secularization, modern philosophies of progress whose content is identifiable with Christian salvationism may be the only legitimate candidates for the label of secularized eschatology. To this extent they should represent the starting point for political religion historians, not an afterthought.

The second gain is that political religion historiography would no longer need to concentrate only on totalitarian and illiberal ideologies. Increased sensitivity to secularization theory reveals that it is just as applicable to liberal narratives of progress. Löwith, Voegelin, Berdyaev, and others responsible for the birth of the secularization thesis in the first half of the twentieth century certainly did not neglect totalitarianism; it had an important place in their analyses.[54] It hardly could have

---

(n.p.: Vrin, 2002). Unfortunately, so far this scholarship has gone unnoticed by contemporary political religion historians.

[53] See, e.g., the repeated tributes to Voegelin in Burleigh, *Third Reich*; idem, *Earthly Powers*; and idem, *Sacred Causes.*

[54] Löwith (*Meaning in History*, 159) made passing references to the Third Reich and the Third International at the end of the chapter on Joachim of Floris, whose historical theology set in motion the gradual bending of biblical eschatology *ad sæculum*, a process that, according to Löwith, culminated in modern irreligions of progress. Throughout his writings, Voegelin similarly subsumed Nazism and Bolshevism in his categories of *ersatz* religion, political religion, and modern gnosticism. Berdyaev insisted that "[Russian Communism] wants to be a religion itself, to take the place of Christianity," adding that "It is a transformation and deformation of the old Russian messianic idea." *The Origin of Russian Communism*, trans. R. M. French (London: Geoffrey Bles, 1937), 158, 187. His remarks may be the more telling because he probably spoke from personal experience: before the Bolshevik Party came to power and turned its revolutionary ideals against him, forcing him into exile, the quasi-Christian nature of the Marxist teachings seduced this famous Russian theologian into brief allegiance.

been otherwise, given the relentless persecution to which they had been subjected by the Nazis and Bolsheviks. Yet totalitarianism was not their only target; they formulated their theories about the idea of progress in general, not merely about its illiberal variants. The context of Löwith's or Voegelin's personal ordeals in the Third Reich is important, but it may take one a step too far in restricting secularization theory exclusively to totalitarianism. After all, Löwith continued to espouse his thesis until his death in the 1970s—against Blumenberg, who understood Löwith to be making a general claim, one applicable to the idea of progress in all its shapes and forms. Noticing contributions to secularization theory by American thinkers such as Tuveson and Becker magnifies the arbitrariness of the secularization-totalitarianism nexus further still. Concerned strictly with the genealogy of the liberal idea of progress in England and America and tracing its eschatological origins in seventeenth- and eighteenth-century French philosophy and English Protestant millennialism, these contributions could indeed generate the impression that secularization theory is fixated on liberal narratives, not illiberal or totalitarian.

It remains to conclude, then, that a careful reading of secularization theory dispels much of the conventional wisdom about its inapplicability beyond irreligious and totalitarian ideologies that quietly governs current political religion historiography. Secularization theory is sufficiently wide to cover American liberal-republican millennialism under its umbrella; neither his Protestantism nor his liberalism poses an obstacle to interpreting Wilson through the prism of secularization. On the contrary, and to reaffirm a point made earlier, these attributes make Wilson's idea of progress all the more suitable for secularization analysis. It is time to commence the task.

CHAPTER THREE

THE ESCHATOLOGICAL ORIGINS OF THE AMERICAN REPUBLIC

Millennialism in Colonial America

In his classic study of the origins and development of American democratic thought, the Yale historian Ralph Henry Gabriel remarked that Woodrow Wilson's domestic and foreign policies rested "on ethical beliefs which in American history were as old as Puritanism."[1] Wilson would have accepted this characterization with enthusiasm. He tended to imagine his quest for the League of Nations in terms of completing, on a worldwide scale, the sacred mission of liberty initiated in the American wilderness by small flocks of Puritan settlers. While attending the Paris Peace Conference, he told a delegation of French Protestants that he was determined to pursue "our common ideal [with] all the perseverance of the Puritans."[2] This self-interpretation makes it highly appropriate to begin the analysis of Wilson with a discussion of the colonial period in American history. Wilson did not refer to the Puritans by accident. A historian by training, he was well acquainted with their ideas about liberty and religion, and his appropriation of them indicates that they represent a potent approach to his thinking.

---

[1] Gabriel, *The Course of American Democratic Thought* (New York: Ronald Press, 1940), 338.

[2] Wilson, "Remarks to French Protestants" (January 27, 1919), in *The Papers of Woodrow Wilson*, ed. Arthur S. Link et al. (Princeton, N.J.: Princeton University Press, 1966–1994) [henceforth *PWW*], 54:283.

As the ensuing pages delve into the Puritan and colonial mind, two broad themes emerge. The first is that colonial Americans, like Wilson later on, comprehended politics and the quest for liberty in moral and religious terms. From initial settlement to the American Revolution, many colonial leaders both civil and ecclesiastical saw America as a spiritual project, one of carrying out God's will. Whatever obstacles they confronted, whether hostile environment or foreign enemies, they interpreted them within an eschatological frame of mind: as divinely ordained trials whose overcoming delineated the pathway to God's reign on earth. This was also and especially true during the American Revolution, perceived by many participants in terms of defending God's cause of liberty against the onslaught of Satan wearing the red coats of the British soldiers. The founding of the United States of America occurred in the context of intense millennial expectations and possessed an identifiable eschatological dimension. Insofar as the Revolutionary ideology couched political liberalism in the language of Protestant millennialism, it constituted a veritable secular (political) eschatology: liberal-republican millennialism. This particularly American brand of liberalism subsequently thrived in the nineteenth century and, at the outset of the twentieth, found expression in Wilson's domestic and international thought.

The second theme is that the nexus of politics and religion in colonial America endowed the pursuit of liberty with totalizing domestic and international tendencies. These surface especially well in the Puritan restriction of political franchise and leadership to an elite vanguard of certified "Saints," their zero tolerance for nonconformist ideas and practices, their ruthless persecution of dissenters, and their plans to conquer the world in order to revolutionize it according to their vision. From day one, American liberalism had a decidedly illiberal underbelly. The same totalizing inclinations later permeated Wilson's liberal-republican millennialism; in subtler forms, he inherited them from the Puritans along with the belief that politics was a religious mission. His foreign policy, it will be seen, was formulated within a black-and-white, Manichean conception of the moral and political universe and amounted to little else than a bid to remake the world order in America's image.

Puritan New England as a Model City of God

Millennial expectations surrounded already the initial sighting of America by Columbus, who interpreted his discovery in the context of the biblical prophecy about the universal diffusion of faith in preparation for the earthly paradise. That God had disclosed the New World to humanity meant that the end of history was near. Columbus thus routinely introduced himself at European courts as the "messenger of the new heaven and new earth of which [God] spoke in the Apocalypse by Saint John."[3]

At the outset of the seventeenth century, the same eschatological hopes that reigned aboard the *Santa Maria* filled the sails of the *Mayflower* and the *Arbella*, two ships on which the first English Puritans fleeing persecution began arriving in America and New England. Like Columbus, they considered the New World a prophesied sign of times: a virgin land set aside by God for his elect. Its discovery was God's summons to the faithful to come out of bondage, settle it, and transform it into the New Israel.

The millennial dimension of New England is apparent from its earliest written history: William Bradford's chronicle *Of Plymouth Plantation*. Bradford belonged to Puritan separatists who referred to themselves as Pilgrim "Saints," crossed the ocean on the *Mayflower* in 1620, and disembarked at Plymouth Rock near Cape Cod. Often considered "the father of American history,"[4] he served as governor of Plymouth Colony from 1621 until his death in 1657. His chronicle reveals not only the events making up the early history of the settlement, but also the lens through which Bradford and his fellow Puritans interpreted them: the lens of eschatological faith in God as the mover of all temporal affairs.

Bradford situates the local history of Plymouth Colony within an overarching narrative of universal history as a progressive battle of Christians against Satan, who receives a major blow during the English Reformation. Having liberated the spirit of Christ from captivity under the Roman Catholic Church, England is for Bradford "the first of nations

---

[3] Charles L. Sanford, *The Quest for Paradise: Europe and the American Moral Imagination* (Urbana: University of Illinois Press, 1961), 40. See also Mircea Eliade, *The Quest: History and Meaning in Religion* (Chicago: University of Chicago Press, 1969), 90–91. Wilson interpreted Columbus's achievement within the same eschatological framework when shortly before the Paris Peace Conference he visited the Italian city of Genoa to lay a wreath at the statue of the famous explorer. In discovering America, the president stated, "[Columbus] did . . . a service to mankind," whose significance was "greater even than was realized at the time it was done." Its full meaning surfaced only with the American victory in World War I, which retrospectively revealed Columbus' true stature as "the man who led the way to those fields of freedom which, planted with a great seed, have now sprung up to the fructification of the world." See Wilson's "Remarks about Christopher Columbus" (January 5, 1919) and "Remarks at the Station in Milan" (Jan. 5, 1919), *PWW* 53:615–16.

[4] Moses Coit Tyler, *A History of American Literature, 1607–1765* (Ithaca, N.Y.: Cornell University Press, 1975 [1949]), 101, 109.

whom the Lord adorned [with the light of the Gospel] after the gross darkness of popery which had covered and overspread the Christian world."[5] Unfortunately, the victory is only temporary: Bradford declares that Satan had recovered, infiltrated English Protestantism, Romanized it, and reversed its spiritual achievements. The promise of the Reformation thus comes to rest entirely with the Pilgrim "Saints," who must sever all ties with England and the Old World in order to preserve it. This, Bradford explains, is the reason why he and his company "shook off this yoke of antichristian bondage, and as the Lord's free people joined themselves (by a covenant of the Lord) into a church estate, in the fellowship of the gospel, to walk in all His ways."[6] The rationale for Plymouth Colony is clear: to realize authentic Christian ideals in historical-political reality.

The eschatological purpose of New England was spelled out even more explicitly aboard the *Arbella*, which arrived from England in 1630, sailed past Bradford's settlement, and dropped the anchor just south, where its Puritan passengers founded the Massachusetts Bay Colony. John Winthrop, their leader, outlined the task awaiting them in a sermon entitled "A Model of Christian Charity." In one of the most celebrated passages in early American literature, Winthrop declared that "we must consider that we shall be as a City upon a Hill, the eyes of all people are upon us; so that if we shall deal falsely with our god in this work . . . and so cause him to withdraw his present help from us, we shall be made a story and a by-word throughout the world."[7] Like Bradford, Winthrop too hints that the trajectory of the Puritan migration across the Atlantic was not only horizontal, from one point to another within the geography of this world, but also and especially vertical: from corruption to purity, from the Fall back to God, from *civitas terrena* to *civitas Dei*, from this world to the American "City upon a Hill." America was in this sense both a geographical and an eschatological destination: both a physical place and the end of history. Piety and hard work, Winthrop and the Puritans believed, would transform the wilderness into a model society shining the spirit of Christ across the oceans and serving as a lighthouse guiding the rest of humanity to the Millennium. Three centuries of political and economic success later, with America risen to the status of a world

---

[5] Bradford, *Of Plymouth Plantation, 1620–1647*, ed. Samuel E. Morison (New York: Knopf, 1952), 1.1.

[6] Bradford, *Of Plymouth Plantation*, 1.1.

[7] Winthrop, "A Model of Christian Charity," in *The Heath Anthology of American Literature*, ed. Paul Lauter et al., 2nd ed. (Toronto: Heath, 1994), 1:233.

power, Woodrow Wilson repeated this belief almost verbatim, characterizing the United States as a beacon radiating the Christian principles of justice, liberty, and altruism across the seas.[8]

Significantly, neither Bradford nor Winthrop was a clergyman, but a lay civil magistrate responsible for the political functioning of his respective colony. That they nonetheless wrote on religious issues and delivered sermons—much as Wilson would too in his various civil offices—underscores the spiritual dimension of colonial politics in early New England. In the Puritan consciousness, "the unity of religion and politics was so axiomatic that very few men would even have grasped the idea that church and state could be distinct. For the Puritan mind it was not possible to segregate a man's spiritual life from his communal life."[9] Politics was sacred in that colonial settlement and administration was a spiritual and redemptive experience; and conversely religious worship was political in that it facilitated communal harmony and prosperity, viewed by Puritans as God's visible rewards for keeping his covenant.[10]

The unity of politics and religion also meant that clergymen ventured into the domain of colonial politics and administration as frequently as civil magistrates ventured into the domain of religion and biblical exegesis. Unsurprisingly, the clergy was even fiercer than the lay leaders in merging history with eschatology, polity with church, and civil with ecclesiastical affairs. Despite their conviction that colonial politics served religious ends, Bradford and Winthrop were also pragmatic men; in running their settlements they remained committed to the rich tradition of English law. In contrast, leading clergymen such as John Cotton or John Davenport showed no such respect.

Cotton, pastor of the First Church of Boston and the most prominent theologian in early New England, proposed that the religious purpose of American colonial politics be made even more explicit by reorganizing the laws and government of Massachusetts in accordance with Mosaic

---

[8] Wilson, "Address to the Federal Council of Churches in Columbus" (December 10, 1915), *PWW* 35:334–36.

[9] Perry Miller, *Errand into the Wilderness* (Cambridge, Mass.: Harvard University Press, 1956), 142.

[10] For Winthrop, covenanting with God meant that "we must be knit together in this work . . . [and] entertain each other in brotherly Affection . . . as members of the same body, so shall we keep the unity of the spirit in the bond of peace." "Christian Charity," in *Heath Anthology*, ed. Lauter et al., 233. For the structure of the Puritan covenant, see Perry Miller, *The New England Mind: The Seventeenth Century* (London: Harvard University Press, 1983 [1939]), 365–462.

Law. He drafted an outline of the scriptural code himself, drawing some chapters (such as on crime) directly from the Bible and annotating the rest with marginal references to show that it too followed God's will.[11] In Cotton's case the drive to unify politics and religion thus reached the extreme form of seeking to transform Massachusetts into a literal Kingdom of God: a theocracy on the model of ancient Israel. Similar attempts to reposition society on biblical law in order to realize the earthly Millennium would keep recurring in America down to the nineteenth century. In Wilson's time they were spearheaded especially by the so-called Kingdom Movement under the leadership of the millennialist preacher George D. Herron, whose secular eschatology the president explicitly endorsed as an accurate summary of his own understanding of history, America's role in the world, and his foreign policy aims.[12]

Winthrop rejected Cotton's proposal, but it was implemented elsewhere: in the nearby New Haven Colony—"the essence of Puritanism, distilled and undefiled; the Bible Commonwealth and nothing else."[13] It was founded by John Davenport, Cotton's fellow minister. Following Winthrop's decision not to pursue the scriptural code in Massachusetts, Davenport left the colony and moved just outside its jurisdiction to start a new, more authentically Christian settlement based on Cotton's proposal. Some of the code's provisions apparently sounded too draconian even for Davenport, his Puritan zeal notwithstanding, but Cotton worked tirelessly to exert influence on his close friend. He repeated to Davenport that "Theocracy, or to make Lord God our Governor, is the best Form of Government . . . which men that are free to choose (and in new Plantations they are) ought to establish."[14] This dispelled Davenport's doubts, and through him Cotton succeeded in molding the government for the strictest of Puritan settlements.[15]

---

[11] Cotton, *An Abstract of the Laws of New-England* (London, 1641).

[12] See Herron, *The New Redemption: A Call to the Church to Reconstruct Society According to the Gospel of Christ* (New York: Crowell, 1893), and idem, *The Christian State: A Political Vision of Christ* (New York: Crowell, 1895).

[13] Perry Miller, review of *The New Haven Colony*, by Isabel M. Calder, *New England Quarterly* 8, no. 4 (1935): 584.

[14] Cotton, *A Discourse about Civil Government in a New Plantation Whose Design Is Religion* (Cambridge, Mass., 1663 [1637]), 14.

[15] Isabel M. Calder, "John Cotton and the New Haven Colony," *New England Quarterly* 3, no. 1 (1930): 82. See also idem, *The New Haven Colony* (New Haven, Conn.: Yale University Press, 1934), esp. chaps. 4 and 5.

The drive to turn New England into a theocracy derived in significant part from a widespread sense of historical urgency: Cotton and Davenport believed that the Millennium was imminent. In this expectation they exemplified the general mindset of most Puritan settlers. Millennial images, especially the apocalyptic prophecies in Daniel and Revelation, represented the fundamental matrix structuring their understanding of the errand into the wilderness.[16] Other mental frameworks for interpreting the New World of America were available, including astrology, natural history, and the meteorology of ancient Greeks and Romans, but the clergy systematically steered all strata of colonial society toward eschatology and millennialism. The effort was spearheaded by the prominent Mather family of theologians, including Richard, Increase, and Cotton, who moved eschatology to the very core of New England Protestantism.[17] In consequence, and much like the Franciscan Spirituals following the teachings of Joachim of Floris in thirteenth-century Italy, most Puritan settlers believed they were living near the end of time. Strange and unknown occurrences, of which the New World was full, were regarded as signs that the Last Judgment was approaching.[18] The clergy's lobbying on behalf of theocracy reflected the desire to prepare for and hasten the onset of the *civitas Dei*. Jeopardizing the process through moral lapses was inadmissible. As Cotton warned his congregation, such behavior

[16] J. F. Maclear, "New England and the Fifth Monarchy: The Quest for the Millennium in Early American Puritanism," *William and Mary Quarterly* 32, no. 2 (1975): 224–25.

[17] See Robert Middlekauff, *The Mathers: Three Generations of Puritan Intellectuals, 1596–1728* (New York: Oxford University Press, 1971). Richard Mather's teaching, for instance, was "shot through with an eschatological expectation" (Middlekauff, *The Mathers*, 375n25).

[18] In the words of David D. Hall, a leading social historian of the early colonial period, "The people of seventeenth-century New England lived in an enchanted universe. Theirs was a world of wonders. . . . The most common meaning that the clergy offered for the wonder [was] that it signified impending judgment." *Worlds of Wonder, Days of Judgment: Popular Religious Belief in Early New England* (New York: Knopf, 1989), 71, 116. John Eliot's engagement with the indigenous inhabitants of the New World, who constituted one of its most intriguing wonders, reveals this understanding well: the "apostle to the Indians" saw them as descendants of the twelve lost tribes of Israel, considered their conversion to Christianity instrumental to the approaching Millennium, and did his part in fulfilling the millennial prophecy by ministering to the Algonquian in their own tongue. See Eliot, *The Glorious Progress of the Gospel amongst the Indians in New England* (London, 1649), and idem, *The Christian Commonwealth* (London, 1651).

would bring them defeat at the coming Armageddon and a thousand years of poverty and nadir.[19]

This eschatologically inspired political activism, and the broader unity of politics and religion illustrated by it, reveals two key points about Puritanism in early colonial New England. The first concerns the difference between Puritans and St. Augustine in their respective views on the relationship between the biblical myth of salvation and secular history. Puritanism absorbed a significant amount of Augustinian theology; indeed, it has been argued that Augustine "exerted the greatest single influence upon Puritan thought next to that of the Bible."[20] Crucially, however, the Puritans shared neither Augustine's definition of salvation as a strictly spiritual event nor his view of temporal history as an irreparable *series calamitatis* without any prospects for improvement.[21] Such a pessimistic posture would have precluded any transformative political action by rendering it *a priori* meaningless; it would have led the Puritans to resign themselves to a life of quiet contemplation in monastic seclusion, lending credence to Blumenberg's claim against secularization theory that eschatological consciousness could not have possibly produced the idea of progress.

Yet Puritans were no hermits, but sea explorers, soldiers, statesmen, and in general very entrepreneurial people tirelessly shaping the material world according to their will, which is to say, according to the will of their God—in excellent illustration of the secularization thesis that the idea of progress sprang up from the notion of divine providence. Translating their piety into sociopolitical practice was essential to them, a stated purpose of their migration to America and one of their main bequests to Wilson, who similarly regarded Christianity as a "work-day religion."[22]

---

[19] See, e.g., Cotton, *The Churches Resurrection, or the Opening of the Fifth and Sixth Verses of the 20th Chap. of the Revelation* (London, 1642), 5–6, 15–21.

[20] Miller, *Seventeenth Century*, 4.

[21] E.g., Bradford, having identified divine providence with earthly progress and imagined salvation in secular-political terms, belongs not in the Augustinian (transcendental) eschatological tradition, but in the Eusebian (historical) one, revived by Joachim in the Middle Ages and inherited by the Reformation. See Robert Daly, "William Bradford's Vision of History," *American Literature* 44, no. 4 (1973): 557–61.

[22] As Winthrop ("Christian Charity," in *Heath Anthology*, ed. Lauter et al., 232) declared, "That which the most in their Churches maintain as a truth in profession only, we must bring into familiar and constant practice." See also Miller, *Seventeenth Century*, chap. 2 on "The Practice of Piety." Maclear ("New England and Fifth Monarchy," 226–29) has identified activism and optimistic expectation of the Millennium as hallmark

Their creed was fundamentally activist; idleness and sloth were cardinal transgressions. Few things were more foreign to them than either the reclusive existence of monastic orders or the leisurely life of the aristocracy. Puritanism was in this sense well aligned with the productive sectors of society and the rising middle class. The belief that God had assigned to each individual a specific calling through which to further the progress of his Kingdom on earth represented the very core of what has been described as the "Puritan Ethic" and declared to have "affected, not to say guided . . . the [American Revolutionary] movement in all its phases, from the resistance against Parliamentary taxation in the 1760s to the establishment of a national government and national policies in the 1790s."[23] Whereas Augustine did not consider heaven on earth possible, Puritans were building it in America.

The second point concerns the implications of the Puritan unity of religion and politics for liberty. Because the Puritans regarded politics as a religious activity, participation was not open to everyone. In Massachusetts and New Haven the right to vote and hold office was available only on the condition of participation in the holy covenant.[24] Cotton stated the requirement directly: *"the power of Civil Administrations is denied unto unbelievers, and committed to the Saints."*[25] His words confirm that seventeenth-century New England was deeply exclusionary based on religious affiliation and church membership, which was in turn restricted by public vetting procedures intended to ascertain the sainthood of those seeking admission. The rigor of these procedures was proportional to the intensity of millennialist anticipations among those in charge of the colony in question. In Davenport's New Haven, the process of gathering the first church took over a year because of the scrutiny in certifying the sainthood of each future administrator.[26]

---

characteristics of Puritanism. For Wilson's essay "Work-Day Religion" (August 11, 1876), see *PWW* 1:176–78.

[23] Edmund S. Morgan, "The Puritan Ethic and the American Revolution," *William and Mary Quarterly* 24, no. 1 (1967): 3. Cf. Perry Miller, *The New England Mind: From Colony to Province* (Cambridge, Mass.: Harvard University Press, 1953), 40: "That every man should have a calling and work hard in it was the first premise of Puritanism."

[24] Edmund S. Morgan, *Visible Saints: The History of the Puritan Idea* (Ithaca, N.Y.: Cornell University Press, 1963), 106–8.

[25] Cotton, *Discourse about Civil Government*, 19; emphasis in original.

[26] Stephen Foster, "English Puritanism and New England Institutions," in *Saints and Revolutionaries: Essays on Early American History*, ed. David D. Hall, John M. Murrin, and Thad W. Tate (New York: Norton, 1984), 32–33.

For those who disagreed with Puritanism there was no place in New England. In Massachusetts, the top duty of Winthrop's government was, according to Miller, "the duty of suppressing heresy, of subduing or somehow getting rid of dissenters—of being, in short, deliberately, vigorously, and consistently intolerant."[27] Religious dissent was unacceptable; non-Congregationalist churches gained a degree of legal foothold in Massachusetts only in the last decade of the seventeenth century, and even then they continued to face discrimination for half a century more. Whenever dissent did arise, the culprits were declared heretics and sentenced to exile, as happened to Gortonists, Anabaptists, Quakers, radical separatists such as Roger Williams, and Antinomians such as Anne Hutchinson. In the case of four Quakers who refused to leave in the late 1650s, the sentence was death by public hanging.[28]

The Puritans thus reproduced and even surpassed many of the same evils for which they denounced and fled England. Victims of persecution in their native land, they became perpetrators the moment they emigrated, gained autonomy, and established government according to their own version of Christianity. The purges were justified on biblical grounds and regarded as expressions of Christian love. In persecuting dissenters, the Puritans claimed to be following the will of God, acting as his agents in the great plan to restore heaven on earth and redeem humanity from oppression, suffering, and evil.

It is precisely this strategy of legitimating violence by claiming to possess a special knowledge (*gnosis*) of the meaning of history that represents a shared element between Puritanism and twentieth-century totalitarian regimes, making it possible to group them together.[29] Like these regimes, the Puritans too expressed fundamental dissatisfaction with existing reality, identified the root of all evil in flawed sociopolitical organization, and proceeded to re-engineer the world according to their vision and manual of choice: the Bible. Getting rid of dissenters and other misfits was part and parcel of the project to chisel the ideal out of the real; the Puritan progress to the Millennium depended on it. Hence New England Puritanism, whose spirit Wilson pledged to continue with such great pride when he arrived in Paris to press for the League of Nations,

[27] Miller, *Errand into Wilderness*, 5.

[28] Patricia U. Bonomi, *Under the Cope of Heaven: Religion, Society, and Politics in Colonial America*, updated ed. (Oxford: Oxford University Press, 2003), 28.

[29] See Eric Voegelin, "Gnostic Revolution—The Puritan Case," chap. 5 in *The New Science of Politics* (Chicago: University of Chicago Press, 1952).

illustrates perfectly Hannah Arendt's dictum that "Terror is lawfulness, if law is the law of the movement of some suprahuman force, Nature or History."[30] From day one, the Puritan quest for liberty in America was synonymous with totalizing and homogenizing attitudes mandating terror and exclusion.

The Myth of Religious Declension in Eighteenth-Century New England

That New England Puritans viewed their colonies and politics in eschatological terms does not yet mean that millennialism also informed the creation of the American republic. The American Revolution did not occur in the seventeenth century, but a century later, in 1776, by which time rationalism had spread across Europe, displaced the religious worldview in France, and penetrated British North America as well. The claim that the American Revolution proceeded in the context of eschatological convictions begs the question whether religion and eschatology survived among the colonists into the eighteenth century in the first place.

At first glance, colonial literature seems to point to a negative answer. Counter to the present argument that eschatology and millennialism survived intact and informed the ideology of the American Revolution, a lengthy record of grudging complaints left behind by Puritan elders appears to indicate that religious faith rapidly declined from one generation to the next until, by the early 1700s, it had vanished completely.[31]

---

[30] Arendt, "Ideology and Terror: A Novel Form of Government," *Review of Politics* 15, no. 4 (1953): 311.

[31] In academic circles, this interpretation had been accepted wisdom up until the early 1960s. Intellectual history of colonial New England was dominated by Vernon Parrington and Perry Miller, both of whom narrated the period spanning initial settlement and the American Revolution in terms of religious decline. Parrington contended in his classic overview of American literature and politics that "The seventeenth century in America . . . was a *sæculum theologicum*, and the eighteenth century was a *sæculum politicum*." *Main Currents in American Thought: An Interpretation of American Literature from the Beginnings to 1920* (New York: Harcourt, Brace, 1927, 1930), 1:vii. Unlike Parrington, Miller no longer relied on simple conceptual dichotomies, and he also cast his net wider, covering politics and literature as much as religion, law, philosophy, and education. Nonetheless, he too interpreted the transition from the seventeenth to the eighteenth century as a story of "declension" from Puritanism of the original settlers toward "confusion" among the successive generations. See especially Miller, *From Colony to Province*, bk. 1 and 2. Miller and Parrington thus effectively agreed that in New England the religious worldview did not endure much beyond the seventeenth century.

Already Bradford voiced concerns that younger settlers had forsaken the piety of the original Pilgrims and deserted God for land and profit accumulation. Confident and jubilant at the outset, his history *Of Plymouth Plantation* ends in the lethargy and confusion of a man convinced that the Puritans had failed in their spiritual quest for the Millennium and fallen out of God's favor.[32] Later Puritan leaders and intellectuals such as the poet Michael Wigglesworth inherited this bleak outlook, except they replaced Bradford's quiet lamentation with increasingly vocal reprimands. Appealing to the Old Testament, especially the verses of Jeremiah, they chastised their fellow settlers for lack of faith and strove to shock them into greater piety by invoking gruesome pictures of the desolation awaiting God's chosen people for having broken the sacred covenant.[33] A genre in its own right, the jeremiad dominated the literature of second-generation Puritans almost to the exclusion of all other literary forms.[34] All of this appears to confirm that whereas in the seventeenth century New England was a *sæculum theologicum*, by the eighteenth it had become a *sæculum politicum*.

However, when one turns from texts written by colonial elites to their social context, introduces the factor of "low" culture, and examines popular religious beliefs, practices, and institutions, the picture suddenly changes dramatically. Notwithstanding the jeremiads of the Puritan leaders, ordinary New Englanders continued to go to church and think eschatologically in stunning numbers even after the turn of the eighteenth century. Congregation formation and church building actually outpaced population growth in eighteenth-century colonial America.[35]

[32] Walter Wenska, "Bradford's Two Histories: Pattern and Paradigm in *Of Plymouth Plantation*," *Early American Literature* 13, no. 2 (1978): 157.

[33] For an especially vivid rendition of the terror of the Second Coming, see Wigglesworth, *The Day of Doom: Or, a Poetical Description of the Great and Last Judgment* (Cambridge, Mass., 1666 [1662]), which depicts sinners suddenly woken up by thunder and lightning in the middle of the night, crying for help, gnawing their tongues in horror, and ending up in a lake of fire and brimstone. See also idem, *The Poems of Michael Wigglesworth*, ed. Ronald A. Bosco (Lanham, Md.: University Press of America, 1989). Among the various offenses committed by the younger Puritans, Wigglesworth included carnality, indifference in faith, dead-heartedness, material excess, pride, luxury, debate, deceit, strife, false-dealing, covetousness, hypocrisy, and sloth. See his "God's Controversy with New England" (1662), in Conrad Cherry, ed., *God's New Israel: Religious Interpretations of American Destiny*, rev. and updated ed. (Chapel Hill: University of North Carolina Press, 1998), 47.

[34] Miller, *From Colony to Province*, 29.

[35] Jon Butler, *Becoming America: The Revolution before 1776* (Cambridge, Mass.: Harvard University Press, 2000), 186.

Microhistories of New England towns written since the 1970s have revealed, contrary to the declension argument, that religion remained alive and well:

> in eighteenth-century America—in city, village, and countryside—the idiom of religion penetrated all discourse, underlay all thought, marked all observances, gave meaning to every public and private crisis. . . . [The] separation of the colonial period into a seventeenth-century *sæculum theologicum* and an eighteenth-century *sæculum politicum* will no longer quite do, even as an epigram. For Americans, the eighteenth century . . . [was] an intermixture of both.[36]

Protestantism remained at the very center of the social universe in New England. Its millennialist tenets underwent important changes in the run-up to the American Revolution, as will emerge shortly, but the key point is that they did not vanish. They continued to structure the colonial Americans' understanding of their political quest for liberty and, when the Revolution arrived, served as the default cognitive matrix for the formulation of the republican ideology.

Only one question thus remains: if no decline in religious vitality took place among the settlers, why did their pastors take to chastising them for impiety and declaring their millennial mission on the verge of collapse? The answer is this: because the Puritans failed to accomplish their original project even despite their utmost spiritual and physical exertion—for reasons that lay entirely beyond their control. When Bradford and Winthrop with their congregations set sail for America, they saw themselves as spearheading a universal process; to recall, Winthrop envisioned the American "City upon a Hill" as a model that eventually would be emulated by the rest of the world, especially England. Unfortunately, just as the colonists succeeded in creating this model, they lost the audience for which the model was intended. In Miller's apt words, "New England did not lie, did not falter; it made good everything Winthrop demanded—wonderfully good—and then found that its lesson was rejected by those choice spirits for whom the exertion had been made."[37] Instead of exiling religious dissenters and hanging them if they came back, as Winthrop did to Quakers in Boston, Cromwell created the New Model Army and set England upon a path toward religious toleration.

---

[36] Bonomi, *Cope of Heaven*, 3, 9. See also Patricia U. Bonomi and Peter R. Eisenstadt, "Church Adherence in the Eighteenth-Century British American Colonies," *William and Mary Quarterly* 39, no. 2 (1982): 245–86.

[37] Miller, *Errand into Wilderness*, 13.

Puritan "Saints" returning to London, hoping to spread the Millennium from the New World to the Old, were dismissed as fanatical zealots and symbols of Massachusetts' retrograde conservatism.[38] Having uncovered the road toward salvation, Bradford, Winthrop, Cotton, and the rest of the Puritan leaders watched in consternation as humanity decided not to follow them, rendering them irrelevant.

The Puritans thus started chastising themselves because they were forced to drop their international ambitions and settle for "Puritanism in one country." In other words, the Puritan vanguard found itself much in the same situation as the Bolshevik vanguard in the wake of the October Revolution in Russia three centuries later. Already within one generation of their political success, the Puritans too became victims of history, which refused to proceed according to what they regarded as foolproof theory. In order to maintain the theory's credibility, they had no other option but to start blaming themselves for failing to live up to it. Their eschatology was sacred; that it did not materialize in secular reality presupposed a culprit; and the jeremiad told them where to find the culprit: in their own ranks, no matter that they were more pious than ever before. In the Soviet Union, the same self-flagellation surfaced in the form of ritual self-criticism and confessions of wrongdoing performed by even the most patently devout Bolsheviks.

Interestingly, in suspending their original international ambitions, "Puritanism in one country" began awakening its proponents to their local attachments. By seeing their ideals rejected in Europe, the Puritans became, for the first time, acutely aware of their separate American identity. Neither Bradford nor Winthrop had considered himself anything other than English; their eyes remained fixated on the Old World even as they sailed away from it. America represented for them only a temporary shelter granted by God to his agents so that in due time they might consolidate, multiply, and return to England, the main theater of the universal struggle between Christ and Antichrist, to strike the decisive blow.[39] Now, however, with England closed off indefinitely, New England was all the colonists had; they were there to stay. "Only with the second generation, and then in terms not of achievement but of shortcoming, does New England begin to be local and domestic."[40] The English émigrés

---

[38] See Maclear, "New England and the Fifth Monarchy," 250, 255.

[39] As Miller (*From Colony to Province*, 5) has noted, "[Puritans] were no refugees ... but English scholars, soldiers, and statesmen taking the long way about in order that someday they, or their children, or at least their friends, might rule in Lambeth."

[40] Miller, *From Colony to Province*, 15.

quietly started to think of themselves as Americans at the same time as they took to scolding themselves for insufficient piety.

In this vein, from the earliest stages of their collective identity Americans measured their domestic success partially in terms of their success abroad: in nautical miles still to be covered on their return journey to the Old World, which it was their divinely appointed task to redeem. Their covenant with God would remain unfulfilled and their status as "Saints" unconfirmed until they—or at least their ideals and institutions—crossed the seas and completed the millennial mission. Woodrow Wilson had no doubt that his voyage to Europe after World War I marked precisely this point and that the League of Nations was going to spread the American Millennium worldwide. He warned his fellow Americans that rejecting the League Covenant would mean betraying the nation's original principles and lowering the light intended to illuminate the paths of liberty; "utter blackness . . . would fall on the world."[41] Joining the League, on the other hand, would end the long Puritan detour through American wilderness and fulfill the original Puritan dream of saving Europe. In returning to Europe to fight and win the Great War, Wilson told the jubilant citizens of Genoa shortly after the Armistice, the American "children of freedom [came back] to their mother . . . to assist her in the high enterprise upon which her heart had always been set."[42]

Millennialism as a General Phenomenon in the Run-Up to the Revolution

Although secular eschatology remained in force throughout eighteenth-century New England, and although it was in this geographic region that the opening shots of the American Revolution were fired in 1776, the rebellion against England involved a number of other colonies. The claim that the Revolution had an eschatological dimension and that the republican cause of liberty was not merely a political cause but also a sacred one in the literal sense of the term necessitates at least a brief examination of other provinces and religious denominations, such as Presbyterianism (dominant in the mid-Atlantic region) and Anglicanism (established in Virginia). To what extent was millennialism a general phenomenon extending beyond Puritan New England?

In the first place, millennialism never was an exclusively Puritan trait. To survey seventeenth- and eighteenth-century English Reformation

---

[41] "Address in Boston" (February 24, 1919), *PWW* 55:243.
[42] "Remarks at the Station in Milan" (January 5, 1919), *PWW* 53:616.

theology is to discover that millennialism, unlike almost every other element of doctrine, was practically exempt from sectarian dispute: Presbyterians, Anglicans, dissenters—all substantially agreed on the meaning of the symbols of Revelation and expected the more or less imminent arrival of an earthly kingdom of goodness.[43] Deep denominational divides existed within and among eighteenth-century American colonies, but millennialism and secular eschatology—exegesis of the biblical myth of salvation in historical rather than strictly spiritual terms—represented a common frame of reference.

The outburst of piety and millennialist fervor between 1739 and 1745 provides an excellent case in point. Usually referred to as the "Great Awakening," it was not the first event of its kind; religious revivals had been occurring regularly throughout the colonies. However, whereas previous awakenings were localized and did not extend beyond the church or town of their origin, the Great Awakening became a genuine intercolonial event. Spread by charismatic preachers such as George Whitefield, who toured regions from Georgia to New England with fiery sermons in hand, it swept through all provinces and constituted a widely shared experience. On the one hand, this experience was one of intense controversy: an unprecedented crisis of the mind and spirit.[44] On the other, however, the crisis laid the foundations for American unity—precisely because the doctrinal disagreements frequently aligned American ministers against the same adversary: European ecclesiastical authority. In this vein, it is no exaggeration that the Great Awakening "was really the beginning of America's identity as a nation—the starting point of the Revolution."[45] Particularly Whitefield's religious rhetoric, "inviting everyone who heard it to adopt a new identity and join the imagined community of believers who embraced the new birth, . . . supplied a common encounter . . . that provided an initial, uniquely American collective experience."[46] Through

[43] Ernest Lee Tuveson, *Redeemer Nation: The Idea of America's Millennial Role* (Chicago: University of Chicago Press, 1968), 37.

[44] Richard Hofstadter, *America at 1750: A Social Portrait* (New York: Knopf, 1971), 216. "Before it subsided," Bonomi (*Cope of Heaven*, 133) has written, "the revival had unsettled the lives of more Americans and disrupted more institutions than any other single event . . . to that time."

[45] William McLoughlin, "The Role of Religion in the Revolution: Liberty of Conscience and Cultural Cohesion in the New Nation," in *Essays on the American Revolution*, ed. Stephen G. Kurtz and James H. Hutson (Chapel Hill: University of North Carolina Press, 1973), 198.

[46] Jerome Dean Mahaffey, *Preaching Politics: The Religious Rhetoric of George*

the religious discourse supplied by Whitefield and others, the different immigrant cultures populating America slowly abandoned their parochial attachments that had heretofore divided them and began to think of themselves as a single people.

On the doctrinal level, the Great Awakening represented the reaction of evangelical pietism against Enlightenment rationalism arriving from English and Scottish universities and gaining influence especially at Harvard, the main institution for the ordination of Protestant ministers in America. Against the emphasis on reason as an essential tool for comprehending God's universe, the Awakeners reasserted the importance of piety, saving grace, and the inner experience of the mystery of conversion. According to them, the rationalist clergy was corrupting the church and threatening to extinguish the spirit of Christ in the colonial society. Gilbert Tennent, one of the leaders of the Great Awakening, famously proclaimed that Americans were living "under the Ministry of dead Men" and urged them to "repair to the living" by a "New Birth."[47] What linked the Awakeners across different colonies was their collective aversion to formalism and scholasticism and their stress on introspection, ecumenical spirit, and vital religion. Their teachings did not make up a systematic theology, but rather embodied a shared mood and spiritual posture.[48] This generic character and dissociation from specific theological doctrines made the evangelical idiom wide enough to accommodate all kinds of content including politics—a key factor facilitating its subsequent availability for framing the ideas of the American Revolution.

The rise of a shared nationalist sentiment throughout the colonies ensued from the doctrinal controversy and was facilitated by a crisis over professional standards, which formed part of this controversy. Seeking to maintain their control over colonial churches, the rationalist clergy showed increasing reluctance to ordain ministers from the ranks of the rebellious Awakeners, effectively banning them from preaching. The Awakeners reacted with an open insurgency against the standing ecclesiastical order, such as by founding separate seminaries for the certification of evangelical preachers. They justified these steps by repeatedly

---

Whitefield and the Founding of a New Nation (Waco, Tex.: Baylor University Press, 2007), 72–73.

[47] Tennent, "The Danger of an Unconverted Ministry" (1740), in *The Great Awakening: Documents Illustrating the Crisis and Its Consequences*, ed. Alan Heimert and Perry Miller (Indianapolis: Bobbs-Merrill, 1967), 73–78, 86.

[48] Winthrop S. Hudson, *Religion in America: An Historical Account of the Development of American Religious Life*, 2nd ed. (New York: Scribner, 1973), 78.

invoking the biblical text in 2 Corinthians 6:14-17: "Be ye not unequally yoked together with Unbelievers. . . . Wherefore come out from among them, and be ye separate." Significantly, in many regions such as the mid-Atlantic the insurgency of pietists against rationalists corresponded to a revolt of younger ministers born and educated in America against older clergy trained in Europe.[49] What started as a religious opposition to rationalizing tendencies within Protestant theology was thus slowly metamorphosing into a political opposition by American ministers against European structures of privilege and order.[50]

It is worth emphasizing the sheer extent to which the Awakeners couched the revival of piety in eschatological terms. Evangelical conversion and resistance to the rationalizing tendencies imported from Europe were declared absolutely necessary if Americans wanted to remain God's chosen people, achieve the New Israel, and thereby fulfill the sacred purpose of the errand into the wilderness initiated by their Puritan forefathers. Jonathan Edwards, the most distinguished theologian of the Great Awakening and one of the towering figures in American religious history, made these points repeatedly throughout his sermons. Commenting on the religious frenzy in Northampton, Massachusetts, Edwards saw it as the material expression of divine providence and the beginning of the Millennium. "[T]his work of God's Spirit," he wrote, "so extraordinary and wonderful, is the dawning . . . of that glorious work of God, so often foretold in scripture, which, in the progress and issue of it, shall renew the world of mankind."[51] To hasten the reign of Christ, Edwards worked tirelessly to convince all churchgoers to undergo spiritual revival, scaring them with extraordinary images of infernal suffering should they remain unregenerate.[52] The urgency of his exhortations reflected his historical exegesis of the Book of Revelation, which led him to periodize universal history as a sequence of seven vials of God's wrath poured out onto seven

---

[49] See Bonomi, *Cope of Heaven*, 139–47; Cherry, *God's New Israel*, 29–30.

[50] Cf. Benedict Anderson's influential thesis situating the origins of nationalism to the Americas and crediting the invention of a new type of consciousness of national "imagined communities" to creole pioneers: elites, above all church functionaries, of pure European descent but born in the colonies and professionally discriminated against by Old World ecclesiastical leaders for that reason. See Anderson, *Imagined Communities: Reflections on the Origin and Spread of Nationalism*, 2nd ed. (London: Verso, 1991), esp. chap. 4.

[51] Edwards, "The Latter-Day Glory Is Probably to Begin in America," in *God's New Israel*, ed. Cherry, 54.

[52] See especially Edwards, "Sinners in the Hands of an Angry God," in *Heath Anthology*, ed. Lauter et al., 1:594.

forms of evil, progressively purging the *civitas terrena* of Antichrist and restoring the *civitas Dei* on earth. The latter was for Edwards a real historical event bound to occur on the American continent when pious men in possession of God's grace ascended into positions of civil and ecclesiastical control.[53]

In its overall effect, the Great Awakening solidified the habit of interpreting the colonial experience within the secular-eschatological framework of Protestant millennialism. This framework became increasingly popular even where millennialist ideas were traditionally less pronounced, such as among Anglicans. In addition, the Great Awakening increasingly predicated spiritual and material progress of the colonies on a rejection of European values and institutions. In both respects the revival of piety in 1739–1745 prepared the ground for the great religious uprising that occurred three short decades later and became known as the American Revolution.

The Eschatological Dimension
of the American Revolution

Unfortunately, the seminal role of eschatological consciousness and the Great Awakening in molding the political cause of American independence has not yet been fully recognized. Indeed, mainstream historiography of the ideological mainsprings of the American Revolution generates the impression that these factors played no part in shaping the event at all.[54] The Revolution tends to be portrayed exclusively as an eruption of Whig ideals and civic humanism: an eminently secular project centered on a rational pursuit of liberty in protest against arbitrary government. Eschatological vocabulary, the story goes, was either entirely absent from the republican ideology or only of secondary importance, serving as a smoke screen for what was really a set of nonreligious propositions. This interpretation not only fails to acknowledge the central position of religion and eschatology in colonial society, but also would have been

---

[53] Tuveson, *Redeemer Nation*, 30.

[54] What is often considered the classic account of the Revolution narrates its ideological origins with almost no regard to religion. See Bernard Bailyn, *The Ideological Origins of the American Revolution* (Cambridge, Mass.: Harvard University Press, 1967). Other leading studies express similar neglect. See, e.g., Gordon S. Wood, *The Creation of the American Republic, 1776–1789* (Chapel Hill: University of North Carolina Press, 1969); and J. G. A. Pocock, *The Machiavellian Moment: Florentine Political Thought and the Atlantic Republican Tradition* (Princeton, N.J.: Princeton University Press, 1975), 506–52.

entirely foreign to Woodrow Wilson, who comprehended the American Revolution first and foremost as a religious event: a signal moment when the spirit of authentic Christianity first broke into the secular world in the form of a new nation exemplary in its devotion to the Holy Scriptures.[55]

One suspects that much of the failure to appreciate the eschatological facet of the Revolution stems from two sources. The first is the disciplinary border between political and religious history, which has prevented political historians of the Revolution from exploring the spiritual significance of the republican ideology and, similarly, screened religious historians from the political ramifications of the millennialist teachings. The second is the aforementioned myth of religious declension, until recently the accepted view of religious life in eighteenth-century British North America. Even in the absence of any disciplinary divide between religious and political history, the millennialist dimension of the Revolution would have remained obscured had the historiography of the colonial period not achieved the recognition that, contrary to the declension thesis, religion in America survived past the seventeenth century. When this recognition took place in the 1960s, it simultaneously clarified that many participants in the American Revolution interpreted their actions in eschatological terms and demanded liberty because it was God's cause. In founding an independent American republic, they were founding the Millennium.

What, then, was the specific relationship between the Great Awakening and the American Revolution? One possible answer, in many ways the default reading of the interplay between the two events, challenges the conventional wisdom that the Revolutionary ideology originated among rationalist liberals. Instead, it suggests that "Liberalism was profoundly conservative, politically as well as socially, and that its leaders, insofar as they did in fact embrace the Revolution, were the most reluctant of rebels."[56] Whereas in the French Revolution rationalism was the progressive worldview, in the American Revolution it constituted the conservative force. The true mainstay of the American Revolution, the progressive side, was not the rationalists, but the evangelical revivalists: the Awakeners. Not John Locke, but Jonathan Edwards is the key intellectual progenitor of the Revolution:

[55] See especially Wilson, "Address in Denver on the Bible" (May 7, 1911), *PWW* 23:20.

[56] Alan Heimert, *Religion and the American Mind from the Great Awakening to the Revolution* (Cambridge, Mass.: Harvard University Press, 1966), vii–viii.

"Evangelical" religion, which had as its most notable formal expression the "Calvinism" of Jonathan Edwards, was not the retrograde philosophy that many historians rejoice to see confused in America's Age of Reason. Rather Calvinism, and Edwards, provided pre-Revolutionary America with a radical, even democratic, social and political ideology, and evangelical religion embodied, and inspired, a thrust toward American nationalism.[57]

This perspective on the relationship between the Great Awakening and the American Revolution thus not only takes it for granted that religion continued to flourish in eighteenth-century America, implying that any talk of spiritual decline is misplaced. By claiming that "what was awakened in 1740 was the spirit of American democracy,"[58] it also casts evangelical millennialism as the dominant ideological origin of the American republic. In this manner, it recovers the eschatological dimension of the American Revolution as a crusade of God's elect against the Antichrist.

Nonetheless, this revisionist reading is not without problems, the chief of which is that it overstates its case. Although it restores the eschatological aspect of the Revolution to its rightful place, it also distorts the role of the rationalists: far from being only "the most reluctant of rebels," some of the nation's leading Founding Fathers came from their ranks, including John Adams and Thomas Jefferson. Adams's cool Arminianism and Jefferson's Anglican affiliation and fondness for the Renaissance did not predispose them against the Revolution at all. In other words, religious positions were not as indicative of political attitudes.[59] The relationship between the Great Awakening and the Revolution was more ambiguous. While it is correct that the revivalists were ardently in favor of the Revolution, this did not mean that the rationalist critics of the Great Awakening supported the English crown. Both sides to the Great Awakening controversy, revivalists *and* rationalists, joined hands in enthusiastic support for the cause of independence.

To understand why and how this was possible, one first has to recognize that in secular eschatology the relationship between the

---

[57] Heimert, *Religion and the American Mind*, vii–viii.

[58] Heimert and Miller, *Great Awakening: Documents*, lxi.

[59] In this respect Heimert's interpretation, according to Edmund Morgan, "[partook] more of fantasy than of history." See Morgan, review of *Religion and the American Mind*, by Alan Heimert, *William and Mary Quarterly* 24, no. 3 (1967): 457–59. In a similar vein, Nathan O. Hatch wrote that Heimert "jumps [too] quickly from the Awakening to the Revolution." *The Sacred Cause of Liberty: Republican Thought and the Millennium in Revolutionary New England* (New Haven, Conn.: Yale University Press, 1977), 26. See also Sidney E. Mead, "Through and Beyond the Lines," *Journal of Religion* 48, no. 3 (1968): 274–88; and Bonomi, *Cope of Heaven*, 161.

eschatological and the secular is not simply one-way, with religious convictions determining political attitudes, but two-way. On the one hand, the myth of salvation structures historical consciousness and political action, but on the other, historical and political developments also shape the exegesis of the salvationist myth. Focusing only on the impact of religion on politics obscures the reverse impact of politics on religion in the period spanning the Great Awakening and the Revolution. During this period, one political event in particular, the French and Indian War, generated important religious consequences that represent the missing link between the account of Revolutionary attitudes as polarized along religious lines and the actual support for the Revolution across the entire religious spectrum.

The first and most important religious effect of the French and Indian War was that by posing a threat to all settlers regardless of religious affiliation, the conflict brought revivalists and rationalists together and substantially mended the rupture from the Great Awakening. Controversies surrounding conversion or professional standards of ministry were abandoned in favor of core affinities. Second, the war stimulated Protestant millennialism. Largely exempt from sectarian disputes, the eschatological interpretation of history was the most solid among the newfound affinities. Revivalists and rationalists readily agreed that in fighting the French they were waging a crusade against the Catholic Antichrist so that God's reign in history might be realized. "More concerned with the common struggle than with divisive questions relating to the spread of vital piety, the clergy found remarkable solidarity in a renewed sense of apocalyptic history."[60] Finally, the French and Indian War not only unified the religious factions within the colonies by directing their attention to their shared eschatological convictions, but also altered the eschatological idiom so that it became practically indistinct from political language.[61] "It is striking," one historian has remarked, "how often the political terms 'liberty' and 'tyranny' appear in the religious pronouncements about the French and Indian War."[62] Satan now referred to an enemy nation, the Millennium to political sovereignty, and vital piety, for Jonathan Edwards an evangelical practice of prayer and mediation, to armed combat. "The art of War," one clergyman thundered, "becomes

---

[60] Hatch, *Sacred Cause*, 40.

[61] Bonomi, *Cope of Heaven*, 155, 166, 186.

[62] Ruth H. Bloch, *Visionary Republic: Millennial Themes in American Thought, 1756–1800* (Cambridge: Cambridge University Press, 1985), 42.

a Part of our Religion."[63] Eschatology became secularized and political struggles sacralized to an extraordinary degree in the colonies just prior to the American Revolution.

When shortly after the French and Indian War England became the main political adversary of American colonists, they adjusted their biblical exegesis to the new political landscape and aimed the machinery of secular eschatology at the new target. England succeeded France as the main agent of the Antichrist, leaving the American colonies as the last remaining bastion of Christ on earth. The substitution often proceeded with astonishing simplicity, as demonstrated by Reverend Samuel Cooper of the Brattle Street Church in Boston. Twenty years after mobilizing his congregation against the French, Cooper recycled his old sermons verbatim to rouse support for the American Revolution, the sole alteration consisting of replacing the French with the English as "our Anti-Christian Enemies."[64] By the 1770s leading colonial clergy, both rationalist and revivalist, north and south, was addressing the political crisis using the language of radical Whigs.[65] Sermon literature had become indistinct from political proclamations.[66]

Just as clerical leaders turned religion into political agitation against England, lay leaders turned the political cause of American liberty and independence into a spiritual event foreshadowing the Millennium. John Adams wrote already in 1765 the following: "I always consider the settlement of America with reverence and wonder, as the opening of a grand scene and design in Providence for the illumination of the ignorant, and the emancipation of the slavish part of mankind all over the earth."[67] Similarly Jefferson, echoing Winthrop's plan to erect a "City upon a Hill," proclaimed in 1801 that "A just and solid republican government maintained here will be a standing monument and example for the aim and imitation of the people of other countries."[68] Even the scientific mind of

---

[63] Samuel Davies, *The Curse of Cowardice* (Woodbridge, N.J., 1759), 2, 304. See also James Cogswell, *God, the Pious Soldier's Strength and Instructor* (Boston, 1757).

[64] See Hatch, *Sacred Cause*, 52n72.

[65] Bonomi, *Cope of Heaven*, 212.

[66] "The large majority of ministers who published sermons during the Revolutionary era," according to Melvin B. Endy, "justified the war effort by a rationale that was more political than religious." "Just War, Holy War, and Millennialism in the American Revolution," *William and Mary Quarterly* 42, no. 1 (1985): 3.

[67] Cited in Tuveson, *Redeemer Nation*, 25.

[68] *The Writings of Thomas Jefferson*, ed. A. E. Bergh (Washington, D.C.: Thomas Jefferson Memorial Association, 1907), 10:217.

Benjamin Franklin apparently imagined the meaning of the American Revolution and the United States in eschatological terms. When on July 4, 1776, the Continental Congress summoned him to design a seal for the new republic, Franklin proposed an image of the Red Sea dividing under the hand of Moses and crushing the pharaoh's chariot, with the slogan "Rebellion to Tyrants Is Obedience to God" inscribed underneath.[69] Political language thus frequently resembled sermon literature as much as sermon literature resembled political language.

The religious dimension of the American Revolution is also clearly apparent from battle symbolism such as regimental flags, many of which bore the motto "An Appeal to Heaven" or the motto that Franklin proposed for the national seal.[70] The call to arms was frequently presented as a soul-cleansing experience, offering the militiamen and Continental Army soldiers the opportunity to earn God's forgiveness for past sins. In return they would acquire the kind of protection promised by God to his repentant children in the Old Testament.[71]

Biblical eschatology was by no means the only optic through which the revolutionaries comprehended their actions; it was interwoven with other powerful cognitive frameworks, especially the ideas of Locke, who had become well known in America by this time. However, as a rationale for sacrifice the Bible tended to be much more familiar and intelligible to the rank and file than English theories of liberty. When years after the Revolution one farmer was asked whether he was defending such theories while fighting at Concord Bridge, he proclaimed that he had never heard of Locke and that his reading consisted entirely of the Bible, the Catechism, a popular psalter, and the Almanac.[72] Colonists participated in combat for a number of reasons, including such perennial motives as material gain and the wish not to let down comrades and officers, but religion and millennial expectations represented an important factor also. "Many did consider the glorious cause to be sacred," it has been noted;

[69] Cherry, "Revolution, Constitution, and a New Nation's Destiny," in *God's New Israel*, 65.

[70] See Bonomi, *Cope of Heaven*, 215–16, and Charles Royster, *A Revolutionary People at War: The Continental Army and American Character, 1775–1783* (Chapel Hill: University of North Carolina Press, 1979), 174.

[71] Perry Miller, "From the Covenant to the Revival," in *The Shaping of American Religion*, ed. James W. Smith and A. Leland Jamison (Princeton, N.J.: Princeton University Press, 1961), 333.

[72] Bonomi, *Cope of Heaven*, 5.

"their war, as the ministers never tired of reminding them, was just and providential."[73]

The success of the Revolution verified the millennial prophecy empirically. In the eyes of many Americans, history confirmed their eschatological teachings, leading them to celebrate their political victory as a visible proof of their unique status as God's chosen people. The birth of the United States was widely perceived as the dawning of the New Jerusalem and immediately generated prophecies of further progress and worldwide redemption under America's lead. Ezra Stiles, president of Yale University and a leading rationalist theologian, saw in George Washington the "American Joshua . . . raised up by . . . the Sovereign of the Universe for the great work of leading the armies of [the] American Joseph . . . to Liberty and Independence."[74] Washington's victory fore-shadowed the tremendous glory that awaited the American Israel in the decades and centuries ahead. For Stiles the true meaning of the Revolution extended beyond its own era and place; it was an event of universal significance. Americans had defeated not just the British monarchy, but monarchy everywhere. In the new American republic, Europe received an image of its own inevitable future.[75]

In conclusion, the extensive eschatological imagery and language of the Revolutionary period indicate that while the ideological origins of the United States of America cannot be understood apart from the influence of Enlightenment humanism, Whig political philosophy and Locke's theories of liberal government are not the whole story or perhaps not even the main part of the story. The other ingredient, almost completely ignored by political historians of the Revolution, was Protestant millennialism, which imbued the colonial struggle for liberty with a utopian, salvationist consciousness. Overall, "religion, republicanism, and liberalism did not compete with one another for ascendancy [but rather] . . . blended together to construct the dominant ideology."[76] This ideology thus constituted a veritable secularized eschatology: liberal-republican millennialism. This ambiguous complex of ideas was neither sacred nor secular but both at the same time. It watered down the biblical myth of

---

[73] Robert Middlekauff, "Why Men Fought in the American Revolution," in *Saints and Revolutionaries*, ed. Hall, Murrin, and Tate, 320.

[74] Stiles, "The United States Elevated to Glory and Honour," in *God's New Israel*, ed. Cherry, 85.

[75] Edmund S. Morgan, *The Gentle Puritan: A Life of Ezra Stiles, 1727–1795* (New Haven, Conn.: Yale University Press, 1962), 454–55.

[76] Mahaffey, *Preaching Politics*, 243.

salvation to the level of a political project while simultaneously elevating the latter to the status of the former. The resulting amalgam of political ideas and Protestant eschatology in Revolutionary America has been referred to as "civil millennialism" or "apocalyptic Whiggism."[77]

Whichever term one prefers, the phenomenon was nothing new. Already the first Puritan magistrates, it was seen, commonly used theological vocabulary, portrayed America as the gathering ground of God's elect, justified their political actions with reference to the Bible, and regarded the material progress of their colonies as an empirical confirmation of their sacred mandate to redeem the world. In endowing the American Revolution with an eschatological dimension, comprehending it as a crusade on behalf of the Kingdom of God, and viewing its success as a verification of the biblical prophecy, its leaders were following an existing tradition.

In the newly established United States, it is about to be seen, interpretations of the eschatological myth in secular terms identical with the political goals of the nation would continue down to Wilson, who in some respects represents the culminating point of American liberal-republican millennialism. His prowess as a pulpit preacher was so extraordinary that he was mistaken for an ordained minister on at least one occasion. He certainly believed that Americans were the vanguard of God, who had assigned them a special destiny, a conviction linking him to seventeenth-century leaders such as Winthrop and eighteenth-century politicians such as Franklin and Adams. America, Wilson famously declared, was the only "spirit among the nations of the world."[78]

---

[77] See, respectively, Hatch, *Sacred Cause*, 22–23, and Tuveson, *Redeemer Nation*, 24. For Tuveson (*Redeemer Nation*, 24), John Adams's apocalyptic Whiggism constitutes "the prototype of what was to be . . . the central American attitude toward government."

[78] "Address on the American Spirit" (July 13, 1916), *PWW* 37:415. According to Tuveson (*Redeemer Nation*, 175), this assertion "gave classic expression to . . . the millennialist vision for the United States."

CHAPTER FOUR

"MANIFEST DESTINY"

Secularized Eschatology in the Nineteenth-Century United States

The failure to comprehend the eschatological dimension of American liberal internationalism and Wilson's statecraft is not due simply to ignorance or inattention; chalking it up to these factors would be a mistake. Rather, it is a symptom of a broader, well-established cultural script maintaining that religion played no significant role in America's history and founding, that the liberal-republican ideology of the American Revolution did not rely on biblical assumptions, and that since its birth the United States has been a secular democracy defined by the constitutional separation of church and state. Forged at the formative stage of American historiography during the Progressive era, when "there was no integration of religious history into American history, no sense that it constituted a 'main theme' in the profession's priorities,"[1] this script remains widely embraced and represents a key ingredient in the contemporary construction of American national identity. The field of international relations, which has been famously dubbed "an American social science,"[2] is not exempt from its influence.

---

[1] Harry Stout, "Religion, Communications, and the Career of George Whitefield," in *Communication and Change in American Religious History*, ed. Leonard I. Sweet (Grand Rapids, Mich.: Eerdmans, 1993), 109.

[2] Stanley Hoffmann, "An American Social Science: International Relations," *Daedalus* 106, no. 3 (1977): 41–60.

Nevertheless, this script obscures as much as it reveals: religion and eschatology figured prominently in colonial politics up to and including the American Revolution. From popular beliefs pervading colonial church and society and from writings by civil and ecclesiastical elites alike, it is evident that in seventeenth- and eighteenth-century America religion and politics were not separate, let alone opposed, but fused together. Their unity was so axiomatic as to make pastor and legislator, sermon and policy agenda, church and state nearly indistinct. Far from disqualifying God from politics, many in the newborn American republic regarded politics as Christianity in practice and deemed themselves God's agents on earth, a nation of saints appointed to fulfill the prophecy of salvation. In this they at once resembled the original generation of settlers and foreshadowed Wilson's own understanding of the relationship between the religious and the political.

Instead of divorcing politics from religion, the powerful revival of piety and millennial expectations that was the American Revolution thus strengthened the role of eschatological consciousness as a framework structuring political ideas and actions. In the nineteenth-century United States, this framework continued to thrive. In the eyes of its participants, the victory of the Revolution verified their shared biblical scheme of history and confirmed America's special role as a redeemer nation: the United States was born a sacred country with a divinely ordained mission to perform in the world.[3] Although purporting to represent a radical break with the past by basing its legitimacy on nothing higher than itself and its human makers, the Constitution immediately became sacralized: millennial expectations and symbolism previously centered on the authority of God were reconfigured, reabsorbed, and put in the service of the republic.[4] The faith in the coming of the Kingdom of God was thereby secularized into a belief in social and political progress—first domestic

---

[3] Hannah Arendt went so far as to proclaim this self-adoration key to the new nation's subsequent survival: "the simple fact that the [American Revolution] succeeded . . . in founding a new body politic stable enough to survive the onslaught of centuries to come . . . was decided the very moment when the Constitution began to be 'worshipped,' even though it had hardly begun to operate." *On Revolution* (New York: Viking, 1965), 199.

[4] In the words of H. Richard Niebuhr, "The old idea of American Christians as a chosen people who had been called to a special task was turned into the notion of a chosen nation especially favored. . . . As the nineteenth century went on the note of divine favoritism was increasingly sounded." *The Kingdom of God in America* (Chicago: Willet, Clark, 1937), 179. Cf. Robert N. Bellah, *The Broken Covenant: American Civil Religion in Time of Trial*, 2nd ed. (Chicago: University of Chicago Press, 1992), 4.

and ultimately international. This belief found its most popular expression in the doctrine of "manifest destiny," which cast America's territorial and ideological expansion as divinely foreordained and hence outside the scope of human choice and political negotiation.

Born in the middle of the nineteenth century, by its end President Wilson would inherit the dogma and language of "manifest destiny"[5] and employ it in the same fashion: to depoliticize the political, to obscure the choice-based and partisan character of his projects, and to (mis)portray his domestic and foreign agenda, including the League of Nations, as inevitable and beneficial to all. In this vein, his religious utopianism in the form of Protestant eschatology was organically intertwined with his political utopianism in the form of liberal internationalism, exemplifying the broader tradition of nineteenth-century American liberal-republican millennialism.

Alexis de Tocqueville on the Nexus of Politics and Religion in American Democracy

The unity of politics and eschatological religion was explicit in the discourse of nineteenth-century American democracy. That the republic owed its birth and progress to God, and that its future destiny was to save the world, whether by passive example or active intervention—these beliefs were ubiquitous and readily apparent to foreign visitors. The nineteenth-century German pastor Philip Schaff, for instance, observed that religion constituted the ethical foundation of American liberalism. "The impulse towards freedom and the sense of law and order are inseparably united," he reported to audiences in Berlin and Frankfurt, "and both rest on a moral basis."[6] Another, more famous visitor, the French politician and historian Alexis de Tocqueville, traveled to the United States in the early 1830s and gained similar impressions. He recorded them in his *Democracy in America*, a work celebrated already by his liberal contemporaries such as John Stuart Mill and nowadays spoken of as "the best book ever written on democracy and the best book ever

---

[5] See his "Annual Message on the State of the Union" (December 7, 1920), in *The Papers of Woodrow Wilson*, ed. Arthur S. Link et al. (Princeton, N.J.: Princeton University Press, 1966–1994) [henceforth *PWW*], 66:485.

[6] Schaff, *America: A Sketch of Its Political, Social, and Religious Character*, ed. Perry Miller (Cambridge, Mass.: Belknap, 1961), 47.

written on America."[7] The praise suggests that Tocqueville grasped the relationship between politics and religion in America with authenticity usually reserved only to insiders, and that his account coincided with their self-imagination.

The reference point against which Tocqueville sketched this account came from his experience of the French national past and politics. Hailing from an old aristocratic family whose several members were executed during the French Revolution for siding with the king, he witnessed the excesses of democracy in France firsthand. When he was born in 1805, the Jacobin terror was still recent and Napoleon Bonaparte was busy conquering Europe. Such events turned Tocqueville into a conservative critic of the new regime, but without necessarily aligning him with the old. Dismayed by the outcome of the French Revolution, he was nonetheless convinced that religious absolutism was dead. Christianity and liberalism were for him opposite ideological forces.

This is why a surprising discovery awaited him on the other side of the Atlantic: here, unlike in France, religion and politics went hand in hand. As Tocqueville described his first days in America, "On my arrival in the United States it was the religious aspect of the country that first struck my mind. As I prolonged my stay, I perceived the great political consequences that flowed from these new facts."[8] Whereas in France after 1789 "the spirit of religion and the spirit of freedom almost always move[d] in contrary directions," in the New World Tocqueville found them "united intimately with one another."[9] Their union was so organic as to make them indistinguishable: "Americans so completely confuse Christianity and freedom in their minds," Tocqueville noted, "that it is almost impossible to have them conceive of the one without the other."[10] American priests, for example, did not "act solely in consideration of the other life . . . [but rather] speak so often of the goods of this world . . . [that] you will be altogether surprised . . . to find the political where you believe you will see only the religious."[11] Tocqueville realized that in early nineteenth-century America religion and above all the King James

---

[7] Harvey Mansfield and Delba Winthrop, introduction to *Democracy in America*, by Alexis de Tocqueville, ed. and trans. Mansfield and Winthrop (Chicago: University of Chicago Press, 2000), xvii.

[8] Tocqueville, *Democracy*, 282.

[9] Tocqueville, *Democracy*, 282.

[10] Tocqueville, *Democracy*, 280–81.

[11] Tocqueville, *Democracy*, 280–81.

Bible performed a political role as guides for legislative, executive, and judicial action; and that in turn liberal principles, codified in the U.S. Constitution and Declaration of Independence, possessed theological significance as divinely prescribed means of national salvation. It was instantly apparent to him that the majority of American citizens comprehended the secular progress of liberty and their republic as an eschatological process unfolding according to a scriptural pattern.

Without referring to "secularization," "secularized eschatology," or "political religion," technical terms developed only later on, Tocqueville thus nevertheless expressed the idea that in America religion, by which he meant primarily Protestantism, was a political institution, just as the polis was a sacred community. What he witnessed around him, supplemented by his reading of colonial histories, led him to declare that "From the beginning . . . politics and religion were in accord, and they have not ceased to be so."[12] History and eschatology, national progress and divine providence, the building of the American republic and the pilgrimage to the Millennium—these were perceived by many nineteenth-century Americans as synonymous. In the United States Tocqueville glimpsed the best expression of what he considered a natural tendency of the human mind to "regulate political society and the divine city in a uniform manner; . . . to *harmonize* the earth with Heaven."[13] In short, he found himself in the midst of a society striving to secularize its vision of salvation. What structured the everyday existence of the United States into a coherent, meaningful national narrative was the vision of a liberal-republican utopia in fulfillment of the biblical prophecy.

Tocqueville made numerous other comments about the nexus of politics and religion in America and about its various implications. The significance of these comments may be summarized in two general points. The first is that by repeatedly highlighting the interlocking of religion and politics in the new American republic, Tocqueville undermines any and all historical representations casting the nineteenth-century United States as a purely secular and political project.[14] The second point is that he

---

[12] Tocqueville, *Democracy*, 275.

[13] Tocqueville, *Democracy*, 275.

[14] Patricia Bonomi, mentioned earlier as one of the leading figures in the new historiography of American church and society, indeed motivated her recovery of the missing religious element in part by the wish to reconcile the standard narrative of American intellectual history with Tocqueville's classic book. See Bonomi, *Under the Cope of Heaven: Religion, Society, and Politics in Colonial America*, updated ed. (Oxford: Oxford University Press, 2003), 222, where she stresses that Tocqueville's declarations in *Democracy in*

documented not only liberal-republican millennialism, but also actions justified by its ostensibly universal rhetoric. *Democracy in America* maps in vivid detail the political functions of the American liberal idea of progress: totalizing and exclusionary practices at home and expansionism and imperialism abroad.

Woodrow Wilson's liberal internationalism served similar purposes in the immediate aftermath of World War I: his religiously inspired language of universal morality and America's predestination to world leadership merely cloaked in seemingly apolitical terms what was, at its core, a ruthless pursuit of narrow self-interest. Tocqueville's passages on the latter point therefore merit further attention, but not before fleshing out the dominant form of secularized eschatology and liberal-republican millennialism in the nineteenth-century United States: the narrative "manifest destiny."

Origins and Meaning of "Manifest Destiny"

The phrase "manifest destiny" was originally coined by John L. O'Sullivan.[15] While today his name is likely to be familiar only to a small circle of American intellectual historians, in the two decades preceding the American Civil War he was a figure of some note. A staunch supporter of President Andrew Jackson, O'Sullivan edited two influential magazines in the 1840s: *New York Morning News* and *Democratic Review*. Readership of the former included members of the U.S. Congress, whereas the latter served as a proxy for the Democratic Party and often contained contributions from leading political and literary figures such as Nathaniel Hawthorne, Edgar Allan Poe, and Senator Lewis Cass.

America make sense only when one grants "religion's . . . unique and respected position . . . in the life of the new republic." Similarly, Henry F. May noted that the narrative of nineteenth-century America as a secular society fails to take into account that "such acute observers . . . as Tocqueville . . . reported to astonished Europeans that religion in America, fragmented and unsupported by government, was healthier than religion in Europe." For May, "this was true during the whole of the nineteenth century, the period when America formed its characteristic way of life and rose to world power. While religion was under powerful attack in several major industrial countries, it continued to pervade and sustain American culture. People in America continued to take it for granted that religious and national values were closely related and indeed almost indistinguishable from each other." *Ideas, Faiths, and Feelings: Essays on American Intellectual and Religious History 1952–1982* (New York: Oxford University Press, 1983), 165.

[15] Julius W. Pratt, "The Origin of 'Manifest Destiny,'" *American Historical Review* 32, no. 4 (1927): 798. See also idem, "John L. O'Sullivan and Manifest Destiny," *New York History* 14 (1933): 213–34.

Both journals gave O'Sullivan a degree of influence on American politics and culture and played an important role in popularizing his notion of "manifest destiny." By his death in 1895, this notion had captured the imagination of many Americans and became a permanent part of the nation's political vocabulary.

O'Sullivan invented the phrase in an editorial contribution to the national debate on the annexation of Texas in 1845. Supporting the annexation, O'Sullivan denounced those opposed to it as unpatriotic and urged all Americans to abandon partisan disputes in favor of national unity on the issue. Rejecting Texas, O'Sullivan contended, would "check the fulfillment of our manifest destiny to overspread the continent allotted to us by Providence for the free development of our yearly multiplying millions."[16] From the first, the phrase "manifest destiny" thus connoted an attempt to justify territorial expansion by portraying it as a predetermined and apolitical logic of history, thereby obscuring the voluntary and fundamentally political nature of the action. O'Sullivan took his argument so far as to proclaim any resistance to territorial expansion meaningless. Americans did not have any choice: "Texas has been absorbed into the Union in the inevitable fulfillment of the general law which is rolling our population westward."[17] In the final analysis, territorial expansion was nonnegotiable, ordered by the Lord of history. By casting it as such, O'Sullivan removed it from the scope of ethical judgment and political negotiation.

The annexation of Texas was already a foregone conclusion when O'Sullivan published the editorial, and so his remarks and phraseology escaped any greater notice. Only a few months later, however, the U.S. government began considering the annexation of another region, Oregon, and the controversy regarding the legitimacy of expansion broke out anew. This time O'Sullivan entered the fray early. For the United States the issue of Oregon posed considerable legal difficulties: the title to Oregon was ambiguous at best and quite possibly belonged to Britain, which possessed territory above the forty-ninth parallel and could claim at least a portion of Oregon on the basis of adjacency, a principle recognized under customary international law. Yet O'Sullivan had no doubt that Oregon, all of it, belonged to the United States, and he furnished his fellow Americans with the following justification, which in his view trumped all others:

---

[16] [John L. O'Sullivan], "Annexation," *Democratic Review* 17, nos. 85–86 (1845): 5.
[17] [O'Sullivan], "Annexation," 7.

we have a still better title than any that can ever be constructed out of all these antiquated materials of old black-letter international law. . . . And that claim is by the right of our manifest destiny to overspread and to possess the whole of the continent which Providence has given us for the development of the great experiment of liberty and federated self-government entrusted to us.[18]

As in the case of Texas, O'Sullivan explained the claim to Oregon with reference to God's grand design, in which the United States represented the chosen nation and instrument of universal salvation. International law posed no serious obstacle, for it represented a vestige of a bygone era and a bygone world: the Old World of Europe governed by corrupt monarchies and unelected rulers. The New World of America, based on liberal principles predestined to reign supreme in the future, was no longer bound by the shackles of this illiberal past.

This time around O'Sullivan's words struck a chord: expansionists and antiexpansionists alike picked up "manifest destiny" almost overnight. The former used it to justify their policy; the latter made it a target of their scathing remarks. Within a week the expression made its first appearance on the floor of Congress. On January 3, 1846, in a speech discussing the resolution to terminate the shared tenancy of Oregon and expel Britain from the territory, Massachusetts representative Robert C. Winthrop mentioned "that new revelation of right which has been designated as the right of our manifest destiny to spread over this whole continent."[19] Referring directly to O'Sullivan's article in *New York Morning News*, Winthrop commented as follows: "It has been avowed in a leading Administration journal that [manifest destiny] . . . is our best and strongest title—one so clear, so pre-eminent, and so indisputable, that if Great Britain had all our other titles in addition to its own, they would weigh nothing against it."[20] To be sure, Winthrop distanced himself from O'Sullivan's argument and even poked fun at it, but his remarks on the congressional floor indicate that for him as well as for O'Sullivan, opponent and proponent of expansion, "manifest destiny" signified the same cluster of ideas. These included the belief that history was progressive and eschatological; that the *eschaton* was secular, having the concrete shape of a liberal republic; that God had chosen America to perform the task of world redemption; and that this position gave the United States the right to spread in disregard of any established legal norms.

---

[18] [John L. O'Sullivan], "The True Title," *New York Morning News*, December 27, 1845, 2.

[19] Cited in Pratt, "Origin of 'Manifest Destiny,'" 795.

[20] Cited in Pratt, "Origin of 'Manifest Destiny,'" 795.

O'Sullivan communicated these convictions even before he used them to justify the expansion of the American republic into Texas and Oregon. In other words, the constitutive ideas of "manifest destiny" predate the term. When he coined the phrase in 1845, he merely put a stamp on a set of views formulated already in the late 1830s. It was in these earlier years, specifically in 1839, that the most elaborate explanation of what would subsequently receive the label "manifest destiny" appeared in an anonymous editorial in *Democratic Review*. Commonly ascribed to O'Sullivan himself, the passage begs to be reproduced in full:

> We are the nation of human progress, and who will, what can, set limits to our onward march? Providence is with us, and no earthly power can. . . . The far-reaching, the boundless future will be the era of American greatness. In its magnificent domain of space and time, the nation of many nations is destined to manifest to mankind the excellence of divine principles; to establish on earth the noblest temple ever dedicated to the worship of the Most High—the Sacred and the True. Its floor shall be a hemisphere—its roof the firmament of the star-studded heavens, and its congregation a Union of many Republics. . . . We must onward to the fulfillment of our mission—to the entire development of the principle of our organization—freedom of conscience, freedom of person, freedom of trade and business pursuits, universality of freedom and equality. This is our high destiny, and in nature's eternal, inevitable decree of cause and effect we must accomplish it. All this will be our future history, to establish on earth the moral dignity and salvation of man—the immutable truth and beneficence of God. For this blessed mission to the nations of the world, which are shut out from the life-giving light of truth, has America been chosen; and her high example shall smite unto death the tyranny of kings . . . and carry the glad tidings of peace and good will where myriads now endure an existence scarcely more enviable than that of beasts of the field. Who . . . can doubt that our country is destined to be *the great nation* of futurity?[21]

Although uttered two centuries later, these hopes and beliefs would have been instantly recognizable to America's original settlers such as William Bradford or Governor John Winthrop, for the main themes running through the editorial merely repeat many of the central tenets of Puritan millennialism: the definition of history as providential progress toward liberty, the notion of America's vanguard role in this process, and the vision of universal salvation defined in secular terms. From the broader perspective of American intellectual history, O'Sullivan was no original thinker. His conception of America's "manifest destiny" reflected a

---

[21] [John L. O'Sullivan], "The Great Nation of Futurity," *Democratic Review* 6, no. 23 (1839): 427, 430.

well-established tradition that had been in wide circulation for several generations and was readily understandable to his contemporaries.

This "destinarian" tradition would remain in wide circulation and readily understandable for at least fifty years more, down to President Wilson. Not all his contemporaries agreed with it, of course. It was with open scorn that the influential newspaper editor Carl Schurz, for example, remarked in 1893, shortly after President Harrison's attempt to take over Hawaii, that "Whenever there is a project on foot to annex foreign territory to this republic, the cry 'manifest destiny' is raised to produce the impression that all opposition to such a project is a struggle against fate."[22] Yet Wilson himself continually affirmed the providential shape of history and America's special destiny, and he did it using the kind of language that, consciously or not, repeated many of O'Sullivan's passages almost verbatim. During a speaking tour of American cities to rally public support for the ratification of the Versailles Treaty, he proclaimed that the "[American] view is to the future"; that America "marches . . . with its eyes lifted to . . . the great events which are slowly culminating, in the providence of God, in the lifting of civilization to new levels and new achievements"; and that the bravery of American soldiers in Europe stemmed from their confident realization that they "owned the ideals and conceptions that will govern the world."[23] Wilson thus not only incorporated the term "manifest destiny" into his vocabulary, but also comprehended it as signifying the same kinds of ideas as O'Sullivan and their shared Puritan ancestors.

Liberal-Republican Millennialism
in the Nineteenth-Century United States

As a particular expression of liberal-republican millennialism that was formulated principally to justify the nation's territorial expansion, "manifest destiny" is only the tip of the iceberg when it comes to secular eschatology in nineteenth-century America. Liberal-republican millennialism was a much wider and general sentiment, and it was used to frame many other important political issues and events. Eschatological interpretations of the American quest for liberty recurred throughout the century and surrounded practically every major juncture in the life of the newborn

---

[22] Schurz, "Manifest Destiny," *Harper's New Monthly Magazine* 87, no. 521 (1893): 737.

[23] Wilson, "Address in the St. Paul Auditorium" (September 9, 1919), *PWW* 63:140, 146.

nation: not just its geographic expansion, but also its Civil War, subsequent Reconstruction, and, later still, budding international ambitions. Protestant ministers spearheaded the framing of these events in eschatological terms.

Geographic expansion became a prominent political issue already in the first decade of the century, following Jefferson's Louisiana Purchase (1803). It was placed in the context of scriptural prophecies about salvation and the Millennium even before O'Sullivan introduced the notion of America's "manifest destiny." Lyman Beecher, a prominent New England clergyman, used the Bible to argue that the American "nation is, in the providence of God, destined to lead the way in the moral and political emancipation of the world" and that "the millennium would commence in America," specifically in the recently obtained western territory.[24] To facilitate the great providential design, it was urgently necessary to Christianize this predestined region, as yet untouched by the bustling commerce and healthy political and religious institutions on the Eastern Seaboard. Failure to do this was not an option; it would discredit America's status as God's chosen nation and the heir of the Reformation.[25] Beecher thus called on his fellow ministers to evangelize the American West and, leading by example, abandoned New England for Ohio, where he founded a theological seminary.[26] This represented his personal contribution to "free, unembarrassed applications of physical effort and pecuniary and moral power to evangelize the world," a project whose ultimate goal was "perpetual and boundless prosperity . . . [in] the City of our God."[27]

When the Civil War broke out in the middle of the century, this project came under a lethal threat, but its framing in eschatological terms remained unaffected. The division of the nation between the North and the South challenged the status of the United States as a single people destined by God to redeem the world to liberty, but liberal-republican millennialism merely became bifurcated according to political loyalties of its proponents. Confederate clergy identified America's providential mission with the Confederate cause threatened by hordes of Yankee

---

[24] Beecher, *A Plea for the West*, 2nd ed. (Cincinnati: Truman & Smith, 1835), 8.

[25] Cf. Ernest Lee Tuveson, *Redeemer Nation: The Idea of America's Millennial Role* (Chicago: University of Chicago Press, 1968), 171.

[26] Conrad Cherry, "Westward the Course of Destiny," in *God's New Israel: Religious Interpretations of American Destiny*, ed. Cherry, rev. and updated ed. (Chapel Hill: University of North Carolina Press, 1998), 114.

[27] Beecher, *Plea for the West*, 8, 40.

infidels.[28] For their part, Northern ministers propounded the opposite view. In a sermon preached on April 14, 1861, two days after Confederate batteries fired on Fort Sumter in the opening move of the conflict, Lyman Beecher's son Henry Ward Beecher interpreted the Civil War as an apocalyptic battle waged by the Union, the last bastion of liberty and Christ on earth, against the Southern Devil.[29]

Such demonization of the Southern adversary was highly effective in rousing Northern support for the war cause, but it became a liability the moment the conflict had ended. Condemnations of the Confederacy as an agent of Antichrist now stood in the way of national reconciliation and reunification. Fortunately, and as America's ministers demonstrated already during the Revolutionary era, when they stirred their congregations against the British in part by recycling sermons originally written against the French during the French and Indian War, it is in the nature of secular eschatology to be flexible and easily adjustable according to the ever-changing shape of the friend-enemy distinction. The solution to the problem of reincorporating the defeated Confederacy into the nation in the wake of the Civil War was therefore simple: another reinterpretation of liberal-republican millennialism. The South was brought back over to the side of God's chosen people, and the religious meaning of the Civil War was retrospectively redefined in terms of a shared experience of suffering and divine punishment.

The July 1865 oration delivered by Horace Bushnell in commemoration of the war dead is instructive in this regard. The Yale clergyman no longer portrayed the Civil War the way Henry Beecher did: in sectional terms, as an apocalyptic battle of Northern saints against the Southern

---

[28] See James W. Silver, *Confederate Morale and Church Propaganda* (New York: Norton, 1967).

[29] Beecher, "The Battle Set in Array," in *Patriotic Addresses*, ed. J. R. Howard (New York: Fords, Howard and Hulbert, 1889), 269–88. According to Conrad Cherry, "Beecher believed Northern war efforts to be the instruments of God himself as the Union prepared to preserve America as the 'chosen refuge of liberty for all the earth' and to stamp out slavery, the last major obstacle to American freedom." "Civil War and National Destiny," in *God's New Israel*, ed. Cherry, 164. This portrayal naturally earned Beecher high honors in the North: it endowed the Northern cause with moral legitimacy and instilled the sense that the immense death toll was not meaningless, but noble and indeed inescapable. Following Northern victory, Beecher became widely believed to have direct access to God's mind, which swiftly turned him into a highly popular clergyman and, according to a recent biographer, the single most famous individual in the nineteenth-century United States. See Debby Applegate, *The Most Famous Man in America: The Biography of Henry Ward Beecher* (New York: Doubleday, 2006).

Devil. Instead, Bushnell used the doctrine of atonement to narrate the event as an act of sacrifice by a single nation so that its messianic purpose may be fulfilled in the future.[30] In this new secular-political exegesis of the salvationist myth, the secession attempt that sparked the Civil War represented "the most horrible, God-defying crime of this world,"[31] and God chastised his chosen people accordingly: by submerging them all, North and South alike, in a sea of blood. The disaster was well deserved by Americans; it was a just reward for their disunity, which threatened to take them off their providential path.

Liberal-republican millennialism thus played an important role in enabling the nation to heal and make sense of its most traumatic collective experience. It facilitated the Reconstruction by mending old Civil War rifts and by exalting the newfound unity. In bleeding Americans white regardless of which flag they followed, the Lord reminded all about their common destiny and allowed them to make amends for the transgression of sectionalism. Prior to the conflict their union was only superficial; in Bushnell's words, the American states were merely "kenneled under the Constitution and not reconciled."[32] The four years of shared suffering that was the Civil War, however, had forged a truly organic republic, whose "Government is now become Providential,—no more a mere creature of our human will, but a grandly moral affair."[33] A qualitative change of universal significance occurred in the identity of the United States during the schism: in abolishing slavery, the fire of the conflict incinerated the last vestiges of Satan, purified the nation, and sanctified its ensuing world-historical mission. "There are too many prophetic signs admonishing us," Bushnell declared before the Civil War, "that Almighty Providence is pre-engaged to make this a truly great nation."[34] The survival of the United States confirmed this prophecy: the building of the earthly Kingdom of God was underway, and the theme of what history still lay ahead would be the spread of the liberal-republican Millennium from America worldwide.

The industrial boom that ensued after the Civil War and rapidly transformed the United States into a world power gave further credence to

---

[30] Bushnell, "Our Obligations to the Dead," in *Building Eras in Religion* (New York: Scribner's, 1881), 319–55, quoted in *God's New Israel*, ed. Cherry, 203–14.

[31] Bushnell, "Our Obligations to the Dead," quoted in Cherry, 211.

[32] Bushnell, "Our Obligations to the Dead," quoted in Cherry, 206.

[33] Bushnell, "Our Obligations to the Dead," quoted in Cherry, 210.

[34] Cited in Tuveson, *Redeemer Nation*, 154.

the eschatological narrative of American politics and history, and in turn this narrative furnished moral grounds for the nation's growing international ambitions. Liberal-republican millennialism was slowly becoming a doctrine of American foreign relations. This development, to which Woodrow Wilson's statecraft during and after World War I would give its ultimate policy expression, reactivated the original universal aspirations of the Puritans.

In the wildly popular periodization of world history developed in the 1880s by the Protestant minister and biblical exegete Josiah Strong, for instance, the United States at the end of the nineteenth century represented the climactic moment in the unfolding of an eschatological movement originating in the Incarnation and flowing through the German Reformation.[35] Strong and his fellow citizens, including Wilson, belonged to a generation of Americans that was the generation of world redeemers: "[To] be a Christian and an Anglo-Saxon, and an American in this generation," Strong declared, "is to stand at the very mountain-top of privilege."[36] This privilege consisted of God's grace, enabling Americans to discern the providential path of history with clarity and to act accordingly. Reading secular history through the lens of his liberal-republican millennialism, Strong stated in words that could be easily mistaken for Wilson's

> that the world is evidently about to enter on a new era, that in this new era mankind is to come more and more under Anglo-Saxon influence, and that Anglo-Saxon civilization is more favorable than any other to the spread of those principles whose universal triumph is necessary to that perfection of the race to which it is destined; the entire realization of which will be the kingdom of heaven fully come on earth.[37]

One of the founders of the so-called Kingdom Movement, a socioreligious current in American Protestantism of the 1890s, Strong called on Americans to fulfill their sacred destiny by spiritually regenerating the nation and extirpating its looming domestic social ills. Strong's colleague

---

[35] Strong, *Our Country: Its Possible Future and Its Present Crisis*, ed. Jurgen Herbst (Cambridge, Mass.: Harvard University Press, 1963), 1. Written in 1885 for the American Home Missionary Society as part of its fundraising effort, this book became immensely popular and sold over 175,000 copies by 1916. See Tuveson, *Redeemer Nation*, 165, and Anders Stephanson, *Manifest Destiny: American Expansionism and the Empire of Right* (New York: Hill & Wang, 1995), 79.

[36] Strong, *The New Era; or The Coming Kingdom* (New York: Baker & Taylor, 1893), 354.

[37] Strong, *The New Era*, 81.

and the other founder of the Kingdom Movement, Reverend George D. Herron, was no less fervent in exhorting Americans to perform their God-given duty, except he focused especially on the nation's foreign policy.[38] When Wilson initiated the quest for the League of Nations, Herron immediately cast the policy in eschatological terms as the final step to complete America's sacred mission of redeeming the world from evil—an interpretation with which Wilson, as will be seen, identified wholeheartedly and enthusiastically.

It is worth stressing that although Protestant clergymen such as Strong, Herron, Bushnell, and the Beechers led the way in narrating politics and the quest for liberty in nineteenth-century America as a religious-eschatological project, they were not alone. Liberal-republican millennialism also appeared among American Jews and Mormons.[39] Even more importantly, and just as in the colonial and Revolutionary periods, as a framework for interpreting domestic and international politics eschatological consciousness was not exclusive to the clergy, but—consistently with Tocqueville's remarks about the unity of politics and religion in America—included lay leaders. President Wilson was but one example. These often outdid their ecclesiastical counterparts in casting events making up the political life of the nation as outward expressions of a divine force propelling America toward the biblically prophesized end of history.

The outstanding religious interpretation of the Civil War, for example, came not from any professional theologian, but from President Lincoln. "Never was the basic theme of God effecting his own purposes in the conflict . . . expressed with more compelling power than by Abraham Lincoln in his Second Inaugural Address."[40] Like his clerical contemporaries such as Bushnell, Lincoln understood the Civil War as God's punishment to Americans for the sinful institution of slavery, which divided the chosen nation and brought it on the verge of betraying its sacred destiny. "American slavery," the president stated, "is one of those offenses

---

[38] For Herron's role in the movement, see Robert T. Handy, "George D. Herron and the Kingdom Movement," *Church History* 19, no. 2 (1950): 99–101.

[39] The Mormon leader Brigham Young, e.g., declared that "America is the land of Zion" and that "Zion will extend, eventually, all over this earth." The U.S. Constitution was for Young a divinely inspired document "dictated by the invisible operations of the Almighty." *Discourses of Brigham Young*, ed. John A. Widstoe (Salt Lake City, Utah: Deseret Book, 1954), 119, 358.

[40] Winthrop S. Hudson, ed., *Nationalism and Religion in America: Concepts of American Identity and Mission* (New York: Harper & Row, 1970), 75.

which, in the providence of God, must needs come, but which, having continued through His appointed time, He now wills to remove . . . He gives to both North and South this terrible war as the woe due to those by whom the offense came."[41] National history was for Lincoln a story of progressive elimination of evil through the pouring out of vials of God's wrath. The Civil War was the latest vial emptied. God had "judged" and neutralized the evil of slavery, purified the flock of his earthly agents, and thereby confirmed their special destiny as the vanguard of liberty.[42] Other lay elites who advanced similar religious interpretations of the nation's secular-political life included Presidents Andrew Johnson and Teddy Roosevelt, historian John Fiske, political scientist John Burgess, naval strategist Alfred Mahan, poet Walt Whitman, or the already discussed journalist John L. O'Sullivan.[43]

Insofar as liberal-republican millennialism was common to them all, transcended their differences, and united them with the clergy, it may be said to have represented a veritable national religion. The dominant note in this religion was Protestantism: its proponents repeatedly invoked the mythology of America's origins in English Puritanism, whose spiritual message guided colonial politics, drove the American Revolution, and distinguished it from the godless French Revolution. However, this Protestant message, especially its eschatological portion, was sufficiently modular so that it gradually bridged traditional denominational divides and enabled the forging of a new type of ecumene defined in secular, patriotic terms: the United States of America. Evangelical Protestantism and American nationalism thereby became indistinct: "The belief in secular progress [of the republic] . . . was completely assimilated to the evangelical preaching of the dawning millennium."[44] The achievement of the Millennium depended fundamentally on whether America, imagined as God's New Israel already by Columbus, would embrace its exceptional status as the pattern for the rest of the world and carry out its "manifest destiny": convert humanity to liberalism, democracy, and Protestant Christianity.

---

[41] Abraham Lincoln, "Second Inaugural Address" (March 4, 1865), in *Inaugural Addresses of the Presidents of the United States* (Washington, D.C.: Government Printing Office, 1965), 128.

[42] Cf. Tuveson, *Redeemer Nation*, 206–7; Cherry, *God's New Israel*, 166–67.

[43] For Fiske, Burgess, and Mahan, see Stephanson, *Manifest Destiny*, 75–87; for Whitman, see Tuveson, *Redeemer Nation*, 187–88, and Cherry, *God's New Israel*, 118–19; for Johnson and Roosevelt, see May, *Ideas, Faiths, and Feelings*, 174–77.

[44] May, *Ideas, Faiths, and Feelings*, 171–72.

When Wilson entered the White House and assumed leadership of the United States at the end of the nineteenth century, he had not the slightest doubt about the answer to that question. A devout Presbyterian elder whose dedication and oratory as a prophet of American liberal-republican millennialism surpassed even those of Abraham Lincoln, Wilson represented "the greatest spokesman of the national faith, a man who embodied all . . . its elements and reflected all of its history."[45] When fighting broke out in Europe in August 1914, halfway through his first presidential term, quickly engulfed the Old World in the flames of the most destructive war ever seen, and gradually began threatening the United States, he saw the infernal conflict as a sign of times: the end of history was near, and America was being summoned to its mission of universal redemption. The time had come for the children of New England's Puritan "Saints" to re-emerge from the temporary shelter of the American wilderness, now transformed into a powerful sovereign country, return to Europe, and complete the grand spiritual project initiated by their fathers.

Turning Liberal-Republican Millennialism into Science

The strong Puritan inspiration behind America's patriotic religion does not mean, of course, that nineteenth-century liberal-republican millennialism was identical to the Puritan interpretation of the biblical myth of salvation. As the century unfolded and the impact of European Enlightenment and modern rationalism worked itself out, important changes occurred. Above all, traditional religious categories increasingly yielded to scientific ones in the discourse of American secular eschatology.

Whereas in Puritan New England the idea of progress to liberty was based entirely on the Bible and represented a product of theological historism, a specific mode of exegesis that invests the categories making up the eschatological myth with secular significance, in nineteenth-century America it was increasingly couched in the language of science. Liberal-republican millennialism was becoming more rational on the surface, with its biblical foundations receding into the silent interior of the discourse: to the realm of unarticulated presuppositions such as that history is a coherent and teleological process to begin with. In the conceptual language of secularization theory developed earlier, partial Puritan secularization was becoming more complete. The scriptural story of salvation was not only being read as a road map depicting the progress of actual

---

[45] May, *Ideas, Faiths, and Feelings*, 177.

secular events and occurrences, as already Bradford or Winthrop comprehended it in the tradition established by Joachim of Floris. In addition, the progressive pattern of history was increasingly being divorced from the Bible and placed on independent footing.

This is not to say, of course, that nineteenth-century American eschatologists were dropping the biblical language entirely, let alone proceeding to turn eschatology antireligious, as Marx did around the same time to the Protestant philosophy of world history developed by his teacher G. W. F. Hegel. Whereas in Marx's dialectical materialism Christianity survived only invisibly and may be detected strictly through hermeneutical analysis, in the American liberal tradition God had never receded from plain sight. Unlike Marx, whose progressive "class principle" forms the heart of an explicitly atheistic philosophy of history that denounces religion as a form of false consciousness, theorists of America's liberal progress always regarded it as originating in the will of the Lord, even if over time he had grown impersonal and clues about his intentions had become less direct: available only in the form of scientific laws left behind by the great Author of Nature.

The shift toward scientific language in the discourse of American liberal-republican millennialism is perceptible already in O'Sullivan's original formulation of "manifest destiny." America's westward expansion to Texas, he alleged, was dictated not only by God, but also by hard scientific factors: demography and geography. The demographic law of population growth—O'Sullivan did the math for his fellow Americans—was bound "within a hundred years to swell our numbers to . . . *two hundred and fifty million*," and this fact made the situation "too evident to leave us in doubt of the manifest design of Providence in regard to the occupation of this continent."[46] The physical geography of North America spoke just as clearly: "That Texas must . . . coalesce into one political unity with the rest of the great Confederacy," O'Sullivan averred, "can scarcely fail to strike the most careless eye that will cast a glance over any map of the continent of North America."[47] This map displayed no random grouping of rivers, plains, and mountain ranges, but a coherent unit drawn up by the finger of God: a territory "symmetrically planned and adapted to its grand destiny, in the possession of the race sent there for the providential purpose."[48] Whatever political borders divided the territory at the time

---

[46] [O'Sullivan], "Annexation," 7.

[47] [O'Sullivan], "The Texas Question," *Democratic Review* 14, no. 70 (1844): 424.

[48] [O'Sullivan], "The Texas Question," 425.

were only temporary, bound to disappear by virtue of North America's topography; the inevitability of bringing Texas and ultimately the entire continent under the U.S. Constitution was for O'Sullivan "a simple geographical fact."[49] Subsequent generations of American expansionists used the argument from geography to justify bids not only for contiguous areas but also for islands, twisting it to lay claim to territories as far away as Hawaii and the Philippines. Like O'Sullivan, they all "assume[d] . . . that reasonable dictates for politics were written in the territorial foundation of national life" and that "nature or the natural order of things destined natural boundaries for nations in general and for the United States, the nation of special destiny, in particular."[50]

Efforts to rationalize nineteenth-century American liberal-republican millennialism and the dogma of the nation's "manifest destiny" to spread its liberal-republican principles worldwide also drew on biology and the "queen science" of physics: the science enjoying the greatest prestige as a system for generating objective knowledge in the modern age. The biological version of "manifest destiny" was the doctrine of natural growth, which analogized the American republic to a newborn organism and explained its progress and expansion as a biological instinct to seek nutrients. Territorial increase was alleged to be as natural for the newborn nation as growth is for any young organic life-form.[51] Expressed in terms of physics, "manifest destiny became a sort of Newtonian theory of international relations, with America as the heaviest object":

> The principle formulated by Newton as a universal law of matter was . . . extended to the . . . sphere of politics and enunciated as a law of nations, under the designation, "the law of political gravitation." From this law . . . the deduction [was made] that adjacent nations within the range of America's attraction would fall to the Union by a process as inevitable as that causing the ripe apple to fall to the earth.[52]

The effect of the Newtonian rendition of America's predestined world mission was the same as that of the biological, demographic, or geographic ones: on all these scientific readings, American expansionism appeared to be entirely amoral and apolitical—beyond the scope of human choice, ethics, partisanship, bargaining, and law. Objecting to it was as pointless

---

[49] [O'Sullivan], "The Texas Question," 425.

[50] Albert K. Weinberg, *Manifest Destiny: A Study of Nationalist Expansionism in American History* (Baltimore, Md.: Johns Hopkins Press, 1935), 43.

[51] Weinberg, *Manifest Destiny*, 191.

[52] Weinberg, *Manifest Destiny*, 225.

and ineffective as objecting to infants nursing at the breast or to ripe apples falling from tree to earth. In each case, nature would have its way.

Liberal-Republican Millennialism in Economics
Laissez-Faire

The drive to rationalize "manifest destiny" employed not only natural sciences, but also social sciences, and above all economics. Cast in the economic idiom, liberal-republican millennialism emerged as the doctrine of *laissez-faire*: a doctrine that figured prominently in post–World War I liberal internationalist thought, was seen by some of its proponents (notably Norman Angell) as a cure-all formula for progress to world peace, and represented an essential component of Woodrow Wilson's statecraft.[53]

In secularizing biblical eschatology into a theory of free-market economics and in sacralizing free-market economics into divine will, nineteenth-century American liberal-republican millennialism followed the lead of one of its main inspirations: Adam Smith, the Scottish Enlightenment philosopher, professor of ethics, and father of modern economics. Religious presuppositions guided already his original statement of *laissez-faire*. In Smith's understanding, the famous "Invisible Hand," a scientific term he had coined to capture the curious way in which markets automatically maximize total welfare by harmonizing individual self-interests, was simultaneously a theological concept—the Hand of God.[54]

Insofar as mainstream nineteenth-century American economic thought comprehended *laissez-faire* and God's providence as two sides of the same coin, it was, therefore, far from original. Protestant clergymen preached *laissez-faire* from church pulpits, and leading economists (many of whom were Protestant ministers) extolled its Christian character in university classrooms.[55] Translating the Bible into a theory of

---

[53] As Lloyd E. Ambrosius has written, Wilson's "liberal internationalism embraced . . . Open Door economic globalization, which favored a competitive marketplace for trade and financial investments across national borders." *Wilsonianism: Woodrow Wilson and His Legacy in American Foreign Relations* (New York: Palgrave Macmillan, 2002), 2.

[54] The connection is fleshed out especially well in Reinhold Niebuhr, "The Religious Assumptions of Adam Smith," *Journal of Theology for Southern Africa* 44, no. 1 (1983): 22–23, arguing that "In Smith we find a clear concept of purpose . . . in the context of the will of Nature and of her Author. . . . For Smith . . . divine purpose rules the world, overriding or making use of the generally selfish actions of men—bringing order out of apparent chaos, and seeking the highest well-being and happiness for all."

economics and vice versa, they jointly propounded *laissez-faire* as a "secularized Protestant ethos of production for an expanding commercial society."[56] In effect, they were forging what has been referred to as "clerical *laissez-faire*":

> For at least a generation and in many institutions far longer, this body of doctrine dominated American economic teaching. . . . [T]aught by clerical professors, [it] constituted part of a general view of a world regulated by Divine Law. . . . Buttressed by the nearly unanimous opinion of academic authorities, sustained by the growing wealth and power of the churchgoing middle class, American Protestantism maintained its support of the combined social and religious orthodoxy. . . . Christian America was . . . guided by the Unseen Hand.[57]

The conviction that *laissez-faire* represented God's will and the means to fulfill America's sacred liberal-republican mission in the world grew especially after the Civil War, in response to the dramatic economic upswing and expansion of the nation's wealth.[58] The drive to interpret America's "manifest destiny" in economic terms frequently combined with justifications using demography, biology, or physics.

Among professional theologians, proponents of clerical *laissez-faire* included such prominent figures as Horace Bushnell, Episcopal bishop of Massachusetts William Lawrence, and Francis Wayland, president of Brown University and author of the most popular political economy textbook in nineteenth-century America.[59] The most passionate advocate was Henry Ward Beecher, whose sermons relentlessly defended economic individualism and competition from any kind of intervention, whether by government or organized labor.[60] From his perspective, material inequality and the vast riches amassed by Carnegie, Cornell, Rockefeller, Vanderbilt, and other American captains of industry were not to be denounced, but celebrated as outward signs of the men's piety. Wealth and morality went hand in hand: religiosity had distinct economic advantages, and prosperity was the outward indication of one's spirituality.[61]

---

[55] Bradley W. Bateman and Ethan B. Kapstein, "Between God and the Market: The Religious Roots of the American Economic Association," *Journal of Economic Perspectives* 13, no. 4 (1999): 249–50.

[56] Martin Burke, *The Conundrum of Class: Public Discourse on the Social Order in America* (Chicago: University of Chicago Press, 1995), 61.

[57] Henry F. May, *Protestant Churches and Industrial America* (New York: Octagon Books, 1963), 14, 21, 62–63.

[58] Cf. Cherry, "National Progress and Wealth," in *God's New Israel*, ed. Cherry, 218.

[59] Wayland, *The Elements of Political Economy* (New York: Leavitt, Lord, 1837).

[60] May, *Protestant Churches*, 67–72.

In the words of Bishop Lawrence, "Godliness is in league with riches."[62]

In the same vein, poverty derived from vice and represented God's just punishment for sloth and other moral lapses. For this reason, alms-giving—often practiced by Christians in other contexts as an expression of Christian love and charity—was discouraged by the discourse of clerical *laissez-faire*: as God's chosen people, Americans were to refrain from this activity as much as from strikes, labor unions, demands for higher wages, or pushes for a shorter workday—any measures, in sum, obstructing the Lord's Invisible Hand. Letting God promote the pious and demote the impious without any human interference represented the shortest and quickest path of America's progress to the Millennium: "until the symbolism of the heavenly state, where the streets are paved with gold," as Henry Ward Beecher averred, "shall be reproduced in the realities and actualities of our life here on earth."[63] In his exegesis, the biblical vision of salvation had become thoroughly secularized into a crass commercial-industrial megalopolis.

Unsurprisingly, American industrialists endorsed clerical *laissez-faire* with enthusiasm. If Beecher secularized God's will into an economic doctrine of freewheeling capitalism, Andrew Carnegie was quick to sacralize freewheeling capitalism into an expression of God's will. Civilization, Carnegie stated, was based on four basic laws: "Individualism, Private Property, the Law of Accumulation of Wealth, and the Law of Competition."[64] While these laws had generated tremendous inequality by concentrating all riches in the hands of just a few men, Carnegie argued vehemently that "this change . . . is not to be deplored, but welcomed as beneficial."[65] Just as Beecher did, Carnegie regarded *laissez-faire* as a divine principle that, if observed rigorously and without intrusion, would ultimately weed out all poverty and impiety and dissolve all social conflicts. Carnegie thus concluded by proclaiming it "the

---

[61] As Henry Ward Beecher stated in his 1870 Thanksgiving Day sermon, "nowhere else does wealth so directly point towards morality and spirituality in religion as in America." *The Original Plymouth Pulpit* (Boston: Pilgrim Press, 1871), 5:203–19. On another occasion he alleged that "Generally the proposition is true that where you find the most religion there you will find the most worldly prosperity." "The Temporal Advantages of Religion," in *Plymouth Pulpit* (New York: 1873), 9:366.

[62] William Lawrence, "The Relation of Wealth to Morals," in *God's New Israel*, ed. Cherry, 251.

[63] Beecher, *Original Plymouth Pulpit*, 5:203–19.

[64] Carnegie, "Wealth," *North American Review* 148, no. 391 (1889): 657.

[65] Carnegie, "Wealth," 653–54.

true Gospel concerning Wealth, obedience to which is destined someday to solve the problem of the Rich and the Poor, and to bring 'Peace on earth, among men Good-Will.'"[66] Thirty years later, the same argument casting capitalism and free-trade competition as the royal highway to everlasting peace reappeared as an integral element of the liberal internationalist drive for the League of Nations, a project Carnegie supported as passionately as Woodrow Wilson, his fellow Scotch American.

The presupposition underlying this argument was the same for the fabulously rich steel magnate as for the stern president and indeed every other proponent of clerical *laissez-faire*, lay or ecclesiastical. They all adhered to the "principle of automatic harmony,"[67] believing that all national and international discords were ultimately temporary and that no essential conflicts existed among people voluntarily embracing Christian ideals. In earlier times, especially during the first few decades following the birth of the United States, this principle performed an important emancipatory role: it suggested that many norms and institutions inherited from the British monarchy were artificial, facilitated their dismantling, and thereby advanced the cause of individual liberty and equality in America. By the second half of the nineteenth century, however, a switch had occurred: the notion of automatic harmony now worked as a decidedly conservative weapon, a vehicle serving the dominant few to justify a social order characterized by rampant oppression and deep inequality.[68]

This brings up the hidden political functions of America's liberal-republican millennialism toward the end of the nineteenth century: functions that catered to the *status quo* and were illiberal, exclusionary, and totalizing to the point of genocidal. Even before E. H. Carr and other classical realist IR critics mercilessly pointed them out as the true substance of Wilson's ostensibly universal liberal internationalism, these functions figured already in the discourse of "manifest destiny," from

[66] Carnegie, "Wealth," 664.

[67] Sidney E. Mead, *The Lively Experiment: The Shaping of Christianity in America* (New York: Harper & Row, 1963), 100. According to Paul Tillich, harmony of interests was the "one presupposition . . . always present, sometimes avowed, sometimes tacit" at the time. "The World Situation," in *The Christian Answer*, ed. Henry P. Van Dusen (New York: Scribner's Sons, 1945), 3.

[68] It came to "mean . . . that no matter what an individual did in following his own selfish desires . . . it would ultimately be seen as in harmony with the best interests of the whole society. This naturally cleared the way . . . for the unrestrained and ruthless exploitation of natural and human resources . . . [by] the new tycoons." Mead, *Lively Experiment*, 101.

which Wilson's ideas about world history and America's special role in it emerged.

A Functionalist Analysis of "Manifest Destiny"

A common thread runs through the different expressions of America's "manifest destiny" to redeem the world to liberty: whether cast in the language of economics, biology, physics, or geography, the doctrine functioned to disguise value as fact. The biological narrative of natural growth, to take one example, "resembled most other versions of destiny in associating an ought-implication with a proposition of fact."[69] Through this simple and oftentimes unconscious move the political character of liberal-republican millennialism was obscured and the goals and interests of its advocates objectified. The language of science placed these goals outside the domain of ethical and political contestability and endowed them with the appearance of natural necessity.

Clerical *laissez-faire* illustrates the political functions of "manifest destiny" well. Although on the surface it sought to maximize material prosperity for the whole nation, in reality it pursued the well-being of only a small segment of society to the exclusion of the rest. The American economy in the late nineteenth century was a playground dominated by a handful of giant monopolies and featuring stunning disparities in wealth between industrial magnates on the one hand and regular wage laborers on the other. In this context, the "Gospel of Wealth" served the elite as a form of ideological power to neutralize any potential dangers to its dominant status and to maintain the existing order. Whenever such dangers did occur, whether in the form of labor unions, strikes, the movement for shorter working hours, or other forms of collective action undertaken by workers to level the playing field, they were denounced as unpatriotic and un-Christian: contrary to national wealth and God's will. When in July 1877 a sudden wage cut on railroads east of the Mississippi River triggered the most violent labor uprising in American history, one threatening to rupture the fragile *status quo*, Beecher condemned the unrest in vociferous terms and called on federal troops to restore order with bayonets and Gatling guns.[70]

---

[69] Weinberg, *Manifest Destiny*, 191.

[70] For this and other examples of church opinion, including excerpts from the *Independent*, *Congregationalist*, and *Christian Union*, the main Protestant magazines at the time, see May, *Protestant Churches*, 92–94.

The dogma of "manifest destiny" was even crueler as a doctrine of territorial expansionism than as a theory of economics. In sanctioning the westward advance of white European immigrants across the continent to the shores of the Pacific Ocean, it became synonymous with the systematic dispossession, relocation, and in some instances mass killing of Native Americans. The intensity of their forced resettlement peaked during the decade following the Indian Removal Act (1830), pushed through Congress by President Andrew Jackson, the Democratic Party leader greatly admired not only by John L. O'Sullivan, the original author of "manifest destiny," but later also by President Wilson. In the most notorious instance, the so-called Trail of Tears in the 1830s, some seventeen thousand Cherokee were rounded up by the U.S. Army and expelled from their homelands in Georgia to inhospitable territories west of the Mississippi River.[71] "Manifest destiny" played a key role in justifying and normalizing such acts of violence.

The moral and legal case for the Indian Removal Act presented by the influential Senator Lewis Cass just before the Act's passage is illustrative in this regard. Cass began by admitting that "[asserting] jurisdiction over the aboriginal tribes of America and . . . a right to the country occupied by them" constituted a claim "at first sight revolting to the common justice of mankind."[72] However, in light of God's will commanding America to spread liberty, civilization, and industry, the policy was entirely appropriate. Existing treaties or moral reservations blocking aboriginal resettlement were valid only insofar as they complied with divine schemes; where they contradicted God's will, they could be ignored.[73] Providence represented the key qualification: "The Indians," Cass asserted in this vein, "are entitled to the enjoyment of all the rights which do not interfere with the obvious designs of Providence."[74]

---

[71] For the Trail of Tears and personal accounts of atrocities committed in its course, see Russell Thornton, *American Indian Holocaust and Survival* (Norman: University of Oklahoma Press, 1987), 114–18, and also M. Annette Jaimes, ed., *The State of Native America* (Boston: South End, 1992). During the march about four thousand Cherokee perished due to disease, exhaustion, starvation, and accident, although Thornton, the leading contemporary scholar on American Indian genocide, has estimated the total death toll at more than twice the number. See Thornton, "Cherokee Population Losses during the Trail of Tears: A New Perspective and a New Estimate," *Ethnohistory* 31 (1984): 289.

[72] [Cass], "Removal of the Indians," *North American Review* 30, no. 66 (1830): 76.

[73] Cass' attitude thus paralleled O'Sullivan's attitude toward international conventions preventing the annexation of Oregon.

[74] [Cass], "Removal of the Indians," 76.

Since according to the senator these designs emphasized agriculture and industrialization, and since the Indians engaged in neither, their title to the land was void. Much like the Puritans before him, Cass had no doubt that "the Creator intended the earth should be . . . cultivated" and that the immense American continent was "evidently designed by Providence to be subdued . . . and become the residence of civilized nations."[75]

As is apparent from these words, the appeal to God's eschatological purposes served Cass and other proponents of "manifest destiny" to defend a whole range of modern Western presuppositions that were essential to the building of a powerful American republic but often all but alien to the continent's original inhabitants. These included a conception of nature as a resource to be harnessed, transformed, and exploited, and an idea of political sovereignty defined in terms of a centrally governed territorial unit. Above all, however, "manifest destiny" allowed Americans of the European stock to feel good about themselves as they went about solving the nation's real estate problem by systematically expelling entire indigenous populations from their ancestral lands. The consciousness of representing God's instruments enabled the immigrants to disavow any agency and ethical responsibility and to perpetrate brutal violence against the Indians with the feeling of complete innocence.

The sheer potency of the dogma of America's providentially sanctioned geographic progress as a form of moral anesthetic is discernible from the thoughts of the same famous visitor to the nineteenth-century United States who had noticed its citizens' propensity to blend politics with religion: Alexis de Tocqueville. As intimated earlier, he left a detailed record of the political functions of America's patriotic religion; his travels in the New World coincided with the Indian Removal Act, and he saw the forced relocations—lines of decrepit men, women, and children marched through the countryside, pausing to cross a frigid river, mute all—firsthand. Yet he did not see any atrocities. In what must count as one of the most astounding passages in *Democracy in America*, he declared that "the Americans of the United States have attained [the conquest of the Indian race] with marvelous facility—tranquilly, legally, philanthropically, without violating a single one of the great principles of morality in the eyes of the world. One cannot destroy men while being more respectful of the laws of humanity."[76] Like the society he was writing about, Tocqueville too comprehended history as inevitable progress

[75] [Cass], "Removal of the Indians," 77.
[76] Tocqueville, *Democracy*, 325.

toward republican democracy, and fighting this process struck him as akin to "struggl[ing] against God himself."[77] It was God, not the European immigrants pouring into the New World, who had sentenced the Indians to annihilation.[78] Tocqueville thus bore witness to their genocide without sensing any injustice or wrongdoing. He was caught up in the same secularized religious hermeneutic as the perpetrators.

The totalizing, exclusionary, and deeply illiberal functions of the providentially mandated quest for liberty in the New World, then, had not remained confined to the colonial period. They were active, perhaps even more intensively, under the auspices of the nineteenth-century discourse of American liberal-republican millennialism as well. This discourse may be summarized by the same dictum as Puritan millennialism, a dictum originally formulated with respect to totalitarianism and capturing the legality of terror in societies committed to ideologies of progress and utopia: "Terror is lawfulness, if law is the law of the movement of some superhuman force, Nature or History."[79] In the nineteenth-century United States, this law, whose deep origin lies in the biblical conception of history as eschatology, was encapsulated in the doctrine of "manifest destiny." Its role in sanctioning American expansionism and racial cleansing has been analogized to the Nazi *Lebensraum* doctrine and atrocities on Jews and Slavs.[80] That the American genocide, in contrast to the German one, has remained unpunished, and that its increasing recognition in American history textbooks has failed to spark any intense *Historikerstreit* such as characterizes Holocaust studies, may very well be due to the fact that the United States, unlike the Third Reich, won its war of conquest.[81]

---

[77] Tocqueville, *Democracy*, 7.

[78] According to Christopher Coker, "Tocqueville had no doubt that history alone should be held accountable for [the Indians'] fate." *War and the Illiberal Conscience* (Oxford: Westview, 1998), 74. Cf. Karl Löwith's comment that "To Tocqueville the march of democracy has . . . irresistible providence, for both those who promote it and those who obstruct it are blind instruments in the hands of a power directing history." *Meaning in History: The Theological Implications of the Philosophy of History* (Chicago: University of Chicago Press, 1949), 11.

[79] Hannah Arendt, "Ideology and Terror: A Novel Form of Government," *Review of Politics* 15, no. 4 (1953): 311.

[80] Ward Churchill, "A Summary of Arguments against the Naming of a University Residence Hall after Clinton M. Tyler," unpublished study (1981), cited in *State of Native America*, ed. Jaimes, 3. See also Churchill, *A Little Matter of Genocide: Holocaust and Denial in the Americas, 1492–Present* (San Francisco: City Lights Books, 1997).

[81] Churchill, "Summary of Arguments," in *State of Native America*, ed. Jaimes, 3; Lilian Friedberg, "Dare to Compare: Americanizing the Holocaust," *American Indian Quarterly* 24, no. 3 (2000): 355–56, 360–61.

From Liberal-Republican Millennialism to Wilson

One would be hard-pressed not to notice the extensive parallels running between, on the one hand, a critical analysis of the hidden political functions of "manifest destiny," and, on the other, E. H. Carr's classical realist reading of Wilson's liberal internationalism. To recall the main thrust of Carr's critique, Wilson's statecraft amounted to much less than his eschatological language of world peace, liberty, and justice suggested on the surface. According to Carr, for all this universal language liberal internationalism was actually highly partial and political. It constituted a form of ideological power and served Wilson and the United States as a weapon for the prosecution of American national interests in freezing the favorable global *status quo* after World War I. Progressive in appearance, it was conservative in substance. It was precisely this "exposure of the real basis of [its] professedly abstract principles" that Carr identified as "the most damning and most convincing part of the realist indictment of utopianism."[82]

The same was true of "manifest destiny" to begin with. Just as liberal internationalism advanced narrow national interests under its claim to represent universal values, so the narrative of "manifest destiny" harbored deeply particularistic goals and purposes under its appeal to God's will. At home, it functioned to maintain social peace and cohesion in the context of massive inequality, exclusion, and revolutionary pressures threatening to pull the country apart. Abroad, as a theory of international relations, "manifest destiny" signified "in essence the doctrine that one nation has a preeminent social worth, a distinctively lofty mission, and consequently unique rights in the application of moral principles."[83] This enabled its proponents to sanctify aggressive American imperialism and colonization and to present them in missionary terms, as altruistic policies to enlighten the rest of humanity and facilitate its progress to the redeeming future based on the American "Model of Christian Charity," to allude to the title of Governor Winthrop's famous seventeenth-century Puritan sermon.

The similarity between Wilson's liberal internationalism and "manifest destiny" is no accident, for as is about to be seen the two were actually one and the same thing: Wilson's diplomatic thought exemplified nineteenth-century American liberal-republican millennialism. In his

---

[82] Carr, *The Twenty Years' Crisis, 1919–1939: An Introduction to the Study of International Relations*, 2nd ed. (New York: Harper & Row, 1964 [1949]), 87.

[83] Weinberg, *Manifest Destiny*, 8.

proposal for the League of Nations, the narrative of the United States as a divinely appointed global leader, which emerged as a specific form of "manifest destiny" in the 1890s, reached its climactic expression.[84] Eschatology was central to Wilson's understanding of international politics and his own statecraft.[85] His conceptualization of World War I and American war aims matched readings proffered by millennialists such as George D. Herron, the aforementioned leader of the Kingdom Movement, who saw the conflict as an apocalyptic battle between American legions of Christ and Satanic armies of Prussia.

It also matched the views of Wilson's cabinet members such as Secretary of State William Jennings Bryan, who recognized in Wilson's wartime foreign policy an attempt to fulfill biblical prophecy in world politics and commended the president on undertaking such a noble endeavor. When Wilson delivered his "Peace without Victory" address, in which he announced to the European powers at war the kind of settlement he was willing to support, Bryan declared that Wilson's aims represented a radically novel conception of international relations that was nevertheless "as old as Christian religion, and . . . the only foundation upon which a permanent peace can be built."[86] A great new era was on the horizon, and Wilson was the one guiding humanity toward it. "Your message is epoch-making," Bryan thus told the president, "and will place you among the Immortals."[87]

---

[84] Weinberg, *Manifest Destiny*, 470.

[85] "Wilson's dogma that America 'can only go forward' toward a destiny of leadership is . . . supported by his faith in Providence." Weinberg, *Manifest Destiny*, 481. Weinberg's critical analysis of Wilson's liberal internationalism as a religiously inspired myth fabricated for the purpose of advancing American national interests displays striking overlaps with Carr's assessment, which raises the intriguing question of Weinberg's relation to the classical realist tradition of IR thought. Although completely unknown to IR specialists today, Weinberg would probably not object to being regarded as one of their early twentieth-century forerunners. At least in his capacity as author of *Manifest Destiny*, written under the auspices of the Walter Hines Page School of International Relations at Johns Hopkins University, he was a student of American foreign policy, specifically its legitimating ideological and ethical frameworks.

[86] Bryan to Wilson (January 26, 1917), *PWW* 41:29.

[87] Bryan to Wilson (January 26, 1917), 29.

CHAPTER FIVE

THE (NOT SO) CONSERVATIVE MILLENNIALIST

Woodrow Wilson and History as Orderly Progress Toward Liberty

Already Wilson's contemporaries realized that he would cast a long shadow over subsequent American statecraft, and they set about mapping his character, ideas, and policies even before his death in 1924. The countless studies that have appeared since then disagree on many points, but an important common thread runs through all of them: the recognition that Wilson's religious faith played an important role in his domestic and international political thought and practice. The journalist Ray Stannard Baker, who knew Wilson personally and authored his first major biography, insisted that Wilson's "career can in no wise be understood without a clear knowledge of [his] profound religious convictions . . . Religion was never incidental with him; it was central."[1] In a similar vein, though much more derisively, John Maynard Keynes stated after meeting Wilson at Versailles that "His thought and temperament were essentially theological, not intellectual."[2] The precepts of American Protestant Christianity represented the essential matrix structuring Wilson's

---

[1] Baker, *Woodrow Wilson: Life and Letters* (Garden City, N.Y.: Doubleday, 1927–1939), 1:68.

[2] Keynes, *The Economic Consequences of the Peace* (New York: Harcourt, Brace & Howe, 1920), 38.

understanding of secular political reality, and he wove Presbyterian covenant theology into every facet of existence.[3]

Given the centrality of Wilson's faith to all areas of his life, including diplomacy, it is curious that contemporary international relations has
failed to grasp the role of biblical salvationism in his political utopianism
and neglected to interpret his liberal internationalist project as secularized eschatology. The following pages rectify this shortcoming. They go
through the different elements of Wilson's political utopianism, such as
the harmony of interests, rationalist epistemology, and the idea of progress, and point out the key role of eschatological religion in Wilson's conception of each—first on the domestic level and then in foreign policy,
which sought to extend his domestic liberal-republican millennialism to
the international arena. What will emerge is that Wilson's national and
international politics amounted to a relentless effort to translate eschatological religion into political practice and to actualize a biblical vision of
society *in hoc sæculo*: within the historical world. Wilson was therefore a
utopian in two different senses of the term: as it is understood both by the
international relations community and by historians of ideas espousing
the secularization thesis.

Wilson's Religious Inheritance and Education

The foundations for the influence of religion in Wilson's life and career
were laid during his youth and upbringing. Born in Staunton, Virginia,
on December 29, 1856, only a few years before the outbreak of the Civil
War, Wilson had been surrounded by Protestant Christianity from the
very beginning. His father, Reverend Joseph Ruggles Wilson, was one
of the founders of the Southern Presbyterian Church in the United States
and a highly respected minister, whose activities extended beyond the
pulpit and included church administration and editorship of the *North
Carolina Presbyterian*. His leadership was just as imposing within the

---

[3] John M. Mulder, *Woodrow Wilson: The Years of Preparation* (Princeton, N.J.:
Princeton University Press, 1978), xiii, 7–8; idem, "Wilson the Preacher: The 1905 Baccalaureate Sermon," *Journal of Presbyterian History* 51, no. 3 (1973): 267. Arthur S.
Link, the leading twentieth-century Wilson scholar, summarized the academic consensus as follows: "Every biographer of Woodrow Wilson has said that it is impossible to
know and understand the man apart from his religious faith, because his every action and
policy was ultimately informed and molded by his Christian faith." *The Higher Realism
of Woodrow Wilson, and Other Essays* (Nashville: Vanderbilt University Press, 1971),
4. Link went so far as to proclaim Wilson "the prime embodiment, the apogee, of the
Calvinistic tradition among all statesmen of the modern epoch." Link, *Higher Realism*, 4.

family circle. Regular worship, Bible study, stories of Scottish Covenanters, and frequent receptions of church dignitaries all formed part and parcel of Woodrow Wilson's childhood. Admitted to the membership of the
First Presbyterian Church of Columbia, North Carolina, at the age of
six, he soon became his father's right hand and acquired a permanent
attachment to the precepts of the Presbyterian faith.[4] It is no exaggeration
that "Wilson knew the polity, laws, and procedures of the Presbyterian
Church long before he knew those of his state and nation."[5] Wilson's
political views would develop within an already well-formed eschatological consciousness and bear its clear stamp.

The substance of spiritual beliefs acquired by Wilson in his formative
years is apparent from his earliest preserved writings: religious essays
written during his undergraduate study at Davidson College and published in the *North Carolina Presbyterian* by his father. These essays
display an unquestioning commitment to the Bible; a stern conviction
that religion should guide all areas of life, including significantly the secular-political one; a black-and-white view of the moral universe; and a
crusading spirit underlain by a strong sense of self-righteousness.

In the Bible, the young Wilson discovered the one and only reliable
compass to navigate him through life: a source of eternal truth, "a trea-
sury of poetry, history, philosophy, laws and morals which will never be
equaled."[6] Youth and adolescence are full of transitory romantic infatua-
tions, but Wilson's love for the Bible was no passing affair. It only solidified over time. In a key address delivered decades later in front of twelve
thousand listeners in the Denver Auditorium, he declared that "the Bible
is without age or date or time. It is a picture of the human heart displayed
for all ages and . . . conditions of men."[7] For him, biblical principles were

---

[4] In his typical fashion, Freud cast this attachment as part of a larger psychological
fixation of Wilson on his preacher-father, whose oppressive example allegedly dominated
Wilson throughout his entire life. See Sigmund Freud and William C. Bullitt, *Thomas
Woodrow Wilson, Twenty-Eighth President of the United States* (London: Weidenfeld &
Nicolson, 1967).

[5] Link, *Higher Realism*, 15.

[6] Wilson, "The Bible" (August 25, 1876), in *The Papers of Woodrow Wilson*, ed.
Arthur S. Link et al. (Princeton, N.J.: Princeton University Press, 1966–1994) [hence-
forth *PWW*], 1:184.

[7] Wilson, "Address in Denver on the Bible" (May 7, 1911), *PWW* 23:16. Elsewhere
Wilson proclaimed the Bible "the noblest body of literature in existence, a body of literature having in it more mental and imaginative stimulus than any other body of writings.
A man has deprived himself of the best there is in the world who has deprived himself of
this." See his "Statement about the Bible" (October 8, 1909), *PWW* 19:406.

divine in origin and represented supreme knowledge and reality. During his years in the White House, Wilson would use the Bible and its myth of salvation as a guide for all his political actions at home as well as abroad.

This brings up the second, and crucial, characteristic of Wilson's religiosity: the resolute view that Protestantism had secular and political relevance. Continuing the tradition of vital religion practiced already by the Puritans, Wilson held that biblical teachings applied not only to ministers and others who had chosen religion as their vocation, but also to businessmen, lawyers, and above all politicians. From his early youth Wilson was deeply disturbed by what he perceived as the growing tendency to confine religion only to some areas of life and exclude it from others, where it was no longer deemed relevant or necessary. He called Protestant Christianity a "work-day religion," and he repeatedly exhorted his audiences to place the image of Christ at the spiritual center of all their daily activities, whether these occurred at home, in the market exchange, or in political office.[8] Coupled with a strong work ethic, allegiance to God represented the cornerstone of Wilson's early conception of the ideal statesman, for whom biblical standards trumped all party loyalties.[9]

The ideal statesman needed to be fortified by Christianity because politics, and history in general, was as an ongoing struggle between the powers of light and the powers of darkness—the third important element of Wilson's religious worldview. Wilson displayed "a dualistic and rigidly moralistic view of the world and human activity in it."[10] Drawing on traditional Christian imagery, he declared that

> the field of battle is the world. From the abodes of righteousness advances the host of God's people under the leadership of Christ. . . . From the opposite side of the field, advancing from the tents of wickedness, come the hosts of sin led by the Prince of Lies himself. The foes meet upon the great battle field of every-day life. . . . [I]n this great contest there is a part for every one. . . . Will any one dare to enlist under the banners of the Prince of Lies, under whose dark folds he only marches to the darkness of hell? For there is no middle course, no neutrality. Each and every one must enlist either with the followers of Christ or those of Satan.[11]

---

[8] Wilson, "Work-Day Religion" (Aug. 11, 1876), and "A Christian Statesman" (September 1, 1876), *PWW* 1:176–78, 188–89.

[9] Wilson, "A Christian Statesman," 188.

[10] Mulder, *Years of Preparation*, 49.

[11] Wilson, "Christ's Army" (August 17, 1876), *PWW* 1:180.

As a nineteen-year-old student still to undergo a more substantive intellectual encounter with American liberalism and constitutional history, Wilson had not yet invested the biblical categories such as "Christ's army," "Prince of Lies," "righteousness," or "wickedness" with political meaning; the Bible led him to conceptualize the world in black-and-white, Manichean terms, but concrete political connotations are unspecified and left open. Over the next few decades, however, Wilson would gradually fill the biblical figures with political content reflecting patriotic American liberal-republican values and interests, and by 1918 he would secularize the allegorical battle between Christ and Satan into a political and military conflict between American liberalism and Prussian autocracy, with the Great War as the Apocalypse, the United States intervention as a crusade by God's people, and the League of Nations as the impending Millennium.

The final important aspect of Wilson's early religious posture is his own imagined role in the Manichean universe. In the great progressive struggle between Christ and Satan, Wilson had stylized himself into a Christian soldier executing a sacred mission. As with his attachment to the Bible, the crusading knight fantasy was no teenage phase, but a theme that would serve Wilson as a constant reference point for many years to come, indeed throughout his entire life.[12] On the one hand, it endowed him with dogged determination and unmatched work ethic. On the other, it surfaced in a hyperinflated sense of moral superiority bordering on arrogance.[13] Although Wilson's moral compass gradually became somewhat more sensitive to the irresolvable ambiguities of life, the propensity to reduce the complexities of human existence to clear-cut categories of good and evil, true and false, or just and unjust, with Wilson always standing on the right side, remained at the core of his character.

The political ideas that would later become the core of his liberal internationalist program began taking shape in Wilson's mind soon after he expressed his biblical view of the universe and his burning eschatological faith in the pages of the *North Carolina Presbyterian*. For example, in a biographical essay on John Bright written at the age of twenty-four,

[12] Mulder, "Wilson the Preacher," 269.

[13] As one of Wilson's closest friends remarked, Wilson's self-confidence was not only his driving virtue, but also his tragic flaw: "the sense of his own rightness and conversely of the wrongness of his opponents began to rob him . . . of his . . . skill in diplomacy, his tact and judgment and patience. He was so sure that the right must prevail that he forgot . . . and underestimated the power of his opponents." Bliss Perry, *And Gladly Teach* (Boston: Houghton Mifflin, 1935), 158–59.

Wilson stated his deep admiration for Bright and Cobden and declared that *"Trade*, indeed, is the great nurse of liberal ideas."[14] Like his religious views, the belief that international trade had a pacifying effect by virtue of ridding its participants of narrow cultural and nationalistic prejudices would animate Wilson's entire subsequent career. In the aftermath of World War I it represented one of the foundations of his efforts to create a new world order. As a principle of international political theory, it constitutes the very heart of the so-called commercial strand of interwar liberal internationalism.[15]

Crucially, this and other early expressions of Wilson's liberal political thought started taking shape within the context of his Christian eschatological presuppositions and bore their clear imprint. The moment Wilson had adopted the idea of free trade, he incorporated it into his religious worldview, sacralizing a political principle into a biblical precept—or, what amounts to the same thing, secularizing his biblical faith into a political doctrine. Free trade became God's cause, and Wilson worshipped it accordingly. When as a Princeton student he entered a debating competition and drew from the hat a piece of paper instructing him to argue against free commerce, he tore it to shreds and forfeited.[16] A noble knight executing a mission from God in a world where there was no middle ground, Wilson would not side with the Prince of Lies under any circumstances—not even as a form of make-believe. During his political and diplomatic career, it was precisely this dogmatic adherence to liberal internationalist principles that prevented Wilson from so much as entertaining the point later made by E. H. Carr in his realist critique: that liberal internationalism, far from representing universal principles, mirrored only the standpoint and national interests of World War I victors. In this vein, much of what Carr diagnosed as the central flaw in Wilson's international thought, namely the lack of critical reflexivity, may be ascribed directly to Wilson's religious presuppositions.

Wilson had never come to doubt his religious beliefs, acknowledged their central role repeatedly throughout his life, and always cherished

---

[14] Wilson, "John Bright" (March 6, 1880), *PWW* 1:610, also reprinted in idem, *America's Greatness* (New York: Wise, 1931), 50. See also idem, "Notes for a Speech Opposing the Protective Tariff" (September 23, 1882), *PWW* 2:139.

[15] See Peter Wilson, "Introduction: *The Twenty Years' Crisis* and the Category of 'Idealism' in International Relations," in *Thinkers of the Twenty Years' Crisis: Inter-War Idealism Reassessed*, ed. David Long and Peter Wilson (Oxford: Clarendon, 1995).

[16] Carl F. Price, "Young Teacher," in *Woodrow Wilson: A Profile*, ed. Arthur S. Link (New York: Hill & Wang, 1968), 28.

the early spiritual education from his father as a truly special gift. On one occasion during his White House years, he remarked privately that "*My* life would not be worth living, if it were not for the driving power of religion, for *faith*, pure and simple. I have seen all my life the arguments against it without ever having been moved by them."[17] On another occasion, when the responsibilities of the presidency proved particularly demanding, he told one of his friends that "If I were not a Christian . . . I should go mad, but my faith in God holds me to the belief that He is in some ways working out His own plans through human perversities and mistakes."[18] The belief in God as the Lord of history enabled Wilson to find hidden purpose even in ostensibly meaningless occurrences. Illustrating the Judeo-Christian response to historical evil, Wilson interpreted such occurrences as expressions of divine providence guiding humanity toward salvation. "There is certainly a Providence overruling all," he wrote to a confidante just a few months before the outbreak of World War I; "I can explain nothing, if there is not."[19]

"The Fine Revealing Light"
Faith as the Path to Authentic Knowledge

After completing his undergraduate education at Princeton University and attending law school at the University of Virginia, Wilson opened a legal practice in Atlanta, Georgia, but his career as an attorney was unsuccessful and short-lived. He promptly returned to academic life, enrolling in a graduate course in history, economics, and political science at Johns Hopkins University. He received his Ph.D. in 1886 and subsequently accepted a string of teaching posts that ultimately brought him back to Princeton. The next twenty years at Princeton from 1890 to 1910, first as professor and from 1902 as president of the university, represent the zenith of Wilson's scholarly and intellectual career. During this time Wilson commented frequently on the nature of knowledge and ways of attaining it. Both what he stated and how he stated it reveal that right reasoning was for him a function of religious belief. In other words, in

---

[17] Mrs. Crawford H. Toy, "Second Visit to the White House," diary entry dated January 3, 1915, manuscript in The Ray Stannard Baker Collection of Wilsonia, Library of Congress, quoted in Arthur S. Link, *Wilson*, vol. 2, *The New Freedom* (Princeton, N.J.: Princeton University Press, 1956), 64–65.

[18] Cary T. Grayson, *Woodrow Wilson: An Intimate Memoir* (New York: Holt, Rinehart & Winston, 1960), 106. Also quoted in Mulder, "Wilson the Preacher," 267.

[19] Wilson to Mary Allen Hulbert (March 22, 1914), *PWW* 29:372.

Wilson's case rationalism, another key element of liberal international-ism, involved biblical faith as the ultimate means to authentic knowledge.

That Wilson regarded truth and authentic reality as accessible only through faith in God is evident from the numerous speeches he had deliv-ered in his capacity as a university pedagogue and administrator. He dis-cussed his epistemology and educational theory openly and frequently, stressing time and again the impossibility of knowledge without faith. In a handwritten note for one of his talks, for example, Wilson declared that "*Vigor of faith* [is] a concomitant of all right thinking and feeling . . . *Things seen in the fine revealing light of faith are the real verities of life*."[20] In another instance, he explained that "There are two sides to every life, the spiritual and the intellectual, which are inseparable. . . . The spirit of scholarship is in the spirit of faith."[21] These comments indi-cate that in Wilson's perspective good education as a pathway to genuine knowledge depended on a sincere commitment to Protestant Christianity. "You know as well as I do that there is no sound learning without true religion,"[22] he reminded members of the graduating class of 1903 dur-ing the baccalaureate service. Their degree certificates were valid only to the extent that they had mastered the skill of interpreting all areas of life through the lens of faith. This reflected Wilson's own conception of Protestantism as a "work-day religion" applicable to all secular events and activities.

Wilson's belief that true knowledge depended on faith in God is also apparent from his vision of a good university. In his perspective, univer-sity education necessarily involved spiritual education; higher learning untouched by Christianity was inconceivable.[23] A curriculum consisting only of arts and sciences was insufficient to prepare students for subse-quent leadership in politics, business, and real-world affairs in general; moral and religious instruction was essential and could not be ignored or

[20] Wilson, "Notes for a Chapel Talk" (November 8, 1896), *PWW* 10:42; emphasis original.

[21] "News Report of a Religious Talk" (October 2, 1903), *PWW* 15:10.

[22] See the first of "Two News Reports" (June 10, 1903), *PWW* 14:484. "Scholar-ship," Wilson elaborated elsewhere, "has . . . been most fruitful when associated with religion; and scholarship has never . . . been associated with any religion except the religion of Jesus Christ. The religion of humanity and the comprehension of humanity are of the same breed and kind; they go together." "Address at the Opening of the American University" (May 27, 1914), *PWW* 30:90.

[23] See "News Report of a Religious Talk: Philadelphian Society" (September 29, 1905), *PWW* 16:189; and also the report of Wilson's address "The True University Spirit" (November 7, 1902), *PWW* 14:201–2.

marginalized. Wilson stated this requirement emphatically in his widely publicized inaugural address as Princeton's president: "I do not see how any university can afford . . . [that] its teachings be not informed with the spirit of religion, and that the religion of Christ, and with the energy of positive faith."[24] It is no exaggeration to say that for Wilson a university was good only to the extent that it simultaneously served as a theological seminary, leading its members to comprehend all facets of existence in biblical terms. Sacralizing reality or, equivalently, secularizing eschatological faith into practical knowledge about history, politics, economics, and other worldly subjects was an essential function of higher learning for Wilson.

The form and style of Wilson's educational activities—that is, where he liked to speak, what kind of idiomatic language he used, or with whom he liked to spend time—are as indicative of the key position of faith in his epistemology as the content of his lectures and addresses. Religion and regular church attendance accounted for most of Wilson's most meaningful intellectual experiences already before his move to Princeton, during his initial teaching appointments at Bryn Mawr College and Wesleyan University. The mutual friendship formed during this period with Azel Washburn Hazen, pastor of the First Congregational Church in Middletown, Connecticut, proved particularly inspiring and long-lived.[25] Wilson and Hazen continued to correspond for years following Wilson's departure from Wesleyan, and Hazen's evangelical preaching served Wilson as a catalyst for his own political thought. A passage from Hazen's sermon made its way into one of the most important addresses of Wilson's early scholarly career. Entitled "Leaders of Men," this address marked Wilson's first explicit use of the language of the King James Bible in his political writing, offering the earliest direct evidence of religious presuppositions in his political philosophy.[26]

With the move to Princeton the defining presence of biblical faith in Wilson's political teachings and lecture style surfaced in full, turning Wilson into a charismatic preacher-teacher or, as one of his biographers

[24] Wilson, "Princeton for the Nation's Service" (October 25, 1902), *PWW* 14:184.

[25] See their numerous letters, such as Wilson to Hazen (June 30, 1891), *PWW* 7:228–29, and Hazen to Wilson (April 1, 1897), *PWW* 10:210–11.

[26] Wilson, "Leaders of Men" (June 17, 1890), *PWW* 6:646–71. Key among these presuppositions was Wilson's belief in the inevitability of political progress driven by the Christian law of love, the only force capable of uniting societies and providing political leaders with proper motives. See Link's editorial note, Wilson, "Leaders of Men," 644–46.

fittingly put it, a "university pastor."[27] Originally a Presbyterian seminary, Princeton was once headed by the great American evangelical theologian Jonathan Edwards, mentioned earlier, whose secularized eschatology included the prophecy that the Second Coming of Christ would occur in the United States. Wilson was appointed to teach jurisprudence and political economy, and his later inauguration as Princeton's president marked the first occasion the university elected an individual who was not an ordained minister. However, neither his lecturing assignment in secular academic subjects nor his lack of professional clerical qualifications kept Wilson away from the pulpit.

On the contrary, Wilson's involvement in religious matters was so extensive that a local newspaper mistakenly referred to him as "Rev. Dr. Woodrow Wilson."[28] He gave regular chapel talks to the Philadelphian Society, the campus religious association, and he delivered numerous other public speeches discussing spiritual issues. Among these the most notable were his baccalaureate sermons, the first of which he delivered in 1904 following a request by the graduating class. He felt greatly honored by this invitation and appropriated the role of a preacher at every subsequent commencement ceremony until his departure from Princeton in 1910, skipping only once because of a stroke. His resonant voice and deep, involved interpretation of the Scriptures left even the most restless undergraduates in awe and brought Wilson immense respect and popularity.[29] He was "a pulpit preacher of moving eloquence and evangelical fervor," and his Princeton sermons "were among the greatest speeches that he ever delivered and . . . some of the greatest sermons of [the twentieth] century."[30] A professor of history, law, and American constitutional government, Wilson nonetheless eclipsed most of Princeton's resident clergy as a moral and religious authority on campus.

By adding sermons and chapel talks to his regular course offerings, and by emphasizing continually that true knowledge of history, politics, economics, and other secular subjects was possible only in the light of biblical faith, Wilson worked relentlessly to bring Princeton as close to his vision of the ideal university as he could. In his estimation, Princeton's

---

[27] Arthur Walworth, *Woodrow Wilson*, 2nd ed. (Boston: Houghton Mifflin, 1965), 84.

[28] Mulder, "Wilson the Preacher," 270. Wilson was mistaken for a man of the cloth on more than one occasion. See John A. Garraty, *Woodrow Wilson: A Great Life in Brief* (New York: Knopf, 1956), 16, 46.

[29] Mulder, "Wilson the Preacher," 270.

[30] Link, *Higher Realism*, 8.

preeminence among America's institutions of higher education derived precisely from its exceptionally close approximation of the perfect Christian community. The intense presence of faith within its ivory towers granted its pious members exclusive access to God's hidden plan for America and the world. In this vein, Princeton was for Wilson primarily a metaphysical entity: a community of eschatological conviction and dedication. Its material aspects such as the ornate academic buildings, brick residences, and campus greens were secondary at best, even irrelevant. "The real Princeton," Wilson told the graduating class of 1907, "is a spirit . . . the spirit of learning . . . the spirit which seeks intimate contact with the springs of motive, and which lifts us into the presence of Christ."[31] Christ was for Wilson the first and deepest source of truth and causation, and infusing Princetonians with Christian faith was the first requirement for turning them into leaders capable of guiding America and the world toward future peace, justice, and prosperity.

Religion and Progress to Individual and National Harmony

Wilson's views on education and the ideal university point to a larger theme in his thought: the role of religion in society and politics. Wilson sought to imbue his Princeton audiences with the Bible not only because of his own deeply entrenched epistemological convictions, but also for more practical reasons. He regarded religious faith as the only antidote to the pernicious consequences of the rise of modern society, which he diagnosed as a process of deepening individual and collective crisis. As part of his larger spiritual mission to revitalize religion in individual and national life, Wilson considered Christianizing the next generation of American leaders at Princeton essential to transforming the United States, in 1890s plagued by social conflict, into a concordant, prosperous, and peaceful nation. In this vein, Wilson's biblical faith and his efforts to secularize it into a "work-day religion" stood at the core of another key element of liberal internationalism: the notion of a fundamental social harmony and the related idea of progress to it. Wilson first elaborated its domestic or national version, which later, after the Great War, became the springboard for his vision of progress and harmony on the international level.

---

[31] Wilson, "Sermon: Baccalaureate Address" (June 9, 1907), *PWW* 17:196.

Much like his European contemporary Nietzsche, Wilson recognized the threat of nihilism and social disorder posed by industrialization and the growth of scientific knowledge over the course of the nineteenth century.[32] Signs of moral decay and social fragmentation were becoming increasingly obvious in the United States during Wilson's tenure at Princeton in the 1890s and early 1900s. Violent clashes between American capital and labor in the railroad and mining industries, the ruthless stranglehold on political appointments by corporations in the form of patronage and the "boss system," and the 1901 assassination of President McKinley all indicated a brewing conflict with the potential to escalate into full-fledged anarchy.[33]

Confronted with the increasing disorder and demoralization of American society, Wilson observed that "The everyday, business rationalization of life produces *a hunger for the mystery*,"[34] and that this "hunger for spiritual things . . . is very marked at the present date."[35] Unlike Nietzsche, however, who proclaimed the death of Christianity and predicted that the spiritual void and hunger for order would be answered with totalitarian ideologies and false idols, Wilson saw the solution in diametrically opposed terms. Whereas Nietzsche had no doubt that science had discredited God once and for all, Wilson insisted that the legitimacy of the Bible as the fountainhead of true knowledge remained intact. For him traditional religion was not dead, only weak. The correct response to the impending social fragmentation and loss of meaning consisted in a religious revival and a renewed effort to inject the biblical message into every walk of life. On both the individual and national level, as on

---

[32] With respect to urbanization and the rise of mass society, for instance, Wilson declared that "the city curtails man of his wholeness, specializes him, quickens some powers, stunts others, gives him a sharp edge, and a temper like that of steel. . . . The huge, rushing, aggregate life of a great city—the crushing crowds in the streets, where friends seldom meet and there are few greetings; the thunderous noise of trade and industry that speaks of nothing but gain and competition, and a consuming fever that checks the natural courses of the kindly blood; no leisure anywhere, no quiet, no restful ease, no wise repose—all this shocks us. It is inhumane." *On Being Human* (New York: Harper, 1916), 12–13.

[33] For a discussion of the most violent strikes and their dramatic impact on social and religious consciousness in the United States at the turn of the century, see Henry F. May, *Protestant Churches and Industrial America* (New York: Octagon Books, 1963), especially the chapter "Three Earthquakes," 91–111.

[34] Wilson, "Notes for a Religious Address at the Second Presbyterian Church in Philadelphia" (December 11, 1903), *PWW* 15:78; emphasis original.

[35] "News Report: Ministerial Club Meeting" (April 27, 1909), *PWW* 19:173.

the international later on, moving from crisis to harmony depended on secularizing Protestant Christianity into a practical ethic and bringing it to bear on every aspect of existence.

According to Wilson, on the individual level a religious revival promised to counteract the debilitating effects of scientific atheism by restoring the key ingredient missing from the increasingly mechanistic accounts of the universe: the individual's sense of purpose. "Godliness not only results in salvation," Wilson stated, "but enables a man to pursue a confident course in this worldly life, like a straight course in the direction of a visible goal."[36] The trivialization of the human being implicit in its demotion from God's creature to a mere *Homo sapiens*, populating a cold universe in which random evil strikes without any deeper significance or explanation, could be reversed by re-enchanting the world in biblical terms.

Wilson elaborated this idea in an important address on the seventy-fifth anniversary of the founding of the Hartford Theological Seminary, the institution where three decades later Karl Löwith would spend his American exile from Nazism and formulate the secularization thesis. Wilson set out by noting the destructive impact of modern science and religious decline on the individual soul: "[It] is typical of the modern intellectual situation [that] we are infinitely restless because we are not aware of the plan."[37] Then he asked the future theologians and clergymen a rhetorical question: "I wonder if any of you fully realize how hungry men's minds are for a complete and satisfactory explanation of life?"[38] In the main part of his address, Wilson issued a powerful call for a religious revival:

> How necessary for our salvation that our dislocated souls should be relocated in the plan! And who shall relocate them, who shall save us by enabling us to find ourselves, if not the minister of the gospel? . . . Religion is the explanation of science and of life. . . . The minister . . . must show men that there is a plan. . . . The business of the Christian Church, of the Christian ministers, is to show the spiritual relations of men to the great world processes, whether they be physical or spiritual. It is nothing less than to show the plan of life and men's relations to the plan of life.[39]

[36] Wilson, "Some Reasons Why a Man Should Be a Christian" (March 1, 1900), *PWW* 11:453.

[37] Wilson, "The Present Task of the Ministry" (May 26, 1909), *PWW* 19:218.

[38] Wilson, "The Present Task of the Ministry," 218.

[39] Wilson, "The Present Task of the Ministry," 218–19.

For Wilson the solution to modern nihilism thus consisted of placing the biblical idea of salvation back at the center of the universe as its hidden meaning, thereby endowing human life and suffering with coherence, purpose, and direction. Returning to God was the only route to genuine happiness: "a man rejoices in his heart not because of worldly triumphs, but because of a true adjustment of his relations to God. Only the law of the Lord can bring peace."[40] By this law Wilson meant above all the law of love and selfless service, embodied in the image of Christ and representing the perfect rule for human life.[41]

Notably, according to Wilson the revival of "work-day religion" would generate positive consequences not only for the individual psyche, but also and especially on the collective level. Embracing Protestant Christianity privately would transform the character of the entire United States and, if the revival were to be carried abroad, of international politics at large. "Christianity," Wilson declared, "gave us, in the fullness of time, the perfect image of right living, the secret of social and individual well-being; for the two are not separable, and the man who . . . verifies the secret in his own living has discovered [also] the best and only way to serve the world."[42] In this vein, Protestant Christianity constituted the secret wellspring of progress to individual, national, and international harmony alike. It was especially in the biblical principle of love and selfless service that Wilson saw the much-needed "stabilizer of the nation"[43] and the key to overcoming the fermenting class conflict, revolution, and anarchy. By instilling this principle in the next generation of politicians and businessmen, as Wilson tirelessly sought through his sermons and chapel talks at Princeton, a road could be paved from the existing social

---

[40] "News Item: President Wilson's Address" (March 27, 1903), *PWW* 14:399.

[41] See Wilson, "Love the Only Motive for Conduct" (November 2, 1899), and idem, "Report of a Religious Talk" (November 3, 1899), *PWW* 11:273–74. See also "God Is Love: News Report of an Address to the Trenton Y.M.C.A." (February 9, 1903), *PWW* 14:354–55.

[42] Wilson, "When a Man Comes to Himself" (November 1, 1899), *PWW* 11:273.

[43] Wilson, "Address to the Annual Baltimore Conference of the Methodist Episcopal Church" (March 25, 1915), *PWW* 32:430–31. Wilson analogized the significance of religion for American society directly to a recent technological breakthrough in airplane design: "You know that somebody has just invented a thing called stabilizer that is used in connection with airplanes, and by some process, . . . this corrects the erratic movements of the machine, so that it . . . determines the plane upon which the machine is to move, and the machine cannot depart from it. Something like that is the function of the great moral forces of the world, to act as stabilizers even when we go up in the air." Wilson, "Address to the Annual Baltimore Conference," 430–31.

disunity to the fundamental but as yet obscured national harmony of interests in America.

Political progress, then, was a function of spiritual enlightenment and religious revitalization in Wilson's mind. Building a peaceful, just, and wealthy American polis depended crucially on uniting the citizenry in a nationwide interdenominational congregation. For Wilson, politics was in this regard fundamentally about translating religious principle into social action.[44] As he summarized it in "The Modern Democratic State," a milestone treatise in his career as a political theorist, "The goal of political development is identical with the goal of individual development. Both singly and collectively man's nature draws him towards . . . a fuller realization of his kinship with God."[45] He viewed the Bible not merely as a religious treatise, but above all as a political manual: a blueprint for resolving all individual and social frictions. If implemented in historical reality—that is, secularized—its principles harbored the potential for dissolving all past and present discords and transforming the United States into the New Jerusalem: Wilson's liberal-republican vision of the Millennium.

Because political progress depended on spreading the Christian spirit to every area of secular existence, for Wilson American churches and clergymen played an even more important political role than actual politicians and government officials. This view was as old as the Puritans, and in advancing it Wilson joined the ranks of most other nineteenth-century American lay and clerical leaders, providing yet another illustration of Tocqueville's perceptive remarks on the alliance of religion and politics in the United States. Although church and state were separate under the American Constitution, in practice preachers were deemed by Wilson to hold the key to the political development of the nation. Wilson indeed understood politics first and foremost in terms of spiritual enlightenment: not the ministers of the U.S. Government, but the ministers of the Protestant church were the main agents of national progress. "The Church is called to a great mission which is to keep the sap in the body politic," he explained; "It is called upon to keep alive the social instinct which is the instinct of unselfishness and cooperation."[46] It is worth adding that since for Wilson the United States was the political expression of

---

[44] Wilson, "*Religion* and *Patriotism*" (January 16, 1898), *PWW* 10:365–66.

[45] Wilson, "The Modern Democratic State" (December 1, 1885), *PWW* 5:90.

[46] "News Report of a Religious Address in Philadelphia" (December 14, 1903), *PWW* 15:98.

the biblical Millennium, its civil government had a spiritual function just as much as the church had a political one. As he stated in his Princeton lectures on public law, one of the main functions of modern democratic government was to "*stand spiritual guardian in . . . the repression of vice* (prostitution, gambling, etc.)."[47]

As will emerge later, Wilson's idea of progress to a harmony of interests in post–World War I Europe extended his idea of domestic progress beyond the national borders and rested on the same religious foundations. Resolving the crisis in a Europe tormented by war depended on spreading the biblical principles under the leadership of the United States, the redeemer nation chosen by God. "There is a mighty task before us," Wilson said to a group of young Americans as early as 1905, well before the outbreak of the Great War, "and it welds us together. It is to make the United States a mighty Christian Nation, and to Christianize the world."[48] By reforming international politics in accordance with American liberal-republican principles, in which the spirit of Christ had assumed its fullest secular expression, Wilson was certain that Europe and the world would progress once and for all from conflict and oppression to freedom, democracy, and peace. Before discussing the eschatological dimension of Wilson's international political thought, however, it is worth scrutinizing in greater detail his idea of history and its theological presuppositions.

Wilson's Conception of American History
The Germ Theory and Frontier Thesis

The study of the past was Wilson's earliest and longest-lasting intellectual preoccupation: for decades prior to entering politics, he was a prominent scholar and historian—one of the leading American historians of his day. His reputation extended beyond the borders of the United States. His name and academic credentials were familiar to such major European scholars as Lord Acton, Regius Professor of Modern History at Cambridge University, who considered Wilson an expert on modern American political history and contacted him to request a chapter on Lincoln and state rights for a multivolume edition then under preparation at Cambridge University Press.[49] At home, Wilson's admirers included

---

[47] Wilson, "Lecture Notes on Public Law" (September 22, 1894), *PWW* 9:24; emphasis original.

[48] "Two News Reports of an Address in New York on Youth and Christian Progress" (November 20, 1905), *PWW* 16:228.

[49] Acton to Wilson (May 10, 1899), *PWW* 11:117–18. Wilson wrote the chapter,

Frederick Jackson Turner, then as now one of the most celebrated American historians. Upon hearing about Wilson's plans to write a detailed history of the United States, Turner stated that the work "will be *the* American history of our time."[50]

Especially in the early stages of his scholarly career, Wilson was an advocate of the germ theory of history. This theory was propounded primarily by Henry Baxter Adams and Richard Ely, whom Wilson met at Johns Hopkins University in the late 1880s. It explained the liberal-republican identity of the United States by constructing a quasi-biological lineage tracing the nation's primordial origins to ancient Semitic and Aryan tribes, thereby emphasizing the racial and genetic continuity between America and Europe. Wilson's treatise *The State* (1889) offers an illustrative example. Adhering to a conception of society as a living organism, Wilson suggested that ancient Greece and Rome, Western European nations including England, and finally the United States represented successive points along a shared evolutionary trajectory with roots in "the primitive politics of the Teutonic races."[51] Implicit in this reading was the notion that democracy and liberalism were biological (rather than cultural and acquired) characteristics. In Wilson's view, the first Teutons possessed in their blood "a very fierce democratic temper," which passed on to their offspring, down subsequent generations, and all the way to nineteenth-century America.[52]

Within this racial metanarrative, Wilson emphasized especially America's connection to its most immediate antecedent: England. "The political institutions of the United States," he contended, "are in all their main features simply the political institutions of England . . . worked out through a fresh development to new and characteristic forms."[53] These new forms were not necessarily better forms. In fact, in his early political writings Wilson went so far as to declare the U.S. Constitution and the republican form of American government inferior to the English model of constitutional monarchy. Unlike the great majority of his fellow

---

which now appears in *The Cambridge Modern History*, vol. 7 (New York: Macmillan, 1902).

[50] Turner to Wilson (December 24, 1894), *PWW* 9:119.

[51] Wilson, *The State: Elements of Historical and Practical Politics* (Boston: D.C. Heath, 1889), 366–67. See also the discussion of Wilson's historical consciousness in Lloyd E. Ambrosius, *Wilsonian Statecraft: Theory and Practice of Liberal Internationalism during World War I* (Wilmington, Del.: SR Books, 1991), 3–13.

[52] Wilson, *State*, 449–73.

[53] Wilson, *State*, 449–73.

citizens, Wilson did not see the first centennial of the American Revolution in 1876 as an occasion to celebrate. On the contrary, he remarked that America would have been much better off had it remained a constitutional monarchy, "the only true form of government," and he declared repeatedly that "The American *Republic* will . . . never celebrate another Centennial."[54]

Wilson later abandoned such rash statements in favor of a much more nuanced and patriotic political philosophy, but he remained an Anglophile throughout his life. Even when asserting the uniqueness of the American spirit and proclaiming his allegiance to it, he did not forget to point out that the peculiar character of the American democracy was due to its special ancestry: "[Its history] is . . . a continuation of the institutional history of England—English institutions developed upon an American scale and with American modifications."[55] During and after the Great War, this view led Wilson to portray America's intervention on the side of England in terms of reestablishing a blood connection severed by a period of exile and geographical separation.[56] This notion of "lost children returning to their mother to redeem her"[57] represents a persistent trait in the history of American eschatological thinking about Europe. It derives from the original Puritan notion of a transatlantic errand into the American wilderness in preparation for spearheading a millennial revolution in the Old World.

The germ theory, however, was not Wilson's final word on the essential shape and meaning of American history. From the late 1880s on, his view of the national past and America's relationship to Europe became increasingly influenced by another interpretation: Frederick Jackson Turner's pathbreaking (though by no means uncontroversial) frontier thesis. Turner first presented it at a special meeting of the American Historical Association at the World's Columbian Exposition in Chicago on July 12, 1893. In opposition to the germ theory, which portrayed America as a vestige of Europe and thus emphasized continuity between the New World and the Old, Turner's reading stressed discontinuity by

---

[54] See his shorthand diary entries dated June 19 and July 4, 1876, *PWW* 1:143, 148–49; emphasis original.

[55] Wilson, "The True American Spirit" (October 27, 1892), *PWW* 8:37.

[56] See, e.g., Wilson's "Remarks at a Stag Dinner" (December 28, 1918), *PWW* 64:490–92, in which he told the British prime minister David Lloyd George that "Heretofore, the tie that bound us was one of language. Hereafter, we shall be one race."

[57] Cf. Wilson, "Remarks at the Station in Milan" (January 5, 1919), *PWW* 53:616.

highlighting the transformative impact of the North American wilderness on the incoming Europeans:

> In the settlement of America we have to observe how European life entered the continent, and how America modified and developed that life and reacted on Europe. Our early history is the study of European germs developing in an American environment. Too exclusive attention has been paid by institutional students to the Germanic origins, too little to American factors. . . . The wilderness masters the colonist. It finds him a European in dress, industries, tools, modes of travel, and thought. It takes him from the railroad car and puts him in the birch canoe. . . . He must accept the conditions . . . or perish. . . . Little by little he transforms the wilderness, but the outcome is not the old Europe, not simply the development of Germanic germs. . . . The fact is, there is a new product that is American.[58]

For Turner the United States was therefore much more unique and original than previously thought; a rupture had occurred between the New and Old Worlds. The American society and government were not simply updated iterations of their Western European, and specifically English, ancestors; a demonstrable qualitative change had taken place.

Whereas Adams and Ely, both of whom were trained at the University of Heidelberg, structured their understanding of the American past around the enduring presence of Teutonic genes, Turner, among the first American historians trained domestically, focused the spotlight on the environment and the American West. As "the line of most rapid and effective Americanization," the western frontier represented for him "the really American part" of the history of the United States.[59] It was here, at the cutting edge of European civilization advancing into the wilderness, that the immigrants (driven by greed, land-hunger, and scorn for authority) escaped the orbit of Europe and became genuinely American: free, independent, and also patriotic, since the shared frontier experience purged them of all preexisting loyalties to their European places of birth. "The existence of an area of free land, its continuous recession, and the advance of American settlement westward," Turner summarized his position in unambiguous terms, "explain American development."[60]

By the time Turner's paper appeared in the Proceedings of the State Historical Society of Wisconsin in December 1893, Wilson had known

---

[58] Turner, "The Significance of the Frontier in American History," in *The Frontier in American History* (New York: Holt, Rinehart & Winston, 1920), 3–4.

[59] Turner, "Significance of the Frontier," 3–4.

[60] Turner, "Significance of the Frontier," 1.

him for several years and developed a strong personal and professional friendship with him.[61] The publication of the frontier thesis had an important impact on Wilson's mature view of the American past. To be sure, he continued to rely on the germ theory and never truly abandoned his conception of the United States as an extension of England, but Turner's influence increasingly led him to recognize that the United States possessed a much greater degree of autonomous identity than he was willing to grant at first. America was a continuation of England, but a continuation *in a new form.*

The two scholars acknowledged this shared understanding both privately and on various public occasions. Even before Turner formulated the frontier thesis, Wilson reflected in one of his letters to him on "our talks in Baltimore on the growth of the national idea, and of nationality, in our history, and our agreement that the role of the west in this development was a very great, a leading, role, though much neglected by our historians."[62] Only a few years later, Wilson endorsed Turner's thesis openly, discussing the decisive impact of the frontier on American institutions in a language that could easily be mistaken for Turner's own. "That part of our history . . . which is most truly national," Wilson wrote, "is the history of the West. Almost all the critical issues of our politics have been made up beyond the mountains. . . . It is this making of the nation in the great central basins of the continent that an outline of [American] history should principally exhibit."[63]

The pertinence of secularization theory to the frontier thesis emerges the moment one notices what forms the heart of this particular narrative of the American past: a clearly defined idea of progress. The frontier thesis represents an excellent example of history as a coherent story unfolding along a linear trajectory toward a final goal: the modern United States as a self-conscious nation on authentic principles independent from its European antecedents. This trajectory has both a temporal and a spatial

---

[61] They had first met in 1889, during Wilson's visiting lectureship at Johns Hopkins, where Turner was pursuing a doctorate in history. Turner attended Wilson's seminars and privately considered him "one of the best historical men in this country." See Turner to Caroline Mae Sherwood (January 21, 1889), *PWW* 6:58.

[62] Wilson to Turner (August 23, 1889), *PWW* 6:369.

[63] Wilson, "Mr. Goldwin Smith's 'Views' on Our Political History" (September 5, 1893), *PWW* 8:354. Turner read the essay and saw in it a "lucid and effective statement . . . of the importance of the Middle Region, and the West," adding that Wilson's focus on "the doctrine of American *development*, in contrast with Germanic *germs*, is very gratifying." Turner to Wilson (December 20, 1893), *PWW* 8:417.

dimension: America's progress toward its distinct national character is measurable both in years of historical time (from colonial settlement to the end of the nineteenth century) and in land miles (from the Eastern Seaboard to the West Coast). The hidden theological presuppositions underlying the frontier thesis surface precisely in this coherent progressive pattern, which is not found in the chaos of historical events but rather has to be imputed to them on the basis of eschatological faith.[64]

In the case of Frederick Jackson Turner, the argument that the frontier thesis represents faith disguised as historical fact must not be taken too far. This is because, even before he published his landmark paper, Turner showed acute awareness that religious and moral presuppositions could not be expunged from historical narratives. As he famously proclaimed in 1891, "*Each age writes the history of the past anew with reference to the conditions uppermost in its own time.*"[65] This statement is exemplary of critical sociology rather than Rankean empiricism, the epistemological approach prevalent in American and European historiography in Turner's day, and it suggests that Turner understood the tentative and ideological character of his conception of the American past. The frontier thesis was just that: *a* thesis, not *the* history of the United States. It encapsulated but one representation, Turner's own, of the essentially chaotic and meaningless past. In this sense, Turner saw nothing inevitable about the idea of progress expressed in the frontier thesis; if in his reading of American history progress seemed like a natural fact, this was only an illusion reflecting his skillful ability to impose on the chaos of events at least a temporary shape and form: that of his own perspective.[66]

---

[64] To be sure, the dogmatic and culturally specific moorings of the frontier thesis also surface in other areas, such as in what this interpretation of America's national past leaves out: it depicts precolonial America as empty and uncivilized wilderness, neglecting the presence of numerous indigenous cultures. This "invisibilization" of American Indians was part already of the earliest colonial mindset displayed by Columbus and the Spanish conquistadors. On this point, see Tzvetan Todorov, *The Conquest of America* (New York: Harper & Row, 1984), especially Todorov's typology of relational knowledge constructed by the conquering European "self" with respect to the savage "other." It was also implicit in the Puritan view of the New World as a gathering place for God's elect and in the nineteenth-century narrative of the American immigrants' "manifest destiny" to overspread the continent. The frontier thesis perpetuates this longstanding myth of a virgin continent.

[65] Turner, "The Significance of History," in *Rereading Frederick Jackson Turner: "The Significance of the Frontier in American History" and Other Essays*, ed. John Mack Faragher (New York: Holt, 1994), 18; emphasis original.

[66] Out of the figures discussed by Löwith in his *Meaning in History: The Theological Implications of the Philosophy of History* (Chicago: University of Chicago Press, 1949),

Wilson's understanding of the frontier thesis, however, was an entirely different matter. Turner's critical reflexivity and skepticism concerning the possibility of any firm foundations for historical knowledge were foreign to Wilson, whose spiritual commitment to the Bible was absolute, leading him to comprehend the progress of the American national project as the unfolding of God's will within the world. Whereas Turner understood that any unifying principle of historical interpretation was itself within history and hence conditional and mutable, Wilson's faith did not allow for such relativistic thinking. His religious convictions were too entrenched to keep at bay, and they determined his historical views. In the words of a recent biographer, "Wilson was not the kind of scholar who first does his research and then draws his conclusions. He was rather the kind who first has a vision."[67] Insofar as this vision was the biblical myth of salvation, Wilson was not a historian, but a theologian engaged in theodicy: manipulating historical events in order to demonstrate the active presence of God in America's national past and in world affairs at large. As is about to become clear, for him the eschatological myth represented the objective meaning of history, and he acknowledged the religious foundations of his philosophy of history explicitly.

The Theological Presuppositions of Wilson's Philosophy of History

As the example of St. Augustine and his skepticism about any lasting improvement in human affairs demonstrates, a devout commitment to the Bible does not automatically imply a belief in progress as the essential theme of temporal history. One can practice the former without adhering to the latter. In Wilson's case, however, the connection obtained: the president secularized his Christian religiosity into an eschatological conception of history. He "believed that God controls history and uses men and nations in the unfolding of His plan according to His purposes,"[68] and he regarded "progress as the organic law of life and the working out of

---

it is arguably Jacob Burckhardt and his "impressionistic historiography" that Turner's intellectual posture resembles most closely. Crucially, Löwith saw in Burckhardt the first modern historian to have liberated himself from the theological presuppositions that had governed Western historical interpretation since the Bible.

[67] Jan Willem Schulte Nordholt, *Woodrow Wilson: A Life for World Peace*, trans. Herbert H. Rowen (Berkeley: University of California Press, 1991), 33.

[68] Link, *Higher Realism*, 76.

the divine plan of history."[69] The idea of progress was a direct outgrowth of his Protestant faith.[70] It underpinned and shaped not only his domestic agenda, but also and especially his foreign policy, which at its core expressed an eschatological fantasy of an international order transformed by America the redeemer nation.[71]

Wilson made no secret of his staunch belief in the progressive character of the general historical process, which served as the backdrop for his idea of national and international progress. As he stated in his 1910 Thanksgiving proclamation, for instance, "it is a very common fact . . . that all life is a struggle against evil. All the evil in the world is antique; it is hoary with age. All the . . . good things . . . are new things. They have come into existence in a long . . . unbroken series with the progress of the ages."[72] His religiously inspired, Manichean conception of the universe divided between good and evil was not static, but dynamic: developing along a straight line. The opposing forces did not coexist in eternal recurrence precluding any hopes for improvement; the pessimism of Augustine and of ancient Greek and Roman historians was utterly foreign to Wilson.[73] On the contrary, they were engaged in an unfolding struggle, with the one element slowly conquering and eradicating the other. Time was in forward motion for Wilson, and its essential theme was the progressive emancipation of humankind from evil. Insofar as by history Wilson meant political history, and insofar as he defined the driving struggle between good and evil in terms of freedom versus oppression, history was for him fundamentally a march toward liberty. "From the dim morning hours of history . . . down to this modern time of history's high noon when nations stand forth full-grown and self-governed," he declared, "the law of coherence and continuity in political development has suffered no serious breach. . . . [The] lines of advance are seen to be singularly straight."[74]

From the perspective of the secularization thesis, the idea of progress alone would have been sufficient to indicate the presence of eschatological presuppositions in Wilson's historical thought—even if he denied them.

[69] Arthur S. Link, *Woodrow Wilson: Revolution, War, and Peace* (Arlington Heights, Ill.: AHM, 1979), 6.

[70] Ambrosius, *Wilsonian Statecraft*, 7, 10.

[71] Gregory S. Butler, "Visions of a Nation Transformed: Modernity and Ideology in Wilson's Political Thought," *Journal of Church and State* 39, no. 1 (1997): 42–43.

[72] Wilson, "Thanksgiving Day Address" (November 24, 1910), *PWW* 22:88.

[73] Ambrosius, *Wilsonian Statecraft*, 7.

[74] Wilson, *State*, 2–7, 17–21, 575–76.

Yet denying them was just about inconceivable to the devout Wilson: in contrast to proponents of ostensibly scientific ideologies of progress, he thus admitted the biblical foundations of his progressive conception of history readily and openly. "Let no man suppose," he said in his famous Denver address on the Bible, "that progress can be divorced from religion, or that there is any other platform for the ministers of reform than . . . the utterances of our Lord and Savior."[75] After returning to his hotel room from the Denver Auditorium late at night, he reaffirmed this point in private: "The Bible," he wrote to an intimate friend, "is undoubtedly the book that has made democracy and been the source of all progress."[76] Wilson's epistemology, which defined truth in terms of reality illuminated by the revealing light of faith, applied to his historical knowledge as well. One could discover the real shape of history only by viewing it through the biblical prism, the key to decoding all existence.

The central position of the biblical myth of salvation in Wilson's historical consciousness also can be demonstrated negatively: by noticing how disturbingly senseless the historical process appeared to him without the eschatological lens. Wilson was incapable of accepting history strictly on its own merits, as an essentially chaotic sequence of random events, and he shuddered at the absence of any purpose or direction. His longtime personal secretary recalled an interesting remark that illustrates Wilson's fear of history as chaos particularly well: "I believe in Divine Providence," Wilson said on one occasion; "If I did not have faith, I should go crazy. If I thought that the direction of the affairs of this disordered world depended upon our finite intelligence, I should not know how to reason my way to sanity."[77] Without faith in God and salvation, man's situation in history apparently terrified Wilson. On one occasion he described this situation in terms of solitude and disorientation: "We speak of a man [lost] in a desert [who] does not know where any beaten path and highway is."[78] The Bible was therefore all-important. According to Wilson, "A man has found himself when he has found his relation to the rest of the universe, and [the Bible] is the book in which those

[75] Wilson, "Address in Denver on the Bible" (May 7, 1911) [henceforth "Denver Address"], *PWW* 23:20.

[76] Wilson to Mary Allen Hulbert Peck (May 7, 1911), *PWW* 23:11.

[77] Joseph P. Tumulty, *Woodrow Wilson as I Know Him* (Garden City, N.Y.: Doubleday, 1921), 335–36. See also Wilson's "Luncheon Address in San Francisco" (September 18, 1919), *PWW* 63:350.

[78] Wilson, "Denver Address," 14.

relations are set forth."[79] Through the story of salvation, history gained purpose and legibility and revealed itself to the interpreter as a reassuring narrative of progress driven by transcendental forces, by which Wilson understood "forces . . . proceed[ing] from the law and providence of God."[80]

Wilson's belief that "The providence of God is the foundation of affairs"[81] endowed his conception of history with all the typical tendencies of Christian historical consciousness. For example, Wilson's faith in God as the Lord of history translated into determinism, the source of Wilson's confidence that his post–World War I proposals were certain to succeed—and of his utter shock when his domestic political opponents, led by Senator Henry Cabot Lodge, rejected them. Another characteristic in common with all other constructions of history erected on implicit or explicit biblical foundations, whether formulated by Augustine, Joachim, Bossuet, Comte, or Marx, was ascetic futurism: the propensity to discount the past and the present in favor of the future as the site of all meaning. As Wilson stated in one of his books, "We think of the future, not the past, as the more glorious time in comparison with which the present is nothing."[82]

In Augustine's case the emphasis on the future did not engender any optimism, since the Doctor of the Latin Church regarded the eschatological moment only as a spiritual and existential possibility, not a historical one. Like Joachim and other representatives of theological historism, however, Wilson understood the prophecy of salvation in historical terms, and so his futurism was fundamentally optimistic—certain of impending great improvements in the secular-political order of existence. Thus a review of Wilson's five-volume *History of the American People* (1902) commented that the narrative radiated "the spirit of one strong in his love for the country and hopeful of its future. This work is full of optimism. . . . The view is always forward, on to better things. . . . The tone is instinct with enthusiasm, confidence and expectation."[83] Everyday events and actions had value for Wilson only to the extent that they hastened his

[79] Wilson, "Denver Address," 14.

[80] Wilson, "Address at the Dedication of a Synagogue in Newark, New Jersey" (September 7, 1911), *PWW* 23:306.

[81] Cited in Link, *Higher Realism*, 13.

[82] Wilson, *The New Freedom: A Call for the Emancipation of the Generous Energies of a People* (New York: Doubleday, 1913), 42.

[83] Charles McLean Andrews, review of *A History of the American People*, by Woodrow Wilson, *The Independent* 54 (1902): 2957–59, reprinted in *PWW* 14:280–83.

vision of the future. He regarded the present and the past as only a sort of dark prehistory to the real history of humankind, whose beginning was still ahead.[84]

It is perhaps unnecessary to point out the role reserved in Wilson's eschatological conception of history for the United States. As scores of American clerical and lay leaders before him, Wilson too considered the United States God's chosen nation. America occupied the same messianic position in his imagination as New England once did in the imagination of Governor John Winthrop: it was a model Christian society providentially destined to serve as a beacon illuminating the path of universal progress. "America was born a Christian nation," Wilson said about the origins of the United States, and it "exemplif[ied] that devotion to the elements of righteousness which are derived from the revelations of Holy Scripture."[85] The divine inspiration set the American republic apart from the rest of as yet unenlightened humanity. Wilson emphasized the exceptional status of his native country on numerous occasions, most notably when he declared that the United States was "the only idealistic nation in the world."[86]

America's responsibility to minister to the world emanated directly from the nation's allegedly sacred origins. As the only nation whose "voice . . . [expressed] the ideal purposes of history," the United States was uniquely positioned to guide humanity toward salvation; if it declined this role, there was no other nation to step in its place.[87] In practical terms, as the discussion of his foreign policy will reveal, Wilson understood this role in terms of converting foreign nations and the structure of international relations as a whole to the founding principles of American democracy. This foreign policy agenda represented the secular expression of what in Wilson's mind was fundamentally a biblical-eschatological mission. Liberty, the main ideal codified in the American Declaration of Independence and the centerpiece of Wilson's liberal internationalism, was religious in origin in his understanding.[88] It derived from the Word of

---

[84] In the words of Ralph Henry Gabriel, Wilson understood "the ultimate reality to be found in the kingdom of the ideal." *The Course of American Democratic Thought* (New York: Ronald Press, 1940), 337.

[85] Wilson, "Denver Address," 20.

[86] Wilson, "Address in the Coliseum in Sioux Falls" (September 8, 1919), *PWW* 63:113.

[87] Wilson, "Address in the Coliseum in Sioux Falls."

[88] Wilson, "Denver Address," 15; see also idem, "The Variety and Unity of History" (September 20, 1904), *PWW* 15:481.

God rather than the Magna Charta. Not the English document sealed by King John in 1215, but the Bible constituted for Wilson the true "Magna Charta of the human soul" and of American freedoms.[89]

Taken together, Wilson's idea of history as liberal progress and his ardent acknowledgment of the Bible as the source of this idea make his philosophy of history an excellent example of partial or incomplete secularization, to use the theoretical language developed earlier. The biblical myth of salvation is secularized only in the limited sense of being interpreted in political-historical terms; the resulting notion of progress remains consciously Christian. This is in contrast to the complete secularization exemplified by Comte or Marx, whose philosophies go one step further and abandon Christianity for scientific atheism; their eschatological foundations are thereby subdued and remain present only covertly and hermeneutically. Notably, and to reiterate one of the conclusions flowing from the Löwith-Blumenberg debate on secularization, products of partial secularization are especially immune to the critique of secularization as a valid tool for understanding the genealogy of modern philosophies of progress. To this extent, from the vantage of secularization theory, prospects are more than favorable for interpreting Wilson's idea of liberal progress as secularized eschatology.

Conservative Millennialism
The Quest for Orderly Progress

Even before turning to Wilson's foreign policy, the role of the Bible as the bedrock of his conceptions of knowledge, education, liberty, the general historical process, America's past, and progress to national harmony points unmistakably to the conclusion that he was a political eschatologist. His domestic political agenda manifested a religious mission to transform the United States into God's kingdom on earth; after all, Wilson defined patriotism as nothing else than Christianity enacted in political practice.[90] However, there remains an important hurdle to drawing this conclusion. In a number of writings and speeches Wilson seems to have furnished solid grounds for just the opposite claim: that he was a pragmatic conservative, not a progressive let alone an impractical religious utopian. Chief among these grounds are Wilson's disdain for revolution as a method of advancement and his emphasis on order as the first condition of liberal-republican government.

---

[89] Wilson, "Denver Address," 15. Cf. Schulte Nordholt, *Life for World Peace*, 47.
[90] Wilson, "Religion and Patriotism" (July 4, 1902), *PWW* 12:474–78.

Wilson's conservatism surfaced on several occasions during his scholarly and political career. An especially clear example occurred in the immediate aftermath of the great economic depression of 1893, which triggered widespread labor unrest (such as the Pullman Strike in May 1894) and threatened to evolve into a national crisis. With the country teetering on the verge of anarchy, Wilson initiated an urgent search for principles capable of shepherding the United States through the cataclysm unscathed.

He discovered them in Edmund Burke. In a key lecture, Wilson used Burke's famous denunciation of the French Revolution to voice his own reaction to the economic, social, and political storm of 1893: "Burke," he stated, "hated the French revolutionary philosophy and deemed it unfit for free men. And that philosophy is in fact radically evil and corrupting. No state can ever be conducted on its principles."[91] Flatly rejecting any calls in America for a radical change to socialism or other visionary models of society, Wilson proclaimed that liberty had always grown slowly and in stages: "governments have never been successfully and permanently changed except by slow modification operating from generation to generation."[92] Reforming the standing American society, not tearing it down in order to create a brand new one, was Wilson's response to the looming national crisis.

His criticism of revolutionary politics drew in part on his notion of society as a living organism evolving through piecemeal accretion of new characteristics.[93] What disturbed Wilson most about French liberals was their conception of government as a contract that could be made over at will.[94] This definition ignored the role of habit, for Wilson one of the key foundations for liberal government. The visionary dreams of Rousseau and other intellectual fathers of the French Revolution struck Wilson as poetic but impracticable and indeed dangerous. For him, it was the sober "masculine and practical genius of the English mind" that represented the only solid "footing . . . for liberty and institutions that make men free."[95] This preference for English liberalism was consistent

---

[91] Wilson, "Edmund Burke: The Man and His Times" (August 31, 1893), *PWW* 8:341.

[92] Wilson, "Edmund Burke," 341.

[93] See Wilson, "Leaders of Men" (June 17, 1890), *PWW* 6:659, in which he argued that "Society is . . . an organism" and that "The evolution of its institutions must take place by slow modification and nice all-around adjustment."

[94] Wilson, "Edmund Burke" (August 31, 1893), *PWW* 8:341.

[95] Wilson, "The Real Idea of Democracy" (August 31, 1901), *PWW* 12:176–77.

with Wilson's germ theory of history, which regarded liberty as a Teutonic and Anglo-Saxon gene.

Another example of Wilson's conservatism is his interpretation of the American Revolution. Much like the majority of American clergymen in 1776, Wilson considered the event a defensive move: not a violent overthrow of a certain political tradition, but a reaction undertaken to preserve a tradition come under a sudden threat. From his vantage point, the term "American Revolution" was a misnomer: "The revolutionists," Wilson stated, "stood for no revolution at all, but for the maintenance of accepted practices, for the inviolable understandings of precedent."[96] In his view it was England that, by abruptly subjecting its colonies to the principle of taxation without representation, betrayed its own longstanding liberal customs and left their defense in the hands of Americans. Not the colonists, but the English were the real rebels by virtue of their attempt to undo accepted, habitually evolved articles of liberal government. As for the American colonists, Wilson was adamant that "Those who framed our federal government had planned no *revolution*: they did not mean to invent an American government."[97] America's Founding Fathers sought "only to Americanize the English government, which they *knew*, and knew to be a government fit for free men to live under, if only narrow monarchical notions could be got out of it and its spirit liberalized."[98] American government was for Wilson a continuation—not subversion—of English institutions.

To Wilson's views on the French and American Revolutions, one could add his famous response to the Russian Revolution as yet a third instance of his conservatism: he rejected the Bolshevik scheme of radical progress, affirmed the existing capitalist order, and argued that the only way to rectify its socially divisive tendencies was through gradual reform and moral education.[99] The upshot of all three examples, however, is the same: taken together, they seem to collide head-on with the present argument that Wilson was an ardent progressive guided by an eschatological vision of society.[100] How, then, if at all, can Wilson's conservatism be reconciled with his political millennialism?

---

[96] Wilson, "The Ideals of America" (December 26, 1901), *PWW* 12:213.

[97] Wilson, "Lecture on Democracy" (December 5, 1891), *PWW* 7:350.

[98] Wilson, "Lecture on Democracy," 350; emphasis original.

[99] Wilson, "The Road Away from Revolution" (July 27, 1923), *PWW* 68:393–95.

[100] The tension between his conservatism and visionary politics has been noted by several scholars. See, for instance, Butler, "Nation Transformed," 44–45, and Simon P.

One possibility is that his conservatism has been exaggerated. It may be a myth, a legacy of biographers who were as wedded to patriotic progressive Protestantism as Wilson—and hence considered the perspective just as pragmatic and realistic as he did in his own mind.[101] Burke's political philosophy may have exercised much less influence on Wilson than commonly assumed. Wilson encountered Burke already in his undergraduate curriculum, but little indication exists that he had found the Irish philosopher particularly interesting until the early 1890s. This suggests that Wilson's attachment to Burke may have been similar to the national crisis that had spawned it in the first place: intense but ultimately passing. In this vein, it is likely that Wilson's "so-called conservative period has been overdrawn."[102]

Even more important to notice is that Wilson was not nearly as contemptuous of radical politics as his organic conception of liberal government cemented by habit appears to imply. It is little known, for instance, that Wilson was not categorically opposed to socialism. Unlike any American president before or since, he had given socialism serious thought and a considerable degree of legitimacy.[103] He considered it "clear that in

---

Newman, "The Hegelian Roots of Woodrow Wilson's Progressivism," *American Presbyterians* 64, no. 3 (1986): 193–94. It is especially pronounced in the writings of Arthur S. Link, Wilson's preeminent biographer. On the one hand, Link has done more than anyone else to map Wilson's eschatological beliefs and their vital bearing on Wilson's domestic and foreign policy. These led Link (*Higher Realism*, 130) to proclaim that "Wilson was not merely an idealist, but a crusading idealist. . . . At times, he [apparently believed] that he was a kind of messiah divinely appointed to deliver Europe from the cruel tyranny of history." On the other hand, however, and with equal resolve, Link (*Higher Realism*, 77) held that "[Wilson] repudiated and condemned utopianism." Indeed, Link wholeheartedly disagreed with Carr, Morgenthau, and other classical realist IR critics who had denounced Wilson's liberal internationalism as utopian. Instead, Link (*Higher Realism*, 130) posited that "Wilson was in fact the supreme realist . . . among all the major statesmen and thoughtful critics of his age."

[101] Cf. Butler, "Nation Transformed," 47–49. Link is illustrative in this regard: like Wilson, he understood the Bible in historical terms, celebrated it as a source of civilization and political progress, and saw America as a nation chosen by God to spearhead this progress in the world. Link's portrayal of Wilson as a supreme realist is therefore in many ways a reflection of Link's own theological presuppositions. These are discernible from Link's definition of realism: "A realist," he stated, "is one who . . . can see realities or truth through the fog of delusion that . . . shrouds the earth-bound individual." *Higher Realism*, 130. This definition assumes the existence and human attainability of an extrahistorical viewpoint—that is, the viewpoint of God.

[102] August Heckscher, *Woodrow Wilson* (New York: Scribner, 1991), 112.

[103] Thomas J. Knock, *To End All Wars: Woodrow Wilson and the Quest for a New World Order* (New York: Oxford University Press, 1992), 7.

fundamental theory socialism and democracy are almost if not quite one and the same."[104] Summarizing socialism as the idea that "no line can be drawn between private and public affairs which the State may not cross at will," Wilson held unequivocally that, "applied to a democratic state, such doctrine sounds radical but not revolutionary. It is only an acceptance of the extremest logical conclusions deducible from democratic principles."[105] As late as 1919, Wilson's sympathies with socialism were extensive enough to prompt private fears by his secretary of state that he was a *de facto* advocate of communism in America.[106]

If there was something about socialism Wilson disagreed with, it was only its envisioned method of change. "My ideal *reverses the order of the socialist*," Wilson explained his differences. "He wants *first* a new constitution for society, new orders of authority and adjustments of organization, in order that thereby a new nature *may be wrought out* for society. I believe that the work must be carried on in the opposite direction. . . . *Organization is a product of character*, not an antecedent and cause of character."[107] Not even this preference for gradual moral reform over rapid social reorganization, however, was absolute in Wilson's thought.[108] This is especially apparent from the ensuing passage, in which his messianic mind revealed its full capacity for violence, persecution, and terror as valid means to achieve the ideal society:

> Leadership does not always wear the harness of compromise. Once and again . . . a *Cause* arises in the midst of a nation. Men of strenuous minds and high ideals come forward . . . as champions of a political or moral principle. . . . They stand alone: and oftentimes are made bitter by their isolation. They are doing nothing less than defy public opinion, and shall they convert it by blows? Yes. . . . [Slowly] masses come over to the side of the reform. Resistance is left to the minority, and such as will not be convinced are crushed.[109]

[104] Wilson, "Socialism and Democracy" (August 22, 1887), *PWW* 5:561.

[105] Wilson, "Socialism and Democracy," 561. Two decades later, Wilson continued to "speak with considerable respect of Socialism as a theory. The abstract theories of Socialism are not easily . . . distinguished from the abstract principles of Democracy. The idea and object of the thoughtful Socialist is to protect every man, to give him the best opportunity, and to serve him in such ways as will be in the general interest and in the interest of nobody in particular. . . . [T]hat is the object of Democracy too." "The Banker and the Nation" (September 30, 1908), *PWW* 18:426–27.

[106] "From a Memorandum by Robert Lansing: Tendency toward Communistic Ideas" (September 1, 1919), *PWW* 62:612–13.

[107] Wilson, "Lecture on Democracy" (December 5, 1891), *PWW* 7:366; emphasis original.

[108] Knock, *To End All Wars*, 8.

[109] Wilson, "Leaders of Men" (June 17, 1890), *PWW* 6:663.

In light of such remarks and the preceding analysis of Wilson's biblical beliefs, describing him as conservative and pragmatic is rather dubious. If the label "conservative" is applicable to Wilson at all, then only in the sense that his political ideas conserved the tradition of Puritan millennialist eschatology and the belief in America as the redeemer nation.[110] Wilson's rejection of the Bolshevik Revolution, for example, may be regarded as a statement of conservative political philosophy only if one ignores that Wilson simultaneously advocated Christianizing the United States to attain his biblically inspired vision of a harmonious and prosperous nation. Wilson's proposed road away from revolution, in other words, was a road of providential progress and salvation; William Jennings Bryan hailed it as a powerful call "to get back to God."[111] In this sense, Wilson's conservatism had very narrow limits: it "[did] not really involve a reverence for what is old . . . it [was] not any kind of traditionalism."[112] Wilson's political consciousness may be characterized as conservative only in its external posture toward alternative political philosophies. In its internal makeup it was thoroughly eschatological.

The importance Wilson ascribed to order must be understood in the context of this eschatological consciousness. Order was dynamic for Wilson. He did not value it as an end in itself, but as a means facilitating the providential progress of history. "The conservatism which commends itself to me," Wilson remarked on this point, "is not the conservatism of inaction. I believe that the law of liberty . . . is also *a law of progress*. Indeed I could not imagine liberty in a world in which there was no progress. But *progress is a march, not a scamper*. It is achieved by advance . . . *under discipline.* . . . *The* [providential] *law of liberty* is a *law of . . . discipline*."[113] Wilson's political philosophy thus relied on a conception of history best described as orderly progress.[114]

This conception of progress certainly differs from the more radical and fast-paced varieties such as are found in the ideologies of the French and Russian Revolutions, but it is no less eschatological. It merely

[110] Butler, "Nation Transformed," 46.

[111] Bryan to Wilson (August 21, 1923), *PWW* 68:407.

[112] Harry Clor, "Woodrow Wilson," in *American Political Thought: The Philosophic Dimensions of American Statesmanship*, ed. Morton J. Frisch and Richard G. Stevens (New York: Scribner, 1971), 208.

[113] Wilson, "Lecture on Democracy" (December 5, 1891), *PWW* 7:363, 365; emphasis original.

[114] Cf. Lloyd E. Ambrosius, *Wilsonianism: Woodrow Wilson and His Legacy in American Foreign Relations* (New York: Palgrave Macmillan, 2002), 31.

allowed Wilson to argue in one of his seminal lectures that political leaders "cannot be of the school of the prophets"[115]—and to reveal himself unwittingly as just such a prophet in the very next moment. "The leader," he stated in the same lecture, "must perceive the direction of the nation's permanent forces, and must feel the speed of their operation."[116] These alleged forces propelling America toward liberty are not demonstrable empirically. Their real origin was Wilson's religious faith and, most fundamentally, the biblical prophecy of salvation.

Social Gospel
Domestic Politics as Religion in Practice

How did Wilson's notion of orderly providential progress surface in specific domestic policies? These often seem to have lacked any religious content, tempting one to view Wilson's national agenda much like contemporary IR scholars view his international agenda: as a purely secular project. However, this is merely an appearance. It dissipates the moment one places Wilson's domestic policies into their proper context and connects them, using secularization theory as a guide, with his eschatological consciousness as it surfaced in the various sermons and religious utterances he was delivering at the same time. To incorporate these into the analysis is to discover that the seemingly innocuous language of, say, Wilson's campaign platforms meant more than it suggests on the surface.

The list of bills initiated and signed into federal law during Wilson's White House tenure from 1913 to 1921 is long. Their number and trailblazing content make Wilson one of the most reformist presidents in United States history and also one whose legacy remains powerfully alive in many contemporary government agencies and institutions. It is worth noting that "The first Wilson administration . . . produced more positive legislative achievements than any administration since the days of Alexander Hamilton."[117] Only World War I, the rapidly growing demands of international diplomacy, and, from 1919 on, Wilson's incapacitation by illness prevented him from extending his phenomenal domestic record even further.

The substance of Wilson's national agenda is clearly visible already from his 1912 presidential campaign, which reflected the recurring social

[115] Wilson, "Leaders of Men" (June 17, 1890), *PWW* 6:660.

[116] Wilson, "Leaders of Men," 660.

[117] Richard Hofstadter, *The American Political Tradition and the Men Who Made It*, 2nd ed. (New York: Random House, 1974), 334.

unrest, labor strikes, financial panics, and economic depressions. The crisis that had been plaguing the United States since the early 1890s remained unresolved. Wilson consequently presented himself as a reform candidate, in keeping with his belief that orderly progress was the only way to avert revolution and anarchy. This belief was shared by many of his supporters, as evidenced by the chants coming from the crowd assembled in front of his residence when the Democratic Party officially confirmed Wilson as its presidential nominee: "We want Wilson and Evolution! It's all that will save us from Revolution!"[118] In his campaign platform, Wilson focused heavily on curbing the excesses of freewheeling American capitalism: rampant monopolies, lack of transparency and social responsibility in corporate behavior, exploitation of labor, and the stranglehold of government by big business patronage. To combat these practices threatening the fabric of the nation, he proposed antitrust and antitariff measures, currency and banking reform, direct primaries, and legislation to protect and empower American workers.[119]

Once elected, Wilson was able to deliver on his promises with unusual success thanks to a sympathetic Democratic majority in Congress. The Underwood-Simmons Tariff Act (1913) greatly reduced average tariff rates and struck a serious blow to American monopolists, who suddenly found themselves exposed to international competition and without sufficient profits to continue political patronage. The Federal Reserve Act (1913) took the control of the nation's money supply out of the hands of a few powerful financiers, whose profit motives often collided with general welfare, and delegated it to a board of presidential appointees. It created the Federal Reserve System to provide flexible currency and act as a lender of last resort. The Clayton Anti-Trust Act (1914) and the Federal Trade Commission Act (1914) targeted trusts directly; the latter law introduced the Federal Trade Commission with broad powers to prevent monopoly practices. Other notable achievements included the Keating-Owen Child Labor Act (1916), which sought to curtail child labor by prohibiting the sale in interstate commerce of goods manufactured by children; the Adamson Act (1916), which established an eight-hour workday for interstate railroad workers; federal workmen's

---

[118] "News Report" (July 2, 1912), PWW 24:527.

[119] See, e.g., his "Planks for a Democratic Platform" (June 16, 1912), *PWW* 24:477–81; "Two Addresses in Buffalo" (September 2, 1912), *PWW* 25:69–92; "Address on the Tariff in Syracuse, New York" (September 12, 1912), *PWW* 25:137–43; "Inaugural Address" (March 4, 1913), *PWW* 27:148–52.

compensation legislation; and the appointment of Louis D. Brandeis, one of the leading critics of big business at the time, to the Supreme Court.[120]

Presenting this domestic political program to the American public, Wilson cast it in the language of emancipation: as a program of progress from oppression to liberty. This is especially clear from a key campaign address delivered one month before the 1912 presidential election, in which Wilson portrayed his candidacy as "New Freedom." "[T]he thing that we are proposing to do," he announced to the masses gathered in Indianapolis, "is to restore the Government of the United States to the people. [T]his issue has arisen because . . . the Government . . . has not been under the control of the people in recent decades."[121] According to Wilson a vast evil conspiracy by monopolists and their government puppets was taking place in America, corrupting the ideals of the Founding Fathers and steering the nation off "the paths of liberty, the paths of peace, the paths of common confidence, . . . the only paths . . . to prosperity and success."[122] In pledging to liberate the American people from the tyranny of big business and special interest politics, Wilson saw himself as spearheading "the re-emancipation of America,"[123] with the 1912 Election Day as a kind of second Declaration of Independence. As he remarked to Bryan at an earlier stage in the campaign process: "We are engaged in a war for emancipation,—emancipation of our institutions and our life,—from the control of the concentrated and organized power of money."[124]

Most of the speeches just cited indeed lack overt biblical references, but this should not make one blind to the eschatological presuppositions structuring Wilson's domestic political project. It must be remembered that for him, concepts such as liberty or progress, no matter how secular in surface appearance, were religious in origin. Political action on their behalf expressed a spiritual mission in facilitation of God's plan of salvation. Wilson's remark to Bryan about the Democratic campaign as a battle for liberty, for instance, may be read as lacking any theological inspiration only if one disregards that three weeks earlier Wilson, speaking to a

---

[120] For Wilson's own summary of his first-term domestic accomplishments, see his "Speech in Long Branch, New Jersey, Accepting the [Second] Presidential Nomination" (September 2, 1916), *PWW* 38:129–30.

[121] Wilson, "Campaign Address in Indianapolis Proclaiming the New Freedom" (October 3, 1912), *PWW* 25:322.

[122] Wilson, "Campaign Address in Indianapolis," 329.

[123] Wilson, "Campaign Address in Indianapolis," 328.

[124] Wilson to Bryan (March 15, 1912), *PWW* 24:249.

different audience, explicitly proclaimed the Christian nature of political liberty.[125] His platform for "New Freedom" was fundamentally an eschatological platform. On occasion, Wilson let his biblical inspiration surface directly, such as during the Underwood-Simmons Tariff Bill signing ceremony: "we have served our fellow men and have, thereby, tried to serve God."[126] Wilson effectively told the assembled Congressmen that reducing tariffs, dismantling protectionism, exposing monopolists to competition, and opening up international trade amounted to obeying the Lord of history.

The eschatological dimension of Wilson's domestic politics becomes even clearer when one recalls that for him politics encompassed far more than office-holding and government legislation. Federal legislation was but one method, and not even the most important one, that he used in the pursuit of "New Freedom." The most important method was moral education: Christianizing big business so that it would curb itself of its own accord, making antitrust and labor laws unnecessary. In this vein, as noted earlier, the progress of liberty in America depended on the spread of Christianity as a "work-day religion," a project initiated by Wilson already at Princeton, well before he assumed any political office. In the self-sacrifice of Christ Wilson saw the ideal spirit through which to make the nation's corporate and political elites, up to now driven strictly by greed, more mindful of general welfare, precisely what was needed to preserve social cohesion.

He taught this spirit not only to his Princeton students during his baccalaureate sermons and chapel talks, but also to leading American bankers, businessmen, and industrialists. In numerous addresses to commercial clubs and similar associations around the country, Wilson urged them time and again to be better Christians, or else class war was imminent.[127] Social harmony was for Wilson a function of turning American hearts and minds to the Bible, a view he shared with other proponents of the Social Gospel movement. For all representatives of this variety of American Protestantism, national progress was predicated on religious

---

[125] Wilson, "Address in Nashville on Behalf of the Y.M.C.A." (February 24, 1912), *PWW* 24:209.

[126] Wilson, "Remarks upon Signing the Tariff Bill" (October 3, 1913), *PWW* 28:352.

[127] Examples include Wilson, "The Government and Business" (March 14, 1908), *PWW* 18:35–51, and idem, "The Banker and the Nation" (September 30, 1908), *PWW* 18:424–34.

revitalization and represented the earthly reward for obedience to God.[128] The liberal agenda bundled up under the banner of "New Freedom" was in this regard a secular expression of an essentially religious mission.

In conclusion, the ways in which Wilson comprehended and implemented his national agenda offer ample grounds for regarding his domestic politics as utopian in the sense delineated by secularization theory. One could take the analysis a step further and argue that his "New Freedom" was utopian also in the sense understood by his classical realist IR critics such as Carr: partial, exclusionary, and representative only of those in power. Just as Wilson's international agenda was anchored in narrow interests of dominant nations in interwar Europe, his national agenda had its real origin in values and goals of dominant social groups in late nineteenth-century America. It too served to normalize and objectify hegemonic ideas and hence represented a tool of oppression. Even a cursory reading of the "New Freedom" program reveals that despite its alleged nationwide scope it continued to deny suffrage to women and perpetuated racial segregation.

Instead of dwelling on Wilson's domestic politics, however, it is time to move on to his liberal foreign policy. The biblical foundations of Wilson's national agenda are now in full view, and it is about to emerge that his international agenda, too, represented secularized eschatology: a manifestation of Wilson's liberal-republican millennialism, this time on a global scale.

---

[128] See especially Henry F. May, *Ideas, Faiths, and Feelings: Essays on American Intellectual and Religious History, 1952–1982* (New York: Oxford University Press, 1983), 177–78; Conrad Cherry, ed., *God's New Israel: Religious Interpretations of American Destiny*, rev. and updated ed. (Chapel Hill: University of North Carolina Press, 1998), 221–22; and Ambrosius, *Wilsonian Statecraft*, 3, 11.

CHAPTER SIX

"TO RELEASE MANKIND FROM THE INTOLERABLE THINGS OF THE PAST"

Wilson's Wartime Statecraft as a Mission to Redeem the World

Although traditionally the secularization thesis about the biblical pre-suppositions of modern historical consciousness has been applied almost exclusively to totalitarian and irreligious ideologies, it is no less pertinent to liberal and religious narratives of progress. Wilson's domestic political ideas and practice offer an excellent illustration: his vision of national progress flowed from his deep religious convictions as their secularized expression. This was no idiosyncrasy in the broader historical context of American liberal thought, whose strong eschatological inspiration had molded it in crucial ways from the Puritan origins down to the nineteenth century.

Wilson's foreign policy was undergirded by the same impulses. The influence of his patriotic Protestant salvationism on his statecraft was pervasive and manifested itself vividly on many different occasions, even though it remains possible to this day to come across scholarship paying practically no attention to it—generating the impression that salvationist religion had no place in his diplomacy.[1] Such an impression not only is

---

[1] An illustrative example is G. John Ikenberry et al., *The Crisis of American Foreign Policy: Wilsonianism in the Twenty-First Century* (Princeton, N.J.: Princeton University Press, 2008).

inaccurate in the sense that it precludes recognizing the narrow, culturally specific character of Wilsonian liberalism internationalism, but also produces a variety of additional problems. For example, it makes it more difficult to notice Wilson's lingering presence in the background of other, more recent doctrines of American statecraft laden with eschatological presuppositions.[2]

Fortunately, owing especially to the recent cultural turn in American diplomatic history, the eschatological moorings of Wilson's statecraft are no longer any secret, even if debates concerning their significance persist.[3] The ensuing discussion contributes to this literature in at least two different ways: it offers new evidence of these moorings, such as by illuminating Wilson's neglected relationship with the American Protestant theologian and millennialist preacher George Davis Herron (1862–1925), and above all it places them in the novel context of secularization theory, heretofore unconnected to Wilson. Insofar as the following pages show that the president's IR utopianism, identified by E. H. Carr in the late 1930s, was simultaneously utopian in the sense of secularized biblical eschatology, theorized by Karl Löwith and other intellectual historians around the same time, they represent the culminating part of this study.

As the mapping of Wilson's crusade to spread the American liberal-republican Millennium worldwide is about to begin, it is worth stressing that neither a detailed nor a comprehensive account of his statecraft is the point here. Rather, the objective is to give compelling evidence of the religious foundations underlying that part of his foreign policy that later became the target of Carr's scathing critique and cries of

---

[2] See Milan Babík, review of *The Crisis of American Foreign Policy*, by Ikenberry et al., *Millennium: Journal of International Studies* 38, no. 2 (2009): 470–73, which makes this point with reference to the neoconservative Bush Doctrine and the 2003 invasion of Iraq.

[3] Among Wilson scholars, representatives of the cultural turn include Malcolm Magee and Frank Ninkovich, although the religious underpinnings of Wilson's politics have been recognized by other historians and biographers also—from Ray Stannard Baker via Arthur S. Link to Lloyd E. Ambrosius. As for the actual impact of Wilson's religious faith on his diplomacy, whereas Baker held that "Religion was never incidental with [Wilson]; it was central," New Left historians such as N. Gordon Levin have tended to downplay its importance and narrate it as mostly a rhetorical cover for what was really a bid for global economic hegemony. This is in keeping with the traditional Marxist view of religion as merely an epiphenomenal expression of weightier, more fundamental forces. See respectively Baker, *Woodrow Wilson: Life and Letters* (Garden City, N.Y.: Doubleday, 1927–1939), 1:68, and Levin, *Woodrow Wilson and World Politics* (New York: Oxford University Press, 1968).

"utopianism" in *The Twenty Years' Crisis*. Therefore, the ensuing discussion largely ignores Wilson's early initiatives such as the Mexican intervention (1914).[4] Instead, it is skewed toward his diplomacy during and after World War I. Moreover, his international ideas and actions come into focus only insofar as they reveal the eschatological dimension of this diplomacy. The religious dimension of his political thought often surfaces most visibly not in his famous official addresses, but in more private settings, such as his less well-known personal correspondence or unpublished notes. Part of the failure by mainstream IR to notice the eschatological facet of Wilson's utopianism is due precisely to ignoring this kind of more discreet documentary evidence and focusing only on Wilson's major policy statements.

George D. Herron and Wilson as a Crusader for Democracy and Christ

It would not be difficult to assume that eschatological motivations played no significant role in Wilson's decision to enter World War I. The trigger for his war message to Congress on April 2, 1917, was the resumption of unrestricted submarine warfare by Imperial Germany, which disregarded American neutrality, cost American lives, stranded international travel and commerce on high seas, and made American goods for Europe pile up on wharves all over the United States.[5] Another cause was the infamous Zimmermann Telegram of January 1917: a German diplomatic dispatch, intercepted by British intelligence and disclosed to Wilson, in which Prussia proposed a military alliance with Mexico against the United States and promised Mexico pieces of American territory as spoils of war. In this vein, one might suggest that in going to war Wilson was driven largely by security and economic considerations.

This is only part of the story. A closer look reveals that Wilson's religious convictions played at least as important a role in setting the stage

[4] This is not to imply, of course, that religion and eschatology played no part in Wilson's Mexican affair. See especially Mark Benbow, *Leading Them to the Promised Land: Woodrow Wilson, Covenant Theology, and the Mexican Revolution, 1913–1915* (Kent, Ohio: Kent State University Press, 2010), which argues that "Wilson demonstrated his ardent belief in the concepts of covenant theology, just war, divine selection, and mission," and that "his actions toward Mexico in his first term illustrated . . . this deeply ingrained theological perspective" (p. 12).

[5] See Wilson, "Address to a Joint Session of Congress" (April 2, 1917), in *The Papers of Woodrow Wilson*, ed. Arthur S. Link et al. (Princeton, N.J.: Princeton University Press, 1966–1994) [henceforth *PWW*], 41:519–20.

for his decision to enter the conflict as economic or security concerns. A good way to introduce their bearing on his wartime foreign policy is through the writings of the theologian George D. Herron, with whom the president became acquainted just as he started mobilizing the United States for war.[6] During the war and subsequent peace negotiations, Wilson was inundated by countless letters, reports, memos, and pamphlets from a wide range of individuals and organizations seeking influence, and it may not be obvious why Herron, whose correspondence represents only a small part of this flood, should be singled out as somehow more important. Yet Herron's views did stick out from the rest and clearly impressed Wilson, so much so that the president elevated the theologian to a formal position at the American legation in Berne and included a number of Herron's books in his personal library.[7]

Born in Montezuma, Indiana, on January 21, 1862, Herron grew up in a poor and pious family and never received any formal education. Nevertheless, this did not prevent him from becoming a theologian, and

---

[6] Recent historiography of Wilson's liberal internationalism is almost entirely silent on Herron; even those scholars sensitive to the role of eschatology in Wilson's statecraft have largely ignored him. The following have failed to notice Herron at all: Robert M. Crunden, *Ministers of Reform: The Progressives' Achievement in American Civilization, 1889–1920* (New York: Basic Books, 1982); Thomas J. Knock, *To End All Wars: Woodrow Wilson and the Quest for a New World Order* (New York: Oxford University Press, 1992); Malcolm D. Magee, *What the World Should Be: Woodrow Wilson and the Crafting of a Faith-Based Foreign Policy* (Waco, Tex.: Baylor University Press, 2008); John Milton Cooper, Jr., *Woodrow Wilson: A Biography* (New York: Knopf, 2009). Jan Willem Schulte Nordholt, *Woodrow Wilson: A Life for World Peace*, trans. Herbert H. Rowen (Berkeley: University of California Press, 1991) mentions Herron once, dismissing him (p. 211) as "Wilson's strange special envoy in Europe." Only Lloyd E. Ambrosius appears to have given Herron some attention, but even in this case the treatment is incomplete and largely parenthetical. See Ambrosius, *Wilsonian Statecraft: Theory and Practice of Liberal Internationalism during World War I* (Wilmington, Del.: SR Books, 1991), 11–12, 127; idem, *Wilsonianism: Woodrow Wilson and His Legacy in American Foreign Relations* (New York: Palgrave Macmillan, 2002), 36, 143; and idem, *Woodrow Wilson and the American Diplomatic Tradition: The Treaty Fight in Perspective* (Cambridge: Cambridge University Press, 1987), 12–13, 119, 129.

[7] See Mark Benbow, review of "George D. Herron and the Eschatological Foundations of Woodrow Wilson's Foreign Policy, 1917–1919," by Milan Babík, *H-Diplo Article Reviews*, no. 342 (2012): 2, available at http://www.h-net.org/~diplo/reviews/PDF/AR342.pdf [accessed March 29, 2012]. The volumes in Wilson's private collection include George D. Herron, *Germanism and the American Crusade* (New York: Mitchell Kennerley, 1918); idem, *The Greater War* (New York: Mitchell Kennerley, 1919); idem, *The Menace of Peace* (New York: Mitchell Kennerley, 1917); and idem, *Woodrow Wilson and the World's Peace* (New York: Mitchell Kennerley, 1917).

in 1884 he was ordained to the Congregational ministry. He first achieved national prominence in the early 1890s. His rise to fame reflected his mesmerizing sermons, fueled by his burning faith, and occurred in the context of the same economic and social crisis that prompted Wilson to urge American political and business elites to practice the spirit of Christ as the only pathway to domestic unity, wealth, and liberty.

Herron's response to this crisis was similar to Wilson's advocacy of Christianity as a "work-day religion." In an attempt to stem the deepening divisions and shepherd the nation through the cataclysm unharmed, growing numbers of Protestant clergymen began shaking off their earlier complacency and placing social and labor issues at the top of the church agenda. Herron spearheaded this effort. In an important address to the Minnesota Congregational Club in 1890, he diagnosed the origins of the crisis in self-interest and competition, rejected these principles as sound foundations for national life, and exhorted American industrialists to follow the teachings of Jesus, especially the law of love and self-sacrifice.[8] The message of Christ constituted the only pathway to national accord, unity, liberty, and prosperity. Thus Herron proposed to solve the crisis and harmonize the nation by secularizing Christianity into a theory of American politics and business. The title of Herron's academic position at Iowa (Grinnell) College is indicative: Chair of Applied Christianity, endowed "for the purpose of developing a social . . . and economic philosophy from the teachings of Jesus; for the application of His teachings to social problems and institutions."[9] Herron pursued this agenda with prophetic zeal, spellbinding oratory, and intense eschatological expectation, rapidly establishing himself as one of the leaders of the earlier-mentioned Kingdom Movement in American social Christianity. This movement strove to turn the Bible into the ultimate social law in order to realize the Kingdom of God on earth.[10]

Although no evidence exists that Wilson, in the 1890s still at Princeton, was familiar with Herron at the time, the future president would have agreed with much of the theologian's analysis of the domestic situation. This is because Wilson's reading of the national crisis broadly paralleled Herron's assessment and reform proposals: Wilson, too, identified the root problem in modern industry and *laissez-faire* capitalism, arguing

---

[8] Herron, *The Message of Jesus to Men of Wealth* (New York: Revell, 1891).

[9] *Annual Report of the President of Iowa College, 1898* (Grinnell, Iowa, 1898), 41.

[10] Robert T. Handy, "George D. Herron and the Kingdom Movement," *Church History* 19, no. 2 (1950): 108.

that these fragmented society by fomenting competition and inequality, trivializing human life, and engendering nihilism, and he, too, advocated a religious revival as a way to reverse these perilous effects. Both Herron and Wilson thus saw America's progress from conflict and anarchy to order and unity as a matter of turning Christianity into a practical, everyday ethic.

Perhaps the only significant difference lay in their respective views on the appropriate pace of the progressive change they both sought. In contrast to Wilson, who favored orderly progress under the rule of law, Herron was a member of the Socialist Party and displayed strong revolutionist tendencies. Showing far less respect for existing social organization, rules, and norms, he advocated a more radical sort of change. "It will doubtless be expedient," he proclaimed on one occasion, "that present . . . institutions progressively pass away, in order that the government of the world by the immediate inspiration of God may . . . be fulfilled."[11] He practiced what he preached in his personal life, criticizing marriage, for example, as a form of slavery and deserting his wife for a wealthy mistress.[12]

Such unconventional views and behavior aroused fears that Herron was an anarchist and quickly led to his downfall. By the late 1890s the mainstream opinion within American churches no longer took him seriously, and in 1901 a clerical council expelled him from the Congregational church for "conduct unbecoming a Christian and a gentleman."[13] Herron and his mistress ended up fleeing to Europe, where he started a new life of leisure, writing, and mingling with literary and intellectual elites.

In 1916 Herron was residing in Geneva, and this is where by sheer coincidence—or divine providence, as he must have thought—the climactic chapter of Herron's life, as his biographer described it, began to unfold.[14] Thanks to a series of articles about Wilson printed in Swiss magazines such as *La Semaine Littéraire*, Herron became rumored in Europe as the American president's unofficial spokesman, as the theologian proudly noted in a letter introducing himself to the White House and

[11] Herron, *The Christian State: A Political Vision of Christ* (New York: Crowell, 1895), 121.

[12] Mitchell Pirie Briggs, *George D. Herron and the European Settlement* (Stanford: Stanford University Press, 1932), 10.

[13] "Dr. George D. Herron Expelled from Church," *New York Times*, June 5, 1901, 3.

[14] Briggs, *Herron and European Settlement*, 12.

offering Wilson his services.[15] The president responded favorably: after familiarizing himself with Herron's views and background, he enlisted Herron in the American diplomatic effort in Europe. Appointed to the Berne legation, Herron soon became one of Wilson's informers and remained in this position through the end of the war.

Herron's significance lies in his interpretation of the Great War and American war aims in Protestant millennialist terms, and even more so in the welcoming attitude with which Wilson acknowledged this interpretation as expressive of his own views and motives. Tomáš Garrigue Masaryk, the founding president of Czechoslovakia, who was in close contact with Wilson during 1917–1919, later recalled that Wilson and Herron "were brought together by Herron's writings, since Wilson regarded [Herron's interpretation] as correct and giving an accurate picture of the situation."[16]

Already the initial encounter with Herron's thought elicited a warm welcome from Wilson. When Herron's New York publisher sent the president a translated collection of Herron's Swiss essays, Wilson replied: "I have read it with the deepest appreciation of Mr. Herron's singular insight into all the elements of a complicated situation and into my own motives and purposes."[17] Notably, the volume is saturated with eschatology, indicating that Herron and Wilson saw American liberal internationalism in similar terms: as the secular expression of the biblical program of salvation.

The backbone of Herron's Swiss essays is an account of the Great War in simple black-and-white, Manichean terms. This account must have been intuitively appealing to Wilson: it chimed well with his own tendency, apparent in his earliest published essays, to simplify moral complexities of existence to clear-cut oppositions such as right and wrong or good and evil. The European conflict, Herron stated, "is . . . a war between light and darkness—a war between a white and a black governing principle, each striving for possession of the world."[18] The principle of light corresponded to "the social principle proclaimed at Jerusalem" and to "the religion of democracy—which, if it be real, is none other than

---

[15] Herron to Charles Ferguson (December 31, 1916), *PWW* 40:542.

[16] Masaryk, *Světová revoluce za války a ve válce, 1914–1918* (Prague: Orbis a Čin, 1925), 375.

[17] Wilson to Mitchell Kennerley (October 1, 1917), *PWW* 44:287. Wilson was referring to Herron, *Wilson and the World's Peace*.

[18] Herron, *Wilson and the World's Peace*, 149.

the acceptance and practice of Christ," whereas the principle of darkness was autocracy: "the religion of Germanism . . . the doctrine of power announced and exercised by Germany."[19]

This characterization effectively repeated Herron's earlier reading of the domestic upheaval in the United States in the 1890s—only now he extended this reading to the international level. The world crisis emanated from the same root conflict as the erstwhile national crisis in America: the conflict between the Christian law of love and cooperation on the one hand, and the Satanic notion of self-interest and competition on the other. The Great War would decide which of these would prevail as the governing principle for international affairs, whether "the competitive struggle and woe" or "the justice of love and its liberating correlatives."[20]

Wilson's position in this decisive conflict was not immediately obvious to Europeans, as Herron knew. He was acutely aware of the ambiguity of American foreign policy in the early stages of the war and of the frustration that this ambiguity caused among the Allies. Wilson's failure to take a firm stand against Germany after the invasion of Belgium and again after the sinking of the *Lusitania* generated a widespread conviction that the American president was weak and possibly pro-German. Condemnations of Wilson for his lack of moral discernment became especially pronounced after his speech to the Senate on January 22, 1917, in which he stated that the only kind of peace he was prepared to support was a peace without winners and losers, without dictate and humiliation: in short, "a peace without victory," since "only a peace between equals can last."[21] To British and French leaders this language seemed to indicate that in Wilson's perspective little ethical difference existed between the Allies and the Central Powers. Clemenceau reacted by declaring that "The moral side of the war has escaped Wilson."[22]

According to Herron, however, Wilson's moral ambiguity was only a surface appearance, and in his Swiss essays he took it upon himself to explain to the distraught Allies that the American leader was decidedly on their side. Herron declared resolutely that Wilson was a man of democracy, meaning that at the most fundamental level he was a man of Christ:

[19] Herron, *Wilson and the World's Peace*, 131.

[20] Herron, *Wilson and the World's Peace*, 4–5.

[21] Wilson, "Address to the Senate" (January 22, 1917), *PWW* 40:536.

[22] M. Clemenceau, *L'Homme Enchainée* as quoted in Robert Edwards Annin, *Woodrow Wilson: A Character Study* (New York: Dodd, Mead, 1924), 222.

Woodrow Wilson believes in the whole length and logic of democracy . . . [He] beholds this vision . . . because he is both sturdily and mystically Christian in his view of our common life's collective possibilities. The uttermost democracy . . . is to him the certain issue of the idea for which Jesus lived and died. This man conceives . . . that . . . the literal and general application of the law of love is the only practicable social basis, the only national security, the only foundation for international peace.[23]

American neutrality was going to end soon, Herron argued while the policy was still in effect and widely regarded as permanent in Europe. He assured everyone that it was only a temporary measure that was carefully calculated and had nothing to do with moral blindness. It merely reflected Wilson's fragile domestic political situation: with his initial presidential term coming to a close in 1916, Wilson first had to get himself reelected in a nation traditionally opposed to involvement in European conflicts. Only then would it become possible for Wilson to rouse America to its sacred destiny and lead the fight on behalf of the Millennium. In short, Wilson's moral ambiguity was merely a clever ruse:

[Wilson] believes that the Sermon on the Mount is the ultimate constitution of mankind; and he intends, by hook or crook if you will, by the wisdom of the serpent and the secrecy of the priest, to get this foundation underneath the unaware American nation. He cunningly hopes, he divinely schemes, to bring it about that America, awake at last to her national selfhood and calling, shall become as a colossal Christian apostle, shepherding the world into the kingdom of God.[24]

Penetrating this ruse, Herron told Europeans, was not altogether difficult; in order to understand the secret intentions behind Wilson's ostensibly neutral and cowardly diplomacy, they had to grasp the president's inner religious and eschatological beliefs. Viewed in their light, Wilson's foreign policy surfaced as activist and farsighted beyond anyone's comprehension. Herron explained that it was only a matter of time for the president to declare war on Prussia and initiate a campaign that would not only end the war, but also propel humanity into an entirely novel era.

Signs of the impending rapture were perceptible already: "I see that the world is instinct with . . . expectancy, with a sense of some near Messianic intervention," Herron prophesized; "a change of upward and universal scope is preparing."[25] The war was no ordinary conflict, according

---

[23] Herron, *Wilson and the World's Peace*, 75–77.

[24] Herron, *Wilson and the World's Peace*, 77.

[25] Herron, *Wilson and the World's Peace*, 44.

to Herron, but a millennial revolution: "a crusade for a democracy . . . [as] an approach to the early Christian idea of the kingdom of heaven."[26] In the flames raging across the battlefields of Europe, the Old World anarchy of sovereign countries competing for survival and power was being purged away in preparation for a New World concert of federate humanity: a harmonious "universal politic . . . so revolutionary, so creative of a different world than ours, that few have begun to glimpse [this] vision."[27]

Wilson represented the spiritual vanguard of this process. Divinely appointed to spearhead the revolution, in Herron's depiction the president was "a determined and tremendous radical" whose diplomacy was no less than a sacred summons to reorganize international politics according to "the mind of God as it was revealed in Christ."[28] Far from a weak statesman incapable of perceiving the moral dimension of the war, Wilson was "a redeemer of democracy" who "has announced that Return which is to be at once the conclusion and the true beginning of history."[29]

Wilson identified wholeheartedly with Herron's interpretation and eventually acted just as Herron had predicted, entering the conflict on the Allied side and couching the American intervention in the same kind of eschatological language. This was the reason why in 1917 rumors began circulating around Europe that Herron was the president's secret spokesman.[30] Herron was not the only commentator at the time predicting that Wilson would enter the war; there were others. That the gossip nonetheless came to center on him might in itself be indicative of the proximity of his views to Wilson's: to the public at large, the two men sounded similar enough to engender speculations that the similarity was no accident.

The relationship between Wilson and Herron did not end with Herron's Swiss essays and Wilson's appreciative response to them. On the contrary, this moment marked merely the beginning of a sustained albeit infrequent stream of correspondence between the president and the one-time leader of the Kingdom Movement. This connection lasted at least until spring 1919, and the notes and reports that Herron sent to Wilson during this time were just as saturated with millennial language as the

---

[26] Herron, *Wilson and the World's Peace*, 142–43, 150.

[27] Herron, *Wilson and the World's Peace*, 68, 125.

[28] Herron, *Wilson and the World's Peace*, 4, 73.

[29] Herron, *Wilson and the World's Peace*, 45, 73.

[30] In the apt characterization by Briggs (*Herron and European Settlement*, 25), the theologian "was in no mean degree a John the Baptist, crying in the wilderness, preparing the way for the American Messiah who was to appear in such beatific splendor to war-torn Europe in 1917."

initial essays. Wilson continued to endorse Herron's eschatological interpretation of the war and American foreign policy objectives with enthusiasm.

In February 1918, for example, the Austrian emperor made informal overtures to Wilson in an attempt to negotiate an early peace with the United States. At the heart of the proposal was an offer by the emperor to give an official pledge to the pope that all national groups within the Dual Monarchy would be granted autonomy, in exchange for which the emperor demanded that Wilson enter into peace talks with Austria-Hungary. Herron played a key role in receiving this proposal and relaying it to Washington.[31] He attached a report with his impressions and recommendations.

In this report, Herron took a firm stand against the emperor's proposal on biblical grounds, noting that he came away from the meeting with the Austrian envoys "feeling that this is a case of Satan appearing as an angel."[32] This may appear as a mere turn of phrase, but Herron meant it in the literal and eschatological sense, as is apparent from the wider context of his intellectual activity at the time. Opposed to a premature peace, Herron vehemently denounced any pacifist proposals—from the Central Powers and peace movements in Allied countries alike—as Satan's last-ditch attempts to prevent the war from running its full course.[33] Entering into official peace talks with Austria-Hungary would mean recognizing the Dual Monarchy, betraying its nations' aspirations for self-determination, and turning away from God just as his divine principles were about to be realized on earth in the form of a world federation of liberal democratic nation-states.

---

[31] Masaryk, *Světová revoluce*, 378–80. See also Štefan Osuský, *George D. Herron, dôverník Wilsonov počas vojny* (Brno: Prúdy, 1925), 44–56.

[32] See Herron's memorandum (February 3, 1918), *PWW* 46:247.

[33] See especially Herron, *Menace of Peace*, 8–9, which argued that "For the war to close, and the world not to know what it has been fighting about, would be the supreme catastrophe of history," and that a compromise such as lay at the heart of the Austrian proposal "would issue in universal mental and moral confusion. . . . The judgment day would have come and gone without our discerning the judgment passed upon us, or even knowing we had been judged." Herron adhered to this position until the end of the war, so that when the pope contemplated another call for early peace in summer 1918, Herron warned Washington against yet another attempt by Satan to hijack the meaning of the conflict *"for the glory of the Catholic Church, for Papal rehabilitation, and for the salvation of the Central Empires."* Herron to Hugh R. Wilson (July 1, 1918), *PWW* 49:193; emphasis original.

To prevent Satan, acting through the invisible alliance of the Catholic Church and the Central Powers, from stealing the outcome of the war and submerging the world in spiritual darkness for a thousand years to come, Herron urged Wilson to seize the initiative and move ahead aggressively with his key foreign policy objective: the League of Nations. Herron demanded that the president proclaim it immediately. "Not in the whole history of mankind . . . has the world turned to one man as it now turns to you,"[34] he wrote to Wilson in May 1918, not long after discouraging him from the Austrian peace proposal. He then summoned Wilson to the messianic task of redeeming the world exhausted by conflict: "no hand but yours can open the door of this unprecedented and predestinative opportunity. Will you open it? If you will, the whole race of man will pass through that door . . . and . . . enter upon a world of such fellowship and felicity . . . as now seems incredible and Utopian."[35] An instant call for the League, Herron alleged, would rouse the German people from "the Great Hypnosis under which they morally sleep," discredit their infernal rulers, win the war for the Allies and Christ, and inaugurate the Kingdom of God on earth. Herron thus implored the president to "speak the word that shall bring the World Society into being. [It] is the appeal of the immediate purpose of God in man to which you attend . . . [and] the whole world . . . will follow you as never Moses was followed by his tribes."[36]

Wilson's response to Herron's memorandum evaluating the Austro-Hungarian proposal was straightforward: "This [report] is, indeed, extremely interesting and confirms my impression of Herron. I agree *in toto* with his analysis and conclusions!"[37] Just as during his initial encounter with the theologian, on this occasion, too, the president enthusiastically approved of Herron's eschatological interpretation of international relations, the Great War, and American foreign policy.

Herron's subsequent appeal that Wilson perform his messianic duty and introduce the League right away probably left an even greater impression on the president. It must have struck an especially powerful chord in Wilson, validating as it did his private self-stylization as a soldier of Christ, a fantasy that, together with his Manichean view of the universe, dated back to his youth. He responded to Herron with an urgent

[34] Herron to Wilson (May 31, 1918), *PWW* 48:212.
[35] Herron to Wilson (May 31, 1918), 212.
[36] Herron to Wilson (May 31, 1918), 214, 217.
[37] Wilson to Lansing (February 16, 1918), *PWW* 46:357.

message stating that he was "deeply moved by [the plea]."[38] Seeing that the president's mind was in tune with his own, Herron wasted no time and repeated his request using the kind of idiom that lets the eschatological flavor of his conception of liberal internationalism surface in full:

> I beg you not to hesitate . . . The destinies of mankind for long centuries to come depend upon your instant decision. Tomorrow may be too late. . . . You can expand our American Declaration of Independence into a declaration of the rights of all peoples—into a declaration of the freedom and unity of humanity. You can speak the word that will pitch the whole crazy history, the whole sojourn of man, upon a new and comparatively divine plane of progress. You can wipe away the tears and the shames, the treasons and defeats of two thousand years of universal disappointment. . . . [By] your immediate initiation of the Society of Nations you will perform the most redemptive and creative act . . . since the paling lips of Him who initiated our era pronounced His work complete.[39]

As a matter of historical record this summons, Herron's most fervent yet, went unanswered; it would take another four months for the war to end, and another year for Wilson to leave the Paris Peace Conference with the League Covenant in hand. Why the president declined to follow Herron's pressing plea is a good question, but explanations may not be terribly difficult to find. For one, Wilson operated in a complex environment that included not only Herron but also a variety of other actors, some of whom harbored deep animosity toward the theologian and worked to suppress his advice.[40] Even more importantly, one must bear in mind the subtle but important difference between Wilson's and Herron's millennialism: whereas Herron was a radical, it is worth recalling that Wilson espoused a slower, more conservative reading of providential progress that placed relatively more emphasis on discipline. Instead of revolutionizing the international order unilaterally and without any regard for public opinion and existing diplomatic institutions and practices, as Herron was suggesting, Wilson deemed it essential that the League be introduced in an orderly fashion: through gradual reform and after a multilateral peace conference. This reflected Wilson's commitment to the rule of law, which in turn reflected his liberal Presbyterian covenant theology.

---

[38] Wilson to Herron (July 1, 1918), *PWW* 48:473.

[39] Herron to Wilson (July 6, 1918), *PWW* 48:540.

[40] A prime example is Colonel Edward M. House, whose aversion to Herron was patent and most likely driven by jealousy: Herron's rise up the ranks of Wilson's favorite advisers coincided with House's fall, which by the end of the Paris negotiations had brought his longstanding friendship with the president to an end.

Wilson's failure to respond to Herron's plea to proclaim the League of Nations thus probably stemmed from their disagreement about the proper pace of the League's achievement, not from a difference in views on its eschatological purpose. After all, as is about to emerge, once the Peace Conference had taken place, Wilson referred to the League in the same millennial terms as Herron.

Unfortunately, by the time of the signing of the League Covenant on June 28, 1919, the president was no longer in touch with Herron; the two had broken off their friendship. If one may trust Colonel House, the split occurred in May 1919, at which point Wilson allegedly uttered in exasperation, "I am through with [Herron]."[41] The falling out occurred over the status of the Adriatic port of Fiume in the new political geography of Europe: whereas Herron adamantly defended the Italian claim to the city, Wilson insisted with equal stubbornness that Fiume be administered by the League of Nations. An additional and perhaps even weightier reason was Herron's sense that during the Paris negotiations much of Wilson's original vision had been compromised and that the final outcome hardly resembled it at all.

Until the split, however, and as demonstrated earlier, Herron's eschatological fantasy that the Great War was a crusade in the literal sense of the term, that Wilson was doing God's work, and that universal redemption from evil was just around the corner elicited a number of positive responses from Wilson. While it is possible that these were merely general pleasantries and as such do not really reveal much about the role of eschatology in the president's mind, there is evidence to the contrary that suggests that Herron belonged in a narrow circle of friends enjoying Wilson's genuine attention during the critical period spanning 1917 and 1919. Štefan Osuský, a Czechoslovak diplomat who worked with Herron in Switzerland, stated that "Professor Herron, unknown to the wider public, . . . [served as] Wilson's informer and man of trust."[42] President Masaryk similarly recalled in his account of World War I that "From fall 1917 and throughout the year 1918 [Herron acted] . . . as Wilson's unofficial confidante."[43] Osuský indeed went so far as to proclaim that Herron's eschatology not only resonated with Wilson, but directly influenced his foreign policy decision-making on at least one important occasion: in

[41] From the Diary of Colonel House (May 12, 1919), *PWW* 59:68.

[42] Osuský, *Herron, dôverník Wilsonov*, 44. Cf. Briggs, *Herron and European Settlement*, 25–27.

[43] Masaryk, *Světová revoluce*, 375.

steering the president away from the aforementioned early peace offers extended by the Austrian emperor.[44]

In light of these testimonies, Herron's theory—or rather theology—of world politics may be considered a good proxy for Wilson's own understanding of the Great War, American foreign policy, and the League of Nations, hinting that Wilson's statecraft possessed a clear religious dimension. In the minds of these two men, the building blocks of liberal internationalism had unmistakable biblical origins: liberty and democracy were outward manifestations of the Christian spirit, progress was by divine decree, and the League of Nations denoted the Kingdom of God come to fruition in international politics. In short, and consistently with the title of Herron's one-time position at Iowa College, liberal internationalism was applied Christianity: biblical utopianism secularized into a theory of international politics. "We shall conclude," Herron stated in his proposed solution to World War I, "that only Utopia is practicable. We shall see that no peace is procurable . . . save in the realization of the ideal. . . . It is Utopia or perdition that awaits the human race in the end: it is the kingdom of heaven or yet deeper hells than the one through which the world is now wading."[45] That Wilson repeatedly affirmed Herron's interpretation as expressive of his own views indicates that the president himself regarded liberal internationalism as Protestant salvationism in political practice.

From Domestic to World Progress
Universalizing America's "Manifest Destiny"

Although Herron represents an outstanding point of access to Wilson's eschatological convictions and their role in his liberal internationalism, they can be demonstrated more directly through examples from the president's own thought and practice. Wilson encountered Herron at a relatively late stage in his presidential career, which is to say that their relationship illuminates only a portion of Wilson's foreign policy. However, liberal-republican millennialism and the eschatological conception of history as providential progress had guided Wilson's thinking from a

---

[44] In Osuský's estimation, Herron thus championed the cause of self-determination for the oppressed nations of the Dual Monarchy like few others, for which he deserved public recognition. This motivated Osuský to write his book about Herron in the first place: to familiarize the Czechs and Slovaks with one of the principal figures behind their achievement of political independence.

[45] Herron, *Wilson and the World's Peace*, 36–37.

much earlier time. In order to understand how, it is necessary to back-track to the period when he began expanding this conception from the domestic level to world affairs.

In Wilson's mature domestic thought, as was seen, the idea of progress took the form of the frontier thesis, structuring his understanding of American national past. According to this thesis, which Wilson shared with Frederick Jackson Turner, American history displayed a clear progressive motif both geographically, from the Eastern Seaboard to the Pacific coast, and politically, from defunct European institutions to liberal democratic government on authentic American principles. Wilson argued repeatedly that "Our national history has, of course, its great and spreading pattern," and that westward expansion was "the great determining movement of our history."[46] Allegedly, "no observant person [could] fail to perceive . . . that there [were] currents of national life . . . running in full tide through all the continent from sea to sea."[47] These currents, Wilson held, emanated from the providential logic of history and lay outside the scope of human agency.

From the critical perspective of secularization theory, of course, no such currents existed or exist at all. The eschatological moorings of Wilson's narrative of American history are worth reemphasizing even before explaining how he extended them to his narrative of world history. As Löwith and other secularization theorists argued forcefully, historical events display no inherent logic or meaning; if Wilson saw the chaotic occurrences making up American history in terms of a "distinctive plan,"[48] this is because he had imputed this plan to them on the basis of his *a priori* biblical presuppositions. In Wilson's case, these presuppositions were not hidden; he acknowledged them openly, identifying American territorial expansion and political progress toward liberty with the will of God. "The history of [the United States]," he held, "is undoubtedly a Providential system."[49] In this regard his conception of domestic history fit the mold of the nineteenth-century myth of America's "manifest destiny."

Wilson's idea of international progress grew out of his idea of domestic progress and rested on the same religious assumptions that

---

[46] Wilson, "The Course of American History" (May 16, 1895), *PWW* 9:259, 264.

[47] Wilson, "The Making of the Nation" (April 15, 1897), *PWW* 10:220.

[48] Wilson, "The Course of American History" (May 16, 1895), *PWW* 9:262.

[49] Wilson, "Address on Patriotism to the Washington Association of New Jersey" (February 23, 1903), *PWW* 14:371.

history was eschatology and America God's chosen people. The impetus for extending these beliefs to the international level came in 1890. That year the national census indicated that the geographical expansion of the United States from east to west had been completed, effectively marking the disappearance of the western frontier.

Since for Wilson the frontier represented the defining feature of American history, the news was of monumental significance: "The old sort of growth is at an end,—the growth by mere expansion,"[50] he declared. From now on, he would de-emphasize the territorial aspect of America's providential progress and shift his attention to the other dimension of the nation's sacred destiny: the intensive rather than the extensive one. "We have now to look more closely to internal conditions," Wilson proclaimed, "and study the means by which a various people is to be bound together in a single interest."[51] Although geographically the American Millennium was complete, morally, socially, and politically it was not; a significant lag existed, as was all too evident from the violent labor strikes, riots, and shootings in the 1890s. "The nation . . . has grown to the proportions . . . of the continent," Wilson summarized the problem, "[but it] lies under our eyes . . . unfinished, unharmonized, waiting still to have its parts adjusted, lacking its last lesson in the ways of peace and concert."[52] Solving the crisis, harmonizing the nation, and thereby completing the prototypical Millennium depended in Wilson's view primarily on religious revitalization. His domestic political thought consequently revolved around the concept of "work-day religion" and the redeeming implications of a widespread turn to the spirit of Christ.

By the end of the troubled 1890s, with the worst strikes and riots over, Wilson gradually became convinced that national morals and institutions had caught up with geography, closing the lag between the extensive and intensive dimensions of America's providential progress. The project of building the "model of Christian charity" initiated by John Winthrop and the Puritans in seventeenth-century New England was now complete. The question thus arose, what did God want his chosen people to do next?

For Wilson the answer was clear: "We have been enjoying liberty. Now we are going to give others liberty."[53] Having fulfilled its "manifest

---

[50] Wilson, "Making of the Nation" (April 15, 1897), *PWW* 10:230.
[51] Wilson, "Making of the Nation," 230.
[52] Wilson, "Making of the Nation," 230.
[53] "Liberty and Its Uses" (January 14, 1900), *PWW* 11:374.

destiny" at home, the United States was being summoned by the Lord of history to spread its liberal-capitalistic principles across the globe, redeeming humankind at large.[54] The nation's frontier had been flung wide open. "The census takers of 1890," Wilson announced in 1901,

> informed us . . . that they could no longer find any frontier upon this continent; that they must draw their maps as if the mighty process of settlement . . . were now ended and complete, the nation made from sea to sea. We had not pondered their report a single decade before we made new frontiers for ourselves beyond the seas. . . . We have witnessed a new revolution. We have seen the transformation of America completed. . . . The nation . . . has now stepped forth into the open arena of the world. . . . We have come to full maturity with this new century . . . and to full self-consciousness as a nation. . . . Here is a new world for us. Here is a new life to which to adjust our ideals. . . . It was by plain destiny that we should come to this . . . [Let] us ponder our duties . . . [and] lift our thoughts to the level of the great tasks that await us, and bring a great age in with the coming day of our strength.[55]

Especially the final passages of this statement, uttered well before his presidency, indicate unmistakably that Wilson began universalizing his philosophy of history: expanding its temporal and geographical scope beyond the domestic context.

The potential for this had been nascent in Wilson's historical thought from the beginning by virtue of his belief in God as the Lord of all history, not merely American national history, and by virtue of his view of the United States as a country founded on authentic Christian principles. Considering these principles valid across all time and space, Wilson was able to contend that "[the flag of America] is the flag . . . of humanity,"[56] adding that America's "only title of distinction is that she has a play on the boards which realizes the rights of man."[57] This "play" was based on the Scripture: just like the first New England Puritans, Wilson held that Americans owed their greatness and supreme position among the peoples

---

[54] In the apt characterization by Ambrosius (*Wilsonian Statecraft*, 74), for Wilson "The acceptance of new global responsibility by the United States . . . represented the natural culmination of this nation's own experience. Its progressive history provided the foundation for a new foreign policy. Because of the frontier's closing in 1890, Americans had turned their attention to the outside world."

[55] Wilson, "The Ideals of America" (December 26, 1901), *PWW* 12:215–16, 226–27. See also idem, "The Significance of American History" (September 9, 1901), *PWW* 12:184.

[56] Wilson, "Fourth of July Address" (July 4, 1914), *PWW* 30:254.

[57] "News Report of an Address in Philadelphia to the Universal Peace Union" (February 19, 1912), *PWW* 24:182.

of the world precisely to their "acceptance of those standards of judgment . . . written large upon [the] pages of revelation."[58] It followed that American foreign policy contained not a speck of material self-interest let alone of imperialism. "Conquest and dominion," Wilson proclaimed, "are not in our reckoning, or agreeable to our principles."[59] On the contrary, he sermonized time and again that the spirit of America was the spirit of Christ come alive on the international stage: pure, altruistic, and dedicated entirely to service and self-sacrifice on behalf of humanity.

From this vantage point, Wilson narrated the policy of expansionism initiated by the United States in the late 1890s as part of God's will demanding that Americans enlighten and bring freedom to "other peoples near at hand less fortunate than themselves."[60] Assuming that countries beyond American borders were dark and evil places plagued by oppression, injustice, and poverty, Wilson considered it America's sacred duty to step forward and begin introducing light into the surrounding darkness. What the populations of these foreign countries frequently condemned as unwelcome intrusion into their internal affairs by a powerful nation seeking to increase its sphere of influence, Wilson considered an act of Christian charity administered by the United States army and navy as instruments of progress and civilization.[61]

Among values to be spread worldwide, Wilson emphasized especially constitutional liberty, whose "development . . . in the world . . . is dearer than anything else to thoughtful men of America."[62] On the most fundamental level, this American-led progress toward liberty involved the spread of Christianity. "The world," Wilson proclaimed, "has advanced . . . as real civilization . . . by spiritual means. . . . We have got to save society . . . by the instrumentality of Christianity in this world."[63] Thus in Wilson's view international progress depended on the same thing as domestic progress: religious revitalization.

---

[58] Wilson, "Address in Denver on the Bible" (May 7, 1911), *PWW* 23:18.

[59] Wilson, "Annual Message on the State of the Union" (December 7, 1915), *PWW* 35:297.

[60] Wilson, "Address in Omaha" (October 5, 1916), *PWW* 38:346.

[61] See, e.g., Wilson's commencement speech at the U.S. Naval Academy (June 5, 1914), *PWW* 30:146.

[62] Wilson, "Address on Latin American Policy in Mobile, Alabama" (October 27, 1913), *PWW* 28:451.

[63] Wilson, "Address to the Federal Council of Churches in Columbus" (December 10, 1915), *PWW* 35:329, 334.

This finding is consistent with Herron's interpretation of Wilson's European statecraft during and after World War I as an approach to the earthly Millennium of republican liberty. However, it is necessary to note that in a number of the utterances just cited, Wilson was not referring to Europe, but to lands lying south and west of the United States. This indicates that eschatological assumptions about the progressive shape of history and America's providential mandate underpinned Wilson's liberal internationalism already in the late 1890s and early 1900s, when he was only just beginning to expand his focus beyond domestic American society—and then not toward Europe, but rather Central and South America and territories across the Pacific. This was, of course, the original geographic orientation of "manifest destiny." When John L. O'Sullivan coined the term in the early 1840s, he did it with reference to the annexation of Texas and Oregon, and half a century later, Turner's frontier thesis reinforced the association of progress with westward expansion by portraying American liberal democracy as the end result of progressive transformation of European institutions en route from the eastern seaboard to the Pacific coast.

In flinging the American frontier wide open and projecting the nation's "manifest destiny" beyond the borders of the United States, Wilson thus initially adhered to its traditional (westward) trajectory. For him, it was the Philippines, seized along with Guam and Puerto Rico from Spain in 1898, that represented America's inaugural station on her sacred mission of world redemption. The next stop would be China, whose 1911 revolution opened her up to the civilizing influence of Christianity arriving in the guise of American liberalism. Tellingly, Wilson proposed that the revolution be "fructified" by Christianity as the "great fountain of all that is just and righteous,"[64] and he approached John R. Mott, leader of the YMCA and various world missionary movements, with an offer of ambassadorship.

Other stations for America's "manifest destiny" included Haiti, the Dominican Republic, and Mexico, all of which Wilson subjected to military intervention during the early phases of his presidency. He justified the involvement by invoking the providential logic of history and portraying America as the obedient servant of God and humanity. Faith and eschatological presuppositions guided his foreign policy in each of the foregoing cases.[65]

---

[64] Wilson, "Remarks to Potomac Presbytery" (April 21, 1915), *PWW* 33:50–51.

[65] As Magee (*Wilson and Faith-Based Foreign Policy*, 47) has written about the

When dealing with countries in the Caribbean and Latin American regions, Wilson often cast his eschatological agenda in the language of the Monroe Doctrine. The original purpose of this doctrine, formulated in 1823, was to shelter new republics in South America from European intrusion, thereby maintaining their liberty and security to pursue self-determination and sovereign political development. Wilson, however, comprehended the doctrine's function differently, regarding it not as a shield protecting Latin American republics against external interference, but as a vehicle for extending America's frontier and promoting its sacred mission of liberty. In this vein, with respect to the United States' Latin American policy at the turn of the nineteenth century, "the ideal of intervention on behalf of liberty had the traditional elements of the dogma of manifest destiny—the notion of America's preeminent moral distinction and that of its representation of Providence by virtue of this distinction."[66] In Wilson's hands this theological notion effectively became a blank check to intervene anytime and anywhere in complete disregard of international law or the given country's sovereignty.[67]

It is worth pointing out that the sentiment that God bade the United States to extend its liberal-republican principles and institutions westward was in no way unique to Wilson. On the contrary, it was widespread and cut across party lines. The Republican senator Albert J. Beveridge, for example, declared in 1900 that America "is the 'empire' of which the prophetic voice declared 'Westward the Star of Empire takes its Way'—the star of the empire of liberty and law, of commerce and communication, of social order and the Gospel of our Lord . . . And today it illuminates our path of duty across the Pacific into the islands and lands where Providence has called us."[68] Even more famously, Wilson's sense of calling and divine election was also espoused by Theodore Roosevelt,

---

Mexican intervention, for instance, it was a perfect "demonstration of . . . Wilson's application of [the theological principle of] antinomy to foreign policy decision making." See also Benbow, *Leading Them to Promised Land*, and Crunden, *Ministers of Reform*, 236–46.

[66] Albert K. Weinberg, *Manifest Destiny: A Study of Nationalist Expansionism in American History* (Baltimore, Md.: Johns Hopkins Press, 1935), 421.

[67] Crunden (*Ministers of Reform*, 240) has paraphrased Wilson's justification of the Mexican intervention as follows: "[The United States] had the right and duty to intervene whenever and wherever it felt the moral urge . . . because of its long-standing divine mission to liberate the world for democracy."

[68] Beveridge, "The Star of Empire," in *The Meaning of the Times and Other Speeches* (Indianapolis: Bobbs-Merrill, 1908), 118–19.

who similarly regarded Christianity as the cornerstone of civilization and hailed the expansion of America's hemispheric influence—imperialism by another name—as a natural right derived from God.[69]

When legitimating American interventionism and expansionism by referring to the providential logic of history and to the United States as the earthly agent of God, Wilson was therefore speaking the language of his time. His self-consciously progressive imperialist mindset, anchored in patriotic eschatological assumptions about America's exceptional status among nations, was shared by and readily comprehensible to his contemporaries.

"Manifest Destiny" Turns Eastward
Europe as America's Final Frontier

When the Great War erupted, Wilson saw it as "the eve of a great consummation."[70] European power politics had gained apocalyptic proportions, and the president, guided by his eschatological convictions about the shape of history, had no doubt that the crisis constituted a providential sign of times for the United States: an order from God to raise arms, take to the final battle against evil, and mount a millennial revolution overthrowing anarchy, balance-of-power competition, and war among nations once and for all. In Wilson's perception, the onset of the European conflict marked the final stage in the divine plan of universal salvation and disclosed America's final frontier. In response to the divine summons, Wilson reversed the traditional course of "manifest destiny" and projected it eastward.

On the one hand, Wilson's view that American intervention in the Great War was inevitable reflected pragmatic considerations, especially his keen sense of interdependence among nations at the outset of the twentieth century. The awareness of extensive commercial and other linkages binding nations in a single web was a common liberal theme at the time. Among its key exponents was the British thinker and peace activist Norman Angell. Writing on the eve of the Great War, Angell used the notion of market interdependence to refute the idea that armed conquest was economically beneficial, a presupposition that undergirded

---

[69] It was under Roosevelt that the United States acquired the Philippine Islands, Puerto Rico, Hawaii, Guam, and a virtual protectorate over Cuba from the wildly popular 1898 war against Spain.

[70] Wilson, "Address in Washington to the League to Enforce Peace" (May 25, 1916), *PWW* 37:116.

militarization in Germany as much as in Great Britain. According to Angell, European nations had become commercially intertwined to such a degree that a decision to go to war was bound to induce economic losses (such as international credit rating deterioration and capital flight) well in excess of any potential benefits. In this vein, Angell argued that "It is a logical fallacy and an optical illusion in Europe to regard a nation as increasing its wealth when it increases its territory."[71]

Wilson shared the same awareness of commercial interdependence as Angell, but he used it in a different way: to argue that once a war had started in one part of the world, the web of linkages was bound to amplify the conflict to other regions. With respect to the European crisis, the president recognized that interdependence made American neutrality impossible in the long run; the United States would be drawn into the conflict whether it wanted or not. In this vein, Wilson told the American Congress at the beginning of his second presidential term that "It has been impossible to avoid . . . matters lying outside our own life as a nation . . . The war inevitably set its mark from the first upon our minds, our industries, our commerce, our politics, and our social action. To be indifferent to it or independent of it was out of the question."[72]

However, economic interdependence and the rising losses to American exports and shipping caused by the European conflict were not the principal justification for why the United States should abandon its neutrality. Wilson based the necessity of American involvement in the Great War much more frequently on metaphysical grounds: on his eschatological conception of history as providential progress and on his belief in America's "manifest destiny" to spearhead this progress. He declared that the national "spirit . . . is going out conquering and to conquer until . . . in the Providence of God . . . a new light is lifted in America which shall throw the rays of liberty and justice far abroad upon every sea, . . . upon the lands which now wallow in darkness and refuse to see the light."[73]

Invocations such as this one in many respects repeated the basic theme of Governor John Winthrop's sermon about America's sacred mission as a "city upon a hill": a community destined by God to illuminate humanity with the redeeming spirit of pure Christianity. In the 1890s Wilson considered this spirit essential to overcoming the domestic crisis

[71] Angell, *The Great Illusion*, 3rd ed. (New York: G. P. Putnam's Sons, 1911), 30–36.

[72] Wilson, "Second Inaugural Address" (March 5, 1917), *PWW* 41:333.

[73] Wilson, "Memorial Day Address" (May 30, 1916), *PWW* 37:128.

and uniting the fragmented American nation. Now, facing a world crisis, he was convinced that Christianity as a "work-day religion" would have the same healing and harmonizing effects in world affairs.

Wilson kept this conviction somewhat subdued during the war. Uncertain about the war's eventual outcome, he tended to convey the eschatological inspiration of his foreign policy only to a few trusted individuals, such as Herron, whose millennialist expectations he knew to be as firm as his own. With the conflict successfully over, however, the president abandoned all scruples. The outcome of the war cemented his belief in American-led providential progress with empirical evidence: Wilson regarded America's triumph in the apocalyptic conflagration as direct proof of God's scheme for the salvation of humankind and of America's "manifest destiny" to facilitate this process. The ecstatic masses welcoming him in Europe reinforced this view further still. In Milan, for instance, Wilson's automobile was deluged with leaflets celebrating the president as "Savior of humanity," "God of Peace," and "The Moses from across the Atlantic."[74] These terms catered directly to Wilson's private self-understanding as a soldier of Christ, an identity he had cultivated since his late teens. He found them utterly delightful, reportedly declaring the reception in Milan "Most superb, stupendous and overwhelming."[75]

In light of this experience, Wilson must have arrived at the Paris Peace Conference imagining himself as the soldier of Christ he had once idolized in his early religious essays: a messianic leader bringing the sacred principles of American liberalism to their final frontier. The old Puritan dream of returning to the Old World from the transatlantic refuge in order to spread the American Millennium worldwide seemed to him on the verge of fulfillment. Wilson alluded to the Puritan mission on at least one public occasion when describing the purpose of his trip to Versailles.[76]

His impression that he was providentially appointed to bring this mission to its conclusion and effect universal redemption transpired in his behavior: at Versailles he became reclusive and paranoid, harboring increasing distrust not just of foreign leaders, but of his own diplomatic team.[77] Danger, conspiracy, and sabotage lurked everywhere, and it was

---

[74] From the Diary of Dr. Grayson (January 5, 1919), *PWW* 53:614.

[75] Diary of Dr. Grayson, 613.

[76] See his "Remarks to French Protestants" (January 27, 1919), *PWW* 54:283.

[77] "His sense of divine election and his position at the center of world politics," according to Magee (*Wilson and Faith-Based Foreign Policy*, 89), "came together to create the feeling that he could not confide in anyone regarding his task."

imperative to take extreme precautions. At the same time, Wilson had no doubts that he was going to complete this task successfully. His foreign policy agenda faced considerable resistance from critics both at home and in Europe, but they stood no chance. "I want to utter this solemn warning," Wilson notified his enemies in the U.S. Senate, for instance, "[that] the great tides of the world do not give notice that they are going to rise, . . . and those who stand in the way [will be] overwhelmed."[78] In the final analysis, any and all opposition to his liberal internationalist principles struck the president as naïve. In his view these were destined to prevail by virtue of representing God's will.

The same convictions surrounded the centerpiece of Wilson's European statecraft during and immediately after the Great War: the League of Nations, about whose achievement the president felt supremely confident. This institution represented the endpoint in his narrative of international progress: the climactic conclusion of the great centuries-long project of realizing the spirit of Christ in the secular order of world affairs. In and through the League, Wilson's notion of Christianity as a "work-day religion," which he originally formulated with respect to domestic politics, would be extended across the entire world, bringing lasting harmony and peace.

That European statesmen would agree to the League was by no means certain when the Armistice was signed on November 11, 1918; in order to achieve it, Wilson had to overcome several obstacles in Paris, such as pressures to negotiate a peace treaty with Germany first and consider the League proposal later on a separate occasion. When he prevailed and returned to the United States with the League Covenant in hand, he regarded his latest—and, unbeknownst to him, final—political success as a definite confirmation that the providential "tides of the world" could not be stopped. Presenting the League Covenant for ratification in the Senate, he portrayed the document as follows:

The stage is set, the destiny disclosed. It has come about by no plan of our conceiving, but by the hand of God who led us into this way. We cannot turn back. We can only go forward, with lifted eyes and freshened spirit, to follow the vision. It was of this that we dreamed at our birth. America shall in truth show the way. The light streams on the path ahead, and nowhere else.[79]

[78] Wilson, "Speech at the Metropolitan Opera House" (March 4, 1919), *PWW* 55:415.
[79] Wilson, "Address to the Senate" (July 10, 1919), *PWW* 61:436.

Wilson disavowed any free will in the historical process and cast American diplomacy, the League Covenant, and international politics as foreordained by God. His language was typical of secularized biblical eschatology in general and of American Protestant millennialism in particular. Half a century after O'Sullivan defined America's "manifest destiny" in terms of spreading the sacred principles of liberal democracy across the North American continent, Wilson extended the doctrine beyond America's borders to define the nation's leading role in the world. In doing so, he reactivated a well-established and instantly recognizable script in American societal and political culture.[80]

When the Senate refused to ratify the Versailles Treaty, causing the United States to opt out of the League and stray off the providential path, it was a tremendous blow to Wilson from which he never recovered. However, not even this disastrous course of events did any damage to his conviction that history was fundamentally a story of progress toward American-style liberal government as the fullest expression of authentic Christian principles in this *sæculum*. His eschatological consciousness remained intact even amidst his greatest political defeat.

Wilson thus continued to believe that the United States was a special nation chosen by God to carry the sacred mission of liberal democracy to every corner of the world. In 1920, this mission had long lain sabotaged by Senator Lodge and others who had voted against ratifying the League Covenant. But Wilson pressed on with his crusade nonetheless. "This is the time of all others when democracy should prove its purity and its spiritual power to prevail," he told the Congress. "It is surely the manifest destiny of the United States to lead in the attempt to make this spirit prevail."[81] With these words Wilson became the first and to this day the only American president to invoke "manifest destiny" in an official address.

The League of Nations as Millennial "Testaments of Liberty"

Just how essential the League of Nations was to Wilson's liberal internationalist agenda is evident already from the resolve with which he continued to cling to it until the very end of his life, well after losing the treaty fight against the Senate and leaving the presidential office. According

---

[80] His words on the Senate floor, as Weinberg (*Manifest Destiny*, 470) put it, once again "set long familiar ideals in vibration."

[81] Wilson, "Annual Message on the State of the Union" (December 7, 1920), *PWW* 66:485.

to Link, however, the League idea drove Wilson's European diplomacy from day one and represented the principal factor behind his decision to enter the war: "The most important reason for [this] decision was his conviction that American belligerency . . . would assure American guarantee of the peace settlement and membership in a postwar league of nations."[82] By the time the war had ended and Wilson arrived at Versailles, he could hardly think of anything other than the League.

His fixation did not escape the notice of direct participants in the negotiations. For instance, Harold Nicolson, who attended the Peace Conference alongside Carr and Keynes as a junior member of the British delegation, later recalled that for Wilson "the League Covenant was his own Revelation and the solution to all human problems. . . . [Before] the Ark of the Covenant he sacrificed his Fourteen Points one by one."[83] European statesmen promptly realized that in dealing with the American president the League constituted their most valuable bargaining chip, and they used it to obtain concessions from him.[84]

Embodying such a large portion of Wilson's statecraft that by 1919 it had become practically synonymous with it, the League idea exemplified the eschatological presuppositions of his liberal internationalism with special intensity. This is evident already from his understanding of the diplomatic process of drafting the League Covenant at Versailles. "World politics," Wilson explained with reference to this process a few months after its conclusion, "[is] the concert of the methods by which the world is to be bettered, that concert of will and of action which will make every nation a nobler instrument of divine Providence."[85] In his view, statesmen convened in Paris in order to remove any artificial obstacles previously blocking the will of God from directing international affairs. By allowing God to guide the world without obstruction, the League would facilitate progress to the millennial harmony of interests, bringing liberty, peace, justice, and prosperity to all nations. This understanding of the drafting process reflected and extended Wilson's definition of domestic politics in that it sought to apply the spirit of Christ to every area of secular or political practice.

[82] Link, *Wilson: Campaigns for Progressivism and Peace, 1916–1917* (Princeton, N.J.: Princeton University Press, 1965), 414.

[83] See Nicolson, *Peacemaking: 1919* (New York: Harcourt, Brace, 1939), 198.

[84] Magee, *Wilson and Faith-Based Foreign Policy*, 95.

[85] Wilson, "Luncheon Address to the St. Louis Chamber of Commerce" (September 5, 1919), *PWW* 63:33.

The notion that in return for embracing God and placing themselves completely at his disposal the nations of the world would receive redemption from war and suffering was reflected in the title of the League's founding treaty, another feature revealing Wilson's underlying eschatological agenda. The very term "covenant" is indicative of his religious motivation. It did not designate the treaty initially. As Jan Christiaan Smuts, the South African statesman heavily involved in the Versailles negotiations, later recalled in a private letter, early drafts referred to the treaty merely as a "convention," but at Wilson's insistence the final document was renamed " 'Covenant' . . . in remembrance of his [Presbyterian] Covenanter descent."[86]

This suggests that Wilson viewed the League not merely as an ordinary diplomatic treaty, but as a monumental spiritual achievement: the final fulfillment of the millennial hopes held by his ancestors. Although then as now the term "covenant" possessed a wide range of meanings, including nonreligious ones, Wilson used it in the specific sense delineated by Presbyterian covenant theology.[87] As such the League Covenant involved at least three interrelated spiritual subcovenants—between each individual member and God, between each individual member and all the other members, and between God and all members collectively—institutionalized in the League as a giant presbytery of nations. In this presbytery Wilson regarded himself as the presiding minister, a new Moses selected by divine providence to explain the modern Tablets of the League Covenant to national leaders. In Paris, as he was fond of recalling, nations large and small flocked to him, "sat at [his] feet . . . and said, 'Teach us the way to liberty.' "[88]

A third aspect of the League revealing its eschatological foundations was its geographic location. Several options were proposed at first:

[86] Cited in Crunden, *Ministers of Reform*, 258. Wilson affirmed this connotation publicly while touring the United States to rouse mass support for the Versailles Treaty against the reluctant Senate. "I have come out to fight for a cause . . . greater than the Senate . . . [and] greater than the government. It is . . . the cause of mankind," he announced in Missouri, concluding his speech by informing the crowds that among his Scotch ancestors "were some of that famous group . . . known as the Covenanters. Very well then, here is the Covenant of the League of Nations. I am a Covenanter!" See his "Address in Convention Hall in Kansas City" (September 6, 1919), *PWW* 63:75.

[87] Magee, *Wilson and Faith-Based Foreign Policy*, 17; Ambrosius, *Wilsonianism*, 36; Harley Notter, *The Origins of the Foreign Policy of Woodrow Wilson* (Baltimore, Md.: Johns Hopkins Press, 1937), 16.

[88] Wilson, "Address in the Des Moines Coliseum" (September 6, 1919), *PWW* 63:79.

Colonel House, for instance, was partial to Lausanne, whereas a number of French and Belgian leaders advocated for Brussels. That the president ended up endorsing Geneva instead was partially due to his and Herron's view that, as Herron had written to him, "Geneva is the real parent of New England. . . . No place upon our planet has such fitting claims to be the meeting place of the League of Nations as Geneva—unless it be Jerusalem."[89] The chosen location reflected the League's status in the imagination of Wilson and Herron as the secular completion of the eschatological program of American Protestant Christianity. Based on this perception, it struck them as logical that the League belonged either to the birthplace of Christianity or the city where Calvin resurrected the spirit of Christ from the darkness of Roman Catholic popery.[90]

The determining influence of Wilson's eschatological faith was not confined merely to the League's geographic location or the title of its founding treaty, characteristics that may be considered symbolic and largely incapable of making any real political difference. On the contrary, his belief that the Bible contained the key to international political harmony and that a universal turn to Christ would have redemptive consequences for world affairs lay at the very heart of the institution as Wilson understood it, and directly shaped some of the key League principles.

An illustrative example is the "cooling off" clause enshrined in Article 12 of the League Covenant. This clause bound participating members to

> agree that, if there should arise between them any dispute likely to lead to a rupture, they will submit the matter either to arbitration or judicial settlement or to enquiry by the Council, and they agree in no case to resort to war until three months after the award by the arbitrators or the judicial decision, or the report by the Council. In any case under this Article the award of the arbitrators or the judicial decision shall be made within a reasonable time, and the report of the Council shall be made within six months after the submission of the dispute.

The progenitor of this "cooling off" clause was William Jennings Bryan.[91] A Presbyterian elder, an even more ardent eschatologist than Wilson, and

---

[89] Herron to Wilson (March 20, 1919), *PWW* 56:121.

[90] Cf. Ambrosius, *Wilson and American Diplomatic Tradition*, 119: "Herron commended Geneva's traditions of religious liberty and democracy and its contributions, especially from John Calvin, to the Scottish Covenanters and English Puritans, and subsequently to the United States. These were persuasive arguments for the Scotch-Irish Presbyterian president."

[91] Paolo E. Coletta, *William Jennings Bryan* (Lincoln: University of Nebraska Press,

together with him and Robert Lansing one of the three principal architects of what Crunden has called "a Presbyterian foreign policy,"[92] Bryan came up with the idea during his pan-American peace initiative when serving as Wilson's secretary of state. Wilson subsequently adopted it for his League initiative, acknowledging his intellectual debt to Bryan and telling Ray Stannard Baker that "some such delay-method must be one of the corner stones of future international relations, if peace [is] to come in the world."[93]

The "cooling off" idea might seem reminiscent of French Enlightenment philosophy, specifically of the Rousseauian distinction between man's "real" and "apparent" interests and the need to create appropriate structures and institutions for the "real" interests to come out. Yet this would overlook the actual way in which Wilson and Bryan devised the principle. In their conception its logic emanated from their biblical historical consciousness: that humans used to live in the Garden of Eden; that by disobeying God they fell into the darkness of the historical world characterized by war, injustice, and suffering; that this world was nonetheless inauthentic and all its disputes and conflicts unnecessary; and that by allocating sufficient time and effort to illuminate these disputes with genuine Christianity the primordial harmony and innocence could be reestablished. Not reason, as Rousseau would have it, but the spirit of Christ represented the key ingredient of progress to redemption.

Wilson explained the sum and substance of the "cooling off" clause as follows, clothing it in quasi-scientific language:

> Whenever any trouble arises, the light shall shine on it for a year before you do anything. . . . [L]ight is the greatest sanitary influence in the world. [It] is a scientific commonplace . . . [that] if you want to make a place wholesome, the best instrument you can use is the sun—to . . . scorch out all the miasma that may lurk there. So with moral light: It is the most wholesome, rectifying, and most revealing thing in the world, provided it be genuine moral light; . . . the light of the man who discloses it in order that all the sweet influences of the world may go in and make it better.[94]

1964–69), 2:239–49; Arthur S. Link, *Wilson*, vol. 2, *The New Freedom* (Princeton, N.J.: Princeton University Press, 1956), 280–83.

[92] Crunden, *Ministers of Reform*, 226. In Crunden's definition, this policy "asserted the virtue of American motives . . . and insisted on the right to export [American] ideals to any unstable area in the world."

[93] "Memorandum by Ray Stannard Baker of a Conversation at the White House" (May 12, 1916), *PWW* 37:33.

[94] Wilson, "Address to the Pittsburgh Y.M.C.A." (October 24, 1914), *PWW* 31:226.

This method, Wilson contended, would allow nations to resolve all their quarrels automatically through arbitration, making armed conflict entirely superfluous. If the sanitary rays of moral light had "shone for a year, it won't be necessary to do anything," he declared; "we will know who was right and who was wrong."[95] War would be abolished by weaving the "cooling off" provision systematically into the fabric of international relations, at which point humankind would conclude its long climb out of the darkness of history and reach "the day when each shall live in the full light which shines upon the uplands, where all the light that illuminates mankind shines direct from the face of God."[96] The glow of Christian religion would sanitize world affairs for good, effectively turning earth back into the primordial Paradise.

Bryan famously commemorated this expectation by having surplus swords from the War Department melted down and recast into miniature plowshares, which he then distributed as lapel pins at State Department functions.[97] One wonders what kind of private reactions this must have elicited among visiting European diplomats and statesmen, but within Wilson's cabinet and American society at large these were serious matters; only uncharacteristically pragmatic individuals would have regarded Bryan as a grotesquely naïve religious zealot and utopian. His millennial vision was certainly shared; he was not alone in espousing it. This is evident not only from Herron's writings, who similarly regarded the League of Nations as the Second Coming of Christ, but also, for instance, from the laudatory message sent to Wilson by the American Federal Council of Churches, which proclaimed the League the "political expression of the Kingdom of God on earth."[98]

Wilson's own belief in the League's radically transformative impact on world history was just as intense and may be regarded as the final and best indication of the eschatological nature of the institution in his imagination. Returning from Paris with the League Covenant in hand, he was convinced that an entirely new era was dawning, one profoundly different from all that preceded it. Introducing the Versailles Treaty for Senate

---

[95] Wilson, "Address to the Pittsburgh Y.M.C.A.," 226.

[96] Wilson, "Address to the Pittsburgh Y.M.C.A.," 228.

[97] Richard Challenger, "Secretary of State," in *William Jennings Bryan: A Profile*, ed. Paul W. Glad (New York: Hill & Wang, 1968), 180–81.

[98] Cited in Conrad Cherry, "American Destiny and World War," in *God's New Israel: Religious Interpretations of American Destiny*, ed. Cherry, rev. and updated ed. (Chapel Hill: University of North Carolina Press, 1998), 271.

ratification, Wilson chose to capture its anticipated effect using the language of spiritual warfare inspired by the Revelation of St. John: he portrayed the old international system based on power politics as a reign of Satan, and he announced that the League was going to bind "the monster that had resorted to arms . . . in chains that could not be broken."[99] Similarly, when presenting the League to masses of ordinary Americans during a national tour a few months later, Wilson repeatedly referred to the Covenant using terms such as "redemption," "salvation," and "a document unique in the history of the world."[100] Many of his eschatological pronouncements have since become canonical, representing some of the highest points in the history of American presidential oratory and serving ensuing generations of Americans as a potent definer of their nation's role in the world. A good example is Wilson's exhortation, only days before a paralyzing stroke effectively ended his political career, that "nothing less depends on us . . . than the liberation and salvation of the world."[101]

As fervently salvationist as his public portrayals of the League were, Wilson's private remarks revealed his millennial expectations even more vividly. In a discreet letter sent to the British prime minister David Lloyd George just a few weeks after the Armistice, the president had written that "The events of the last five years have been the greatest in all recorded times, and the final triumph of civilization over savagery, the victory of right over might, makes of this day and hour an epoch beside which all history is dimmed. . . . Hereafter . . . the history of mankind will be put into two grand divisions only, that before, and that after, this great world conflict."[102] The historical world was about to be revolutionized so dramatically, Wilson held, that people living in the new epoch would rewrite the traditional liturgical calendar and view everything prior to 1918 as mere prehistory to the real history inaugurated by the League of Nations.[103] The birth of the League, marking the completion of the progressive realization of Christ's spirit on earth, would replace the birth of Christ as the central event of world history.

---

[99] Wilson, "Address to the Senate" (July 10, 1919), *PWW* 61:434. Cf. Magee, *Faith-Based Foreign Policy*, 105.

[100] See, e.g., Wilson, "Address to the Columbus Chamber of Commerce" (September 4, 1919), *PWW* 63:7–10, and idem, "Address in the San Diego Stadium" (September 19, 1919), *PWW* 63:382. Cf. Cherry, *God's New Israel*, 224–25.

[101] Wilson, "Address in the City Auditorium in Pueblo, Colorado" (September 25, 1919), *PWW* 63:512.

[102] Wilson, "Remarks at a Stag Dinner" (December 28, 1918), *PWW* 64:491.

[103] Cf. Herron, *Wilson and the World's Peace*, 45.

From the perspective of the Augustinian conception of history, this expectation was fundamentally misplaced. This is because Augustinian eschatology is not historical, but only spiritual and transcendental, harboring no illusions that the human world is progressively emancipated from evil or that salvation may occur in the temporal order of existence. Augustine's attitude toward secular events effectively reaffirmed the skepticism of ancient Greek and Roman philosophers, who regarded all progress in the world as temporary and subject to inevitable cyclical reversal.

Wilson, however, had not the least doubt that history was an inherently linear and civilizing process and that salvation from evil and war as the cardinal expression of evil in international affairs was a real sociohistorical possibility. In the League Covenant he had glimpsed the redeeming "testaments of liberty . . . the things we must do in order that mankind might be released from the intolerable things of the past."[104] This conviction had come about through the process of secularization, in whose course Wilson, following in the footsteps of Joachim of Floris and generations of Protestant theologians and exemplifying nineteenth-century American Protestant progressivism, oriented the transcendental *eschaton* of Augustinian theology *ad sæculum* and reinterpreted it in this-worldly terms: as a future goal of political, economic, and social progress.

---

[104] Wilson, "Address in the St. Paul Auditorium" (September 9, 1919), *PWW* 63:148.

(RE)INTEGRATING THE TWO UTOPIANISMS

Wilsonian Liberal Internationalism
as Secularized Eschatology

"Utopianism" is a term that enjoys widespread use, but its meaning varies dramatically across different epistemic communities. Placed side by side, the academic fields of international relations (IR) and intellectual history offer an excellent example: each of these two areas of intellectual activity has conceptualized utopianism in relative isolation from the other. In contemporary IR discourse, the category refers primarily to Woodrow Wilson's liberal internationalism: a set of ideas formulated during and immediately after World War I, driven by the vision of permanent peace, and institutionalized in the Treaty of Versailles and the League of Nations. In acute contrast, intellectual history has framed utopianism above all in terms of modern historical consciousness, specifically the idea of progress as a secularized expression of biblical eschatology.

While each of these definitions has undeniable merit and contributes valuable knowledge, neither one alone does full justice to Wilson's self-understanding, in which "the distinction between *secular* and *religious* . . . simply did not exist."[1] Politics was a spiritual mission in his

---

[1] Malcolm D. Magee, *What the World Should Be: Woodrow Wilson and the Crafting of a Faith-Based Foreign Policy* (Waco, Tex.: Baylor University Press, 2008), 13; emphasis original.

comprehension: he conceived of his liberal internationalism within an eschatological mindset shaped by his patriotic Presbyterian faith. If the backbone of his "New Diplomacy" was the idea of progress to a new world order based on collective security and the League of Nations, the backbone of this idea of progress in turn was a set of deeply entrenched theological assumptions, such as that history was a redemptive process, with America as the savior nation. Wilson would have been the first to point this out. That the religious inspiration of his diplomacy is not common knowledge today is an unfortunate result of disciplinary specialization in the twentieth century, over whose course religion and eschatology have been factored out of the study of foreign policy and international affairs.[2]

Before this specialization took hold, the gap between the two definitions of utopianism was much smaller. Indeed, it hardly existed at all. To take a second, closer look at the original classical realist IR critics of Wilson is to discover that they clearly understood the religious foundations of his international political thought. This is true not only of E. H. Carr, but also of Hans Morgenthau and Reinhold Niebuhr, all three of whom possessed broad minds unencumbered by subject divisions and spanning multiple fields, in contradistinction to today's specialists. Morgenthau thus saw in Wilsonian slogans such as the "last war," the "war to end war," and the "culminating and final war for human liberty" unmistakable "expressions of an eschatological hope deeply imbedded in the very foundations of liberal foreign policy."[3] Carr and Niebuhr went even further in arguing that liberal internationalism flowed from biblical presuppositions, each of them dedicating extensive passages and indeed entire volumes to making this point. Religion and secularization theory therefore had a firm place in the original analysis of Wilsonian statecraft. To this extent, integrating the two distinctive meanings of utopianism into a single definition may be viewed as a recovery procedure: an act of reviving an insight that was familiar early on but subsequently forgotten.

---

[2] The call to factor them back in and enrich the historiography of U.S. foreign policy with religion has been made by, for instance, Andrew Preston, "Bridging the Gap between the Sacred and the Secular in the History of American Foreign Relations," *Diplomatic History* 30, no. 5 (2006): 783–812.

[3] Morgenthau, *Scientific Man versus Power Politics* (Chicago: University of Chicago Press, 1946), 52.

Synthesizing Religious and Political Utopianism
as a Recovery Procedure

The forgetting required considerable effort, for Carr discussed Wilsonianism as a secularized vestige of Judeo-Christian eschatology quite conspicuously already in the very treatise introducing the concept of utopianism to IR: *The Twenty Years' Crisis*. "The modern school of utopian political thought," he described its genealogy, "must be traced back to the break-up of the mediaeval system, which presupposed a universal ethic and a universal political system based on divine authority."[4] This ethical and political system of medieval Christianity entered a deep crisis during the Renaissance, according to Carr, but in the course of the seventeenth and eighteenth centuries it reemerged in a new form and on a new foundation: natural law philosophy. Carr thus sounds the familiar theme of secularization theory that modern rationalism did away with Christianity only partially and on the surface, whereas in its functions and hidden presuppositions about the nature of history modern philosophy remained committed to the biblical-eschatological worldview. Laws of nature took the place of divine providence, reason that of faith, and science that of religion. "Enlightenment was the royal road to the millennium,"[5] Carr pronounced. "In France," he added, "[utopianism] became associated with a secular, in England with an evangelical tradition."[6]

Carr's thesis that the liberal idea of progress is a product of secularization is even more manifest when one probes beyond *The Twenty Years' Crisis* and examines those of his writings dealing specifically with philosophy of history. Of special note here are his Trevelyan Lectures, delivered in the University of Cambridge in 1961 and subsequently published under the title *What Is History?* This book represented Carr's "second blistering attack on the liberal establishment. This time it was on the liberal historical establishment, as opposed to the liberal establishment . . . in international relations."[7] Carr, who saw himself primarily as a historian, dedicated the entire sixth lecture to the notion of history as progress, and his critical analysis of this notion echoes much that Löwith and other

---

[4] Carr, *The Twenty Years' Crisis, 1919–1939: An Introduction to the Study of International Relations*, 2nd ed. (New York: Harper & Row, 1964 [1949]), 22.

[5] Carr, *Twenty Years' Crisis*, 23.

[6] Carr, *Twenty Years' Crisis*, 23.

[7] Peter Wilson, "Radicalism for a Conservative Purpose: The Peculiar Realism of E. H. Carr," *Millennium: Journal of International Studies* 30, no. 1 (2001): 124.

secularization theorists had to say about the hidden biblical foundations of modern historical consciousness.

Like Löwith, Carr saw the ancient Greco-Roman civilization as essentially unhistorical, captured within a cyclical consciousness of time, and he ascribed the birth of linear time and progressive history to Judaism and Christianity:

> It was the Jews, and after them the Christians, who introduced an entirely new element by postulating a goal towards which the historical process is moving—the teleological view of history. History thus acquired a meaning and purpose, but at the expense of losing its secular character. The attainment of the goal of history would automatically mean the end of history: history itself became theodicy.[8]

The Renaissance revived Greek rationalism, Carr went on, but this revival was only partial: the founders of the modern age failed to revert back to the cyclical consciousness of time. From the Renaissance to the Enlightenment, philosophers remained spellbound by the biblical (eschatological) idea of history and merely translated it into a new idiom: "History became progress towards the goal of the perfection of man's estate on earth."[9] Carr was consequently explicit that modern liberal progressivism in this sense remained premodern and religious, despite all its scientific pretensions. "The presumption of an end of history," he stated, "has an eschatological ring more appropriate to the theologian than to the historian."[10] These words could be mistaken for Löwith's. In aiming them at liberal historians, Carr did not single out Wilson by name, but he doubtless had him, among others, in mind. After all, Wilson was not just the preeminent liberal internationalist statesman, but also a distinguished professor of history and one-time president of the American Historical Association. He was, in short, a member of both liberal establishments attacked by Carr.

In Niebuhr's appraisal of American liberal internationalism, secularization theory played an even more central role than in Carr's and converged with Löwith's thesis practically to the point. Niebuhr's realist critique of Wilsonian statecraft represented but one particular subset of his general critique of modern progressivism as a whole, whose genealogy he interpreted much the way Löwith did. Like the German

---

[8] Carr, *What Is History?* (New York: Knopf, 1962), 145–46.
[9] Carr, *What Is History?* 146.
[10] Carr, *What Is History?* 152.

secularization theorist, the American theologian was keenly aware of the pervasiveness of the idea of progress throughout all modern thinking about time and history. As he put it in *Faith in History*, which came out the same year as Löwith's *Meaning in History*:

> A single article of faith has given diverse forms of modern culture the unity of a shared belief. Modern men of all shades of opinion agree in the belief that [history] is a redemptive process. . . . Faith in history is the dominant note in modern culture. . . . Though there are minor dissonances the whole chorus of modern culture learned to sing the new song of hope in remarkable harmony.[11]

Leibnitz and Herder, Hegel and Marx, Bentham and Kant diverged dramatically on many philosophical questions, but according to Niebuhr, underneath these differences they all agreed that the essential shape of history was progress. This belief represented a common denominator of modernity—"a unity which transcends warring social philosophies."[12] As for its origins, here the American theologian concurred with Löwith also: they derived from the biblical story of salvation and its portrayal of temporal events as flowing forward to a significant future. "Christian faith," Niebuhr proclaimed in this vein, "is indeed the soil out of which modern historical consciousness grew," and the various philosophies of progress preserved it in their silent structural presuppositions: "Every larger frame of meaning, which serves the observer of historical events in correlating the events into some kind of pattern, is a structure of faith rather than of science."[13]

The only notable difference setting Niebuhr's diagnosis of the idea of progress apart from Löwith's is the extent to which Niebuhr trained the optic of secularization specifically at American liberalism and liberal internationalism. Though he occasionally did comment on other ideologies, such as Soviet Bolshevism, his musings on the eschatological origins of modern historical consciousness are above all the musings of an introspective critic of the American liberal tradition, who dedicated his entire career to a ruthless scrutiny of its moral foundations and political aspirations both at home and abroad.[14] His writings on foreign

---

[11] Niebuhr, *Faith and History: A Comparison of Christian and Modern Views of History* (London: Nisbet, 1949), 1–2, 7.

[12] Niebuhr, *Faith and History*, 4.

[13] Niebuhr, *Faith and History*, 42, 135.

[14] This scrutiny did not shy away from figures at the very heart of the liberal pantheon. See, e.g., Reinhold Niebuhr, "The Religious Assumptions of Adam Smith," *Journal of Theology for Southern Africa* 44, no. 1 (1983): 6–23. For Niebuhr's secularization

policy gave special attention to the progressive Wilsonian conception of American statecraft as a moral crusade for universal peace and justice, which Niebuhr regarded as "soft utopianism."[15] This conception was dangerously misguided in Niebuhr's view, and his vehement opposition to it targeted precisely the nature of liberal internationalism as secularized eschatology rooted in the myth of America's "manifest destiny" to redeem the world to liberty. Such ambitions struck Niebuhr as arrogant, blasphemous, and recklessly forgetful of the warning issued by his main spiritual and philosophical guide, St. Augustine: that the *civitas terrena* and the *civitas Dei* have separate destinies, that salvation occurs only through the grace of God, and that projects designed to bring it about through human efforts alone merely end up perpetuating the history of suffering, oppression, and war.[16]

It is precisely on the basis of this assessment that contemporary IR regards Niebuhr as a leading realist opponent of liberal internationalism. He exercised deep influence on both Carr, who cited him repeatedly throughout *The Twenty Years' Crisis*, and Morgenthau, who named him among the authors of his ten favorite books.[17] In this vein, it may be no exaggeration to say that Niebuhr's "range, depth, and complexity

---

analysis of Soviet Bolshevism, see his article "The Religion of Communism," *Atlantic Monthly* 147 (1931): 462–70, in which he noted that "Communism is ostensibly a highly scientific and irreligious social philosophy" and subsequently argued that "In reality it is a new religion" (p. 462). What set the Bolsheviks apart from traditional religion, Niebuhr went on, was their replacement of divine providence with the class principle: "The *deus ex machina* which [Communism] trusts is not the God of religious devotion, but a law imbedded in the processes of history" (p. 463). See also Reinhold Niebuhr, "The Religious Assumptions of Karl Marx," *Journal of Theology for Southern Africa* 44, no. 1 (1983): 24–41.

[15] As such it represented the same kind of religion of progress as the "hard utopianism" of Russian Communism, except it was more tolerant of dissent and trusted in gradual reform rather than rapid revolution. See Niebuhr, "Two Forms of Utopianism," in *A Reinhold Niebuhr Reader: Selected Essays, Articles, and Book Reviews*, ed. Charles C. Brown (Philadelphia: Trinity Press International, 1992), 43–45.

[16] Commenting on "the American Messianic dream" and its counterparts in utopian visions of other nations, especially the Soviet Union, Niebuhr stated that "The illusions about the possibility of managing historical destiny . . . always involve . . . miscalculations about both the power and the wisdom of the managers and of the weakness and the manageability of the historical 'stuff' which is to be managed." *The Irony of American History* (New York: Scribner, 1952), 72.

[17] Christoph Frei, *Hans J. Morgenthau: An Intellectual Biography* (Baton Rouge: Louisiana State University Press, 2001), 113. Morgenthau specified Niebuhr's *Nature and Destiny of Man* and included Carr's *Twenty Years' Crisis* as well.

make [him] without question the most profound thinker of the modern realist school."[18] The main thrust of Niebuhr's realism was nothing else than the secularization thesis applied to the liberal internationalist idea of progress. The sophistication with which Niebuhr propounded this thesis flowed from his training in theology, matched that of Löwith, and earned him his recognition. It also led Niebuhr to notice the German philosopher and express enthusiastic approval of him in turn: the two had read each other's principal work on the eschatological foundations of modern historical consciousness and exchanged favorable reviews.[19] Their intellectual affinity was likely one of the main reasons why Niebuhr, member of the influential International Rescue Committee during World War II, intervened on Löwith's behalf and helped him arrange his American exile from Nazism.

Straddling the contemporary disciplinary divide between IR and intellectual history as a preeminent political realist and a leading secularization theorist in one, Niebuhr thus demonstrates the central role of secularization analysis in the early framing of the liberal internationalist vision of world progress exceptionally well. For him as much as for Carr and, to a lesser extent, Morgenthau, utopianism did not have two separate meanings, one referring to Wilsonian statecraft, the other to secularized eschatology, but only one synthetic definition: Wilsonian liberal internationalism as secularized eschatology. It was only later that this definition gradually became bifurcated and its secular-political facet discussed apart from its religious-eschatological one. In the process, vital parts of Carr's and Niebuhr's intellectual heritage were swept under the carpet.

Implications for Intellectual History

Why are these parts worth retrieving? After all, that it is possible to recover the forgotten eschatological facet of liberal internationalism does not automatically mean that it is also desirable: one may get the impression that it is a purely academic exercise. Yet this impression would be wrong: to reintegrate political and religious utopianism back into a single organic definition is to generate important implications for, among other things, the secularization thesis; the psychology of legitimating violence,

---

[18] Michael Joseph Smith, *Realist Thought from Weber to Kissinger* (Baton Rouge: Louisiana State University Press, 1986), 99.

[19] See Reinhold Niebuhr, review of *Meaning in History*, by Karl Löwith, *Journal of Religion* 29 (1949): 302–3; and Karl Löwith, review of *Faith and History*, by Reinhold Niebuhr, *Theology Today* 6 (1949): 422–25.

expansionism, and war in liberal societies; and the nature and function of liberal internationalism as a foreign policy approach and a theory of international relations. One way to tease out these implications is with reference to the disciplinary divide between intellectual history and IR, showing the gains accruing to each side in turn.

Within intellectual history, the recovery of the eschatological pre-suppositions of Wilson's liberal internationalism furnishes a new case study in support of the secularization thesis as a particular narrative of the origins and genesis of modern historical consciousness. This thesis, stated most forcefully by Löwith, is not the only available framing of the transition from Judeo-Christian to modern historical imagination; it sits alongside and competes against numerous others, including the counter-thesis proposed by Hans Blumenberg. Yet if Blumenberg's interpretation of the lineage of the modern idea of progress represents the main alternative, the way in which Wilson derived this idea affirms Löwith's point of view and invalidates much of what Blumenberg had to say.

The Löwith-Blumenberg debate about the foundations of modern historical consciousness in many ways boiled down to the question of whether biblical eschatology and the modern philosophy of progress shared any substance of ideas; demonstrating a common ideational gene was crucial for describing their relationship along the lines proposed by Löwith, as a genealogy. Blumenberg denied any overlap, alleging instead that profound differences set eschatology and progressivism far apart: whereas believers in progress imagine the end of history as nascent within the world and go about excavating it with boundless optimism, believers in God's providence imagine salvation as an otherworldly event and merely await it with passive humility and fear. Wilson's conception of history, however, flies in the face of this argument. His Protestant exegesis of the biblical myth of salvation led him to envision and engage with history in terms exactly opposite those predicted by Blumenberg: the *eschaton* was for Wilson a decidedly real and this-worldly occurrence, and he strove to accelerate its onset through domestic and foreign policies inspired by genuine faith. Far from letting his religion stupefy him with fear of the impending Last Judgment, Wilson clung to it as his best assurance that historical progress was inevitable, fuelling his expectant activism and progressive political reforms. To this extent Wilson's historical consciousness represents an outstanding example of Löwith's secularization thesis.

Despite the close fit between Wilson's liberal internationalist idea of progress and secularization as a tool for understanding its origins and structure, however, historians such as Michael Burleigh, Emilio Gentile, Roger Griffin, and others who use secularization theory today have failed to pay any attention to Wilson. This brings up a second implication of Wilsonianism as secularized eschatology for intellectual history: in aiming secularization theory exclusively at illiberal and totalitarian movements, students of early twentieth-century Western political ideologies have gone astray. Their fixation on totalitarianism is not wholly unwarranted: it follows precedents established by, among others, Waldemar Gurian, Raymond Aron, and Carl Friedrich, conservative Cold War thinkers who regarded totalitarianism and secular religion as parallel concepts. Yet to conduct a critical survey of the original secularization literature and the Löwith-Blumenberg debate is to discover two things: that secularization theory encompasses the modern idea of progress in general, meaning that as a criterion for case study selection totalitarianism is arbitrary; and that nonreligious and antireligious progressivisms, while still within the orbit of secularization theory, are not as ideally suited for secularization analysis as religious progressivisms. In this vein, the next wave of secularization analysis should redirect attention to those visions of progress and utopia that were both liberal and self-professedly Christian. Wilson's liberal-republican millennialism constitutes an especially fruitful terrain for investigation and an ideal departure point for this research effort.

This recommendation becomes amplified the moment one recalls the underlying purpose of secularization theory: to flesh out the ideational sources of regime appeal. Notions such as *"ersatz* religion," "secular religion," "political religion," and "palingenesis" have been introduced by their authors primarily to illuminate the ways in which German Nazism, Soviet Bolshevism, and Italian Fascism garnered legitimacy for their policies of exclusion, genocide, and war in the first half of the twentieth century. Much of the secularization historiography of totalitarianism first posits that these regimes enjoyed more popular support than has been generally recognized, and this support is then explained with reference to the crisis of traditional religion induced by modern scientific knowledge, triggering an intense search for new utopias capable of reendowing everyday existence with deeper meaning.[20] In the final analysis, the true

---

[20] See, e.g., Emilio Gentile, "The Sacralization of Politics: Definitions, Interpretations and Reflections on the Question of Secular Religion and Totalitarianism," trans. Robert Mallett, *Totalitarian Movements and Political Religions* [henceforth *TMPR*] 1, no. 1 (2000): 30–31; and Roger Griffin, "The Palingenetic Political Community: Rethinking the Legitimation of Totalitarian Regimes in Inter-War Europe," *TMPR* 3, no. 3 (2002): 24–43.

origins of the ideological mass appeal of the Third Reich or the Third International thus lie in unexpended religious faith, which the Nazis and Bolsheviks successfully harnessed for their own ends. Such is the core dynamic driving the totalitarian "psychology of justification."[21]

However, if the motivating purpose of secularization theory is to illuminate this "psychology of justification," which simultaneously facilitated social unity and sanctioned political violence, exclusion, and war in the West between 1914 and 1945, a case can be made that early twentieth-century American liberal internationalism, and Wilson as its finest representative, constitutes a far more interesting subject for analysis than its illiberal and totalitarian counterparts. The real litmus test of the value of secularization as a tool of historical understanding is not totalitarian and authoritarian regimes, but the liberal ones—precisely because here the masses followed their leaders with the least amount of overt coercion. It was in liberal societies such as the United States where social cohesion and consent to violence and sacrifice were most spontaneous. In the case of totalitarian dictatorships such as Hitler's Germany and Lenin's and Stalin's Soviet Union, terror-backed compulsion is bound to remain part of the equation, and the key one at that. Explaining mass support for these regimes with reference to unexpended faith and thirst for greater purpose is much less necessary because there already exists a powerful alternative explanation: fear of persecution should one prove indifferent or, God forbid, openly opposed to the official ideology.

Secularization analysis of Wilson's liberal ideology of domestic and international progress reveals that it was driven by the same psychological dynamic as formed the core of totalitarian regimes. Wilson recognized the threat of nihilism and social fragmentation posed by the growth of modern science and industry, and he openly acknowledged the signal role of eschatological rhetoric in achieving social unity and mass support in the context of a liberal democratic polity. "Oratory [is] essential in a country governed by public opinion," he concluded very early on in his intellectual development, adding that in order to be effective this oratory had to induce "*moral elevation* in its subjects . . . [and be] directly aimed at something . . . *definite*. To inspire, its noise must be the noise of *battle*."[22]

---

[21] Hans Maier, " 'Totalitarismus' und 'politische Religionen': Konzepte des Diktaturvergleichs," *Vierteljahrshefte für Zeitgeschichte* 43, no. 3 (1995): 405.

[22] Editorial note on Wilson's "Government by Debate" (September 23, 1882), in *The Papers of Woodrow Wilson*, ed. Arthur S. Link et al. (Princeton, N.J.: Princeton University Press, 1966–1994) [henceforth *PWW*], 2:155; emphasis original.

The need for strong executive leadership fortified by charismatic eschatological language and a promise of future perfection became especially
urgent during the two principal upheavals he witnessed in his adult life:
the national crisis between American workers and industrialists in the
1890s and the international crisis of 1914–1918. Wilson regarded both
as manifestations of the same root cause: the decline of Christianity in
the modern era, engendering moral disorientation and disappearance of
love as a principle of social and political cooperation. His proposed rem-
edy, politics as a form of religious awakening, reflected this diagnosis.
Whether appealing to warring American citizens or European nations,
Wilson sought peace by moralizing them: exhorting them to adopt his
eschatological vision, unite behind his agenda of redemptive transformation, and accept any sacrifices demanded by this agenda.[23] On both
the domestic and international level, cooperation, cohesion, and progress
from anarchy to order depended on revitalizing the spirit of Christ and
the promise of the future Millennium.

In this vein, Wilson's liberal ideology sought to garner popular support
by performing the same sort of religious function as its illiberal counterparts did elsewhere in the post-Christian West according to contemporary
secularization historiography. His Protestant narrative of orderly progress
appeared too in the context of deep spiritual disenchantment, reflected the
widespread longing for the meaning of history, and proposed to reverse
the debilitating moral, social, and political consequences of modern science and industry with an eschatological vision of utopia.

Implications for International Relations

The implications generated by the recovery of the eschatological facet
of Wilson's liberal internationalism are no less significant for the study
of international affairs. First of all, this recovery negates any and all portrayals of Wilson's international thought in universal terms: as a set of
principles divorced from a unique standpoint in time and place and free
of any cultural biases weighing it down and limiting its applicability.
From the perspective of secularization theory, Wilson's ideology reflects
its sociohistorical context, especially the narrow patriotic religious myths
animating late nineteenth-century American societal culture. The origins

---

[23] For an illustrative example of Wilson's use of the Bible to chastise both American
labor unions and big business in order to ease tensions between them, see his "Baccalaureate Address" (June 13, 1909), *PWW* 19:242–51.

of the idea of progress at the heart of Wilson's statecraft cannot be understood without reference to American Protestantism; if Löwith's thesis is valid, it would have been impossible for the president to conceive of progress at all without a number of biblical presuppositions about the nature of the historical process. To this extent eschatological religion represents an irreducible element of Wilson's international thought.

A second and related implication concerns any and all representations of Wilsonian liberal utopianism as a reason-based approach to foreign policy and international relations, one associated with "scientific humanism," characterized by "pervasive rationalism," and stressing "rational international organization."[24] These representations are misleading. Secularization analysis reveals that Wilson's international thought contained a strong nonrational component. Reason and knowledge had no value for him unless they were situated within and illuminated by religious faith. To claim that Kantian philosophy and late eighteenth-century Enlightenment thought about human perfectibility are the "most obvious origins [of liberal utopianism] as a perspective on international politics"[25] is therefore inaccurate. Since the notion of human perfectibility derives from the Judeo-Christian notion of salvation and merely "rebuilds the Heavenly City of Augustinian eschatology with updated materials," to paraphrase Carl Becker's version of secularization theory, the real origins of Wilson's liberal utopianism are not modern and rational but premodern and religious: located in the Bible.

Insofar as one of the main culprits responsible for the forgetting of the eschatological dimension of liberal internationalism is disciplinary specialization, the recovery of this dimension undermines the status of IR as an independent field of scholarly activity—a third implication worth highlighting. Division of intellectual labor certainly has an important virtue: it allows one to isolate discrete subjects and study each in autonomy from the others on the basis of the *ceteris paribus* assumption. Yet this virtue is simultaneously a vice: in the process of carving up the totality of sociohistorical reality into smaller, more manageable pieces, complex phenomena

---

[24] These characterizations come from, respectively, Samuel Barkin, "Realist Constructivism," in *Perspectives on World Politics*, ed. Richard Little and Michael Smith, 3rd ed. (New York: Routledge, 2006), 417–18; Ian Clark, "World Order Reform and Utopian Thought: A Contemporary Watershed?" *Review of Politics* 41, no. 1 (1979): 100; and Robert Jackson and Georg Sørensen, *Introduction to International Relations: Theories and Approaches*, 2nd ed. (Oxford: Oxford University Press, 2003), 38.

[25] Kimberly Hutchings, *International Political Theory: Rethinking Ethics in a Global Era* (London: SAGE, 1999), 7.

become disaggregated and invisible. In its specialist IR definition, liberal internationalism thus represents only a barely recognizable fragment of what it encompassed in Wilson's mind; the rest has been amputated. Salvaging and reviving the original meaning in its entirety require adopting a holistic perspective spanning IR, intellectual history, American history, religious studies, and so on. After all, Wilson's idea of international progress was merely the outermost extension of his idea of domestic progress, which in turn was an extension of still more fundamental ideas about the eschatological shape of secular history and America's exceptional role in it—ideas inherited from a venerable tradition of patriotic Protestant exegesis established by New England Puritans in the sixteenth century and perpetuated by John L. O'Sullivan and other proponents of America's "manifest destiny" in the nineteenth century. IR specialists not familiar with this exegetical tradition will have difficulty grasping the full significance of Wilson's diplomatic addresses and proclamations.

The final implication may be the weightiest and most revealing of them all: the myth of history as eschatology and of America's providentially mandated vanguard role in it endowed Wilson's liberal internationalism with decidedly illiberal and totalizing tendencies and attitudes. Because the current IR framing of American liberal internationalism does not incorporate eschatology and patriotic millennialism, it cannot address these tendencies and attitudes: it effectively hides them from view and critical scrutiny. Insofar as this amounts to facilitating and normalizing them, IR, in defining liberal internationalism the way it does, may be regarded as serving the needs of American power in world affairs: as a discourse rationalizing this power. Even though "scholars do not like to think about their intellectual dependence on the status of their country, and on the ambitions of its political elite . . . the link exists."[26] National purposes and interests seep into their analysis and shape it accordingly.[27] The current (mis)conception of liberal internationalism illustrates this dynamic well: stripped of its cultural presuppositions, Wilson's approach appears as a cluster of noble principles such as national self-determination, disarmament, multilateralism, collective diplomacy, and international law.[28]

---

[26] Stanley Hoffmann, "An American Social Science: International Relations," *Daedalus* 106, no. 3 (1977): 49.

[27] Cf. E. H. Carr's discussion of the relationship between purpose and analysis in political science in *The Twenty Years' Crisis*, 2–5.

[28] See, e.g., the essays by Thomas J. Knock and Anne-Marie Slaughter in *The Crisis of American Foreign Policy: Wilsonianism in the Twenty-First Century*, by G. John

Yet to bring Wilson's patriotic eschatology back into the picture is to expose the dark underbelly of his diplomatic thought: his belief that Americans, and he as their leader, possessed unique knowledge or *gnosis* of the meaning of history fueled militarism, imperialism, unilateral interventionism, and condescending attitudes toward existing rules and norms of international relations. His liberal internationalist "New Diplomacy" was neither liberal, internationalist, nor new. As a secularized outgrowth of American Protestant millennialism, it was highly provincial, unable to cope with the diversity and plurality of the world beyond America's borders, and intent on homogenizing this world by converting it to American principles in a *de facto* bid to extend the nation's empire beyond its confines in Central and South America. In this sense, Wilson's liberal internationalism represented a traditional approach to statecraft, one anchored in the pursuit of power and control over other nations.

Wilson's militarism surfaced on several different occasions and did not escape the attention of his critics at the time, such as the socialist leader Eugene Debs or the American Union against Militarism. Although the president maintained neutrality during the initial years of World War I and, responding to pacifist and isolationist sentiments among the electorate, based his 1916 reelection campaign on the pledge to keep the United States out of the fight, he swiftly reversed his position soon thereafter: with the second presidential term safe in his pocket, he set about convincing the American public to support the war cause. His desire to intervene in Europe followed his earlier military expeditions such as the brazen Mexican intervention and was part of a well-established pattern in his foreign policy: "Wilson was arguably the first president to use military force systematically to bring about certain kinds of political results."[29] Readying his country for World War I, the self-declared prophet of peace, justice, and liberty sitting in the White House thus initiated a massive arms buildup and simultaneously signed laws such as the Espionage Act

---

Ikenberry et al. (Oxford: Princeton University Press, 2008), 25–52, 89–117, which define Wilsonianism primarily with reference to multilateralism, common counsel, and self-determination; or Michael Mandelbaum, *The Ideas That Conquered the World: Peace, Democracy, and Free Markets in the Twenty-First Century* (New York: Public Affairs, 2002), 17–39, which postulates a "Wilsonian Triad" of principles including popular government and restraints on armaments.

[29] Thomas J. Knock, " 'Playing for a Hundred Years Hence': Woodrow Wilson's Internationalism and His Would-Be Heirs," in *Crisis of American Foreign Policy*, by Ikenberry et al., 31.

(1917) and the Sedition Act (1918), which were used to suppress dissent and put antiwar activists such as Debs in prison.

That these practices sat ill at ease with his noble rhetoric escaped Wilson: from his patriotic eschatological perspective, neither the arms program nor the curbing of civil liberties was in any way incongruous with his principled vision. On the contrary, the policies emanated from this vision: America's "manifest destiny" to redeem humanity to liberty and democracy warranted, indeed dictated, entering the war and adopting whatever measures necessary to wage the fight successfully—whether this meant building arms or silencing antiwar elements. Wilson held that the intervention stemmed from the logic of the national past, was predetermined by God, and that he had very little to do with it; the carnage and sacrifices were a matter of historical inevitability. "The armies of the United States," he stated, were "crusaders . . . [for] the spiritual purpose of redemption."[30] They shed "sacred blood."[31] Considering that what was being decided on the battlefields of Europe was the final outcome of the entire drama of human history, keeping out of the fight was not an option.

Moreover, once in the fight, failure was not an option. The eschatological presuppositions of liberal internationalism fuelled not only the desire to war, but also the determination to use any means necessary to attain victory. To achieve God's cause, in principle anything was permitted—even if it transgressed accepted norms of combat. Much as other (illiberal) political religions, American liberal internationalism, by virtue of its salvationist aspirations, encouraged total warfare. Manichean depictions of the European crisis such as the one provided by George D. Herron, who narrated the Great War as an apocalyptic all-or-nothing crusade of American "Saints" against Satanic Prussians, dehumanized the enemies and made their destruction psychologically bearable and morally just. To perform this destruction efficiently and achieve the Millennium of liberty and peace in the least amount of time, modern science and technology were brought onto the battlefield.[32] As in times of peace, so in

---

[30] Wilson, "Address in the San Diego Stadium" (September 19, 1919), *PWW* 63:382.

[31] "Press Release" (May 10, 1920), *PWW* 65:264.

[32] Cf. Omer Bartov's thesis concerning World War I that "the ideology of progress . . . was a recipe for destruction, violence, loss, and pain." "Progress and Catastrophe," *Tikkun* 14, no. 6 (1999): 42. For the origins and development of mechanized warfare in the context of modern science and technology, see Daniel Pick, *War Machine: The Rationalization of Slaughter in the Modern Age* (London: Yale University Press, 1993), although the study largely neglects the ideational facet of the process.

times of war, too, Americans employed industry to increase the glory of God, giving rise to mechanized killing. In this the Great War resembled the American Civil War.

Militarism was not the only unsavory foreign policy effect flowing from the eschatological presuppositions of liberal internationalism, such as the myth of America's divine status as the redeemer nation. Another was a strong appetite for unilateral interventionism tending toward imperialism. Wilson's efforts to promote Mexican democracy by deposing the dictator Victoriano Huerta represent a prime example. They culminated on April 21, 1914, when Wilson dispatched American marines to seize and occupy the port of Veracruz.[33] Insofar as the immediate purpose of the deployment was to prevent a German ship from delivering weapons to Huerta's arsenal, it may seem that Wilson acted in the spirit of the Monroe Doctrine and that the operation actually expressed an anti-imperialist and anti-interventionist sentiment: a desire to block any European interference in the affairs of sovereign countries lying in the Western Hemisphere. However, this interpretation overlooks the concealed function of the Monroe Doctrine, which it possessed by virtue of being steeped in the dogma of America's "manifest destiny." Although ostensibly formulated to guarantee Central and South America unimpeded political development, the Doctrine effectively served the purpose of American expansionism: "[The] very conception of the United States as a protector . . . was to encourage actual intervention in Latin America."[34] Wilson's real motivation for intervening in Mexico was emblematic of this function. It had nothing to do with safeguarding the country's independence. Rather, as he infamously stated, he intended to "teach the South American Republics to elect good men."[35]

The readiness with which Wilson sent troops to Mexico—or, for that matter, seized the Dominican Republic or applauded President McKinley for taking the Philippines and Puerto Rico—hints at a third consequence of the eschatological or "destinarian" dimension of American liberal internationalism: a distinctly reticent, often openly dismissive posture toward international norms and conventions, including the time-honored

---

[33] The classic study of the incident remains Robert E. Quirk, *An Affair of Honor: Woodrow Wilson and the Occupation of Veracruz* (Lexington: University of Kentucky Press, 1962).

[34] Albert K. Weinberg, *Manifest Destiny: A Study of Nationalist Expansionism in American History* (Baltimore, Md.: Johns Hopkins Press, 1935), 417.

[35] Quoted in Burton J. Hendrick, *The Life and Letters of Walter Hines Page*, 3 vols. (Garden City, N.Y.: Doubleday Page, 1924–1926), 1:204.

principle of sovereignty. This posture was articulated already by the original author of the doctrine of "manifest destiny," John L. O'Sullivan, who had explicitly rejected all legal obstacles to America's annexations of Texas and Oregon as irrelevant on the simple grounds that international law was no match against the will of the Lord of history. Wilson's convictions about the providential logic of history matched O'Sullivan's: after Americans had completed their expansion to the Pacific coast by 1890, God bade them to extend their sacred principles abroad. Like O'Sullivan and other American liberal-republican millennialists, Wilson thus respected international rules such as Mexico's political autonomy and territorial integrity only to the extent that they did not hinder America's "manifest destiny." Owing to his patriotic eschatological consciousness, his ultimate loyalty was to standards that were not of this world.

Some have suggested that the Mexican intervention, which cost American lives but failed to produce any meaningful results and ended in an embarrassing stalemate, taught Wilson a hard lesson and discouraged him from engaging in unilateralism and democratization by force ever again, including during his World War I diplomacy, which represents the core of his liberal internationalist statecraft.[36] However, Wilson's deep-seated eschatological beliefs about historical progress and America's sacred destiny to act as its engine continued to generate unilateralist urges, totalizing tendencies, and other illiberal effects even during his subsequent European intervention and the quest for the League of Nations, normally defined in terms of multilateralism, legalism, collective diplomacy, and national self-determination. In 1917, for example, as Wilson was preparing for war and making repeated proclamations that the United States stood for the interests of all neutral nations, Max Eastman, editor of the magazine *The Masses*, observed that the president did not even bother to consult the foreign governments on whose behalf he alleged to be speaking, let alone obtain their permission to represent them.[37] Wilson's persisting unilateralism is even more evident from the

---

[36] For the claim about the sobering effect of the Mexican misadventure, see Lloyd C. Gardner, "Woodrow Wilson and the Mexican Revolution," in *Woodrow Wilson and a Revolutionary World, 1913–1921*, ed. Arthur S. Link (Chapel Hill: University of North Carolina Press, 1982), 3–48, and Knock, "Wilson's Internationalism," in *Crisis of American Foreign Policy*, by Ikenberry et al., 32.

[37] "Address to the President by Max Eastman" (February 28, 1917), *PWW* 41:306. Thanks to this and other similar comments, Eastman became the target of relentless harassment: Wilson's postmaster general promptly denied *The Masses* mailing rights, causing the magazine to shut down, and Eastman was tried twice under the Sedition Act.

official status under which he committed the United States to the European crisis: as an Associate (not Allied) Power. This status reflected his view, ubiquitous throughout American liberal-republican millennialism, that the United States was morally superior not just to Satanic Prussia, as a matter of course, but to the entire Old World of Europe, including the Allies. In this context, the Associate designation would enable America to get involved on the side of the French and British while remaining apart from them: unique and unconstrained. "[America] would participate in the wicked world and yet keep its hands pure."[38]

At Versailles, the noxious effects of Wilson's patriotic millennialism surfaced in full, resulting in glaring incongruities between his universalistic rhetoric and parochial practice. Already his negotiating style was indicative. Despite calling in the first of his Fourteen Points for "open covenants of peace, openly arrived at, after which there shall be no private international understandings of any kind,"[39] in Paris Wilson personified the spirit of secret diplomacy. The press corps covering the Peace Conference was so appalled by the lack of transparency that American journalists charged Wilson with hypocrisy and threatened to quit their assignments and leave town.[40] Their frustration was justified; Wilson's participation at the Peace Conference amounted to an almost uninterrupted series of closed-door sessions within restricted clubs such as the Council of Four, which usually met in his private study and rarely counted more than five individuals: Wilson, Clemenceau, Lloyd George, Orlando, and an interpreter. This approach reflected Wilson's tacit assumption that "great powers alone should draft the League Covenant, and only then give the small states the opportunity to review it,"[41] and moreover that among the great powers, the United States was the *primus inter pares*. Accordingly, Wilson monopolized the drafting process and relinquished a small degree of control only to his closest

---

[38] Jan Willem Schulte Nordholt, *Woodrow Wilson: A Life for World Peace*, trans. Herbert H. Rowen (Berkeley: University of California Press, 1991), 172. In the same vein, Lloyd E. Ambrosius has commented that "Wilson's liberal internationalism incorporated the traditional American desire for isolation from Europe." *Wilsonian Statecraft: Theory and Practice of Liberal Internationalism during World War I* (Wilmington, Del.: SR Books, 1991), 98.

[39] Wilson, "Address to a Joint Session of Congress" (January 8, 1918), *PWW* 45:536.

[40] Margaret MacMillan, *Peacemakers: The Paris Conference of 1919 and Its Attempt to End War* (London: John Murray, 2001), 65–66.

[41] Lloyd E. Ambrosius, *Woodrow Wilson and the American Diplomatic Tradition: The Treaty Fight in Perspective* (Cambridge: Cambridge University Press, 1987), 66.

ally: Great Britain. His diplomacy was thus not only secretive, but also highly authoritarian and exclusionary: " 'Multilateralism' was . . . a code word for American hegemony."[42] Guided by his eschatological histori-cal consciousness and staunch belief in America's divine purpose and moral preeminence, Wilson naturally reserved the task of crafting the new democratic world order for himself and the United States.

If Wilson's patriotic eschatology and domineering statesmanship flowing from it raised eyebrows within the Council of Four, made up of Western imperial powers, the shock was far worse among the publics at large, especially those in the non-Western colonial world. It was here that the ostensibly universal principles of liberal internationalism engen-dered the greatest expectations, its narrow cultural presuppositions sur-faced most acutely, and the resulting gap between rhetoric and practice opened to its maximum width. Wilson's exaltation of liberty and national self-determination excited high hopes in oppressed peoples everywhere, but as codified by the League Covenant self-determination had limited applicability conditional on standards of civilization. Article 22 alleged that many of the recently freed nations in Africa and elsewhere were "not yet able to stand by themselves," stated that "the well-being and devel-opment of such peoples form a sacred trust of civilization," and went on to place them under the mandate of "advanced nations who by reason of their resources, their experience or their geographical position can best undertake this [sacred trust]." From the vantage point of Wilson's patri-otic eschatology, this provision encapsulated a marvelous act of Christian charity: providentially chosen to guide the world toward God and lib-erty, the United States—working through the proxy of the League and its civilized members, such as the British Empire—was going to expand its sacred ministry from Central and Latin America to new nations. After all, their leaders were eager for enlightenment and, as Wilson liked to recall the Peace Conference, practically begged him for guidance.

From the colonial vantage point, however, this was nothing but a self-serving fairy tale: in what amounted to a transfer of colonial posses-sions from the vanquished powers to the victors of World War I, one for-eign administration simply replaced another.[43] In Africa and the Pacific,

---

[42] Tony Smith, "Wilsonianism after Iraq: The End of Liberal Internationalism?" in *Crisis of American Foreign Policy*, by Ikenberry et al., 63.

[43] This transfer was especially swift in the case of Africa: at Versailles "the issue of Africa's right to control its own affairs was not even broached." William R. Keylor, ed., *The Legacy of the Great War: Peacemaking, 1919* (Boston: Houghton Mifflin, 1998), 14.

the League mandate system was nothing but an old-fashioned land grab under a more innocuous, benevolent-sounding name.[44] The mandates "served only . . . as a fig leaf for the desire of the great powers . . . to annex territories formerly owned by the defeated powers."[45] Wilson's rhetoric of liberty worked only as an ideological cover. In its thin guise, the totalizing and homogenizing consequences springing from the patriotic religious underbelly of his "New Diplomacy" preserved and indeed intensified colonialism, imperialism, and war as hallmark features of the old international order. It is therefore quite appropriate to refer to the Versailles Treaty using terms such as "imperialism in new clothes" or "a peace to end all peace."[46] Touted as inaugurating a new world order of peace based on justice, freedom, and equality among self-determined nations, the Treaty ended up becoming yet another chapter in the long history of hate, oppression, and plunder in world affairs.

This bleak outcome, so much at odds with the radiant proclamations surrounding it, turned off even someone as ardently supportive of Wilson's program as his fellow patriotic millennialist George D. Herron, who reacted to the results of the Peace Conference with unbridled fury and broke all contacts with the president.[47] The question of whether Wilson personally deserved this fury is, of course, apt: the extent of his personal responsibility for the practical achievements of the Peace Conference is debatable. One might even attempt to exonerate him by suggesting that his ideals were compromised by Old World statesmen, whose shrewd *Realpolitik* the American president was ill-equipped to prevent, control, or even so much as understand. In other words, Wilson might have been an "ingenious visionary hoodwinked by the wily Welsh wizard Lloyd

---

[44] MacMillan, *Peacemakers*, 115–16.

[45] Alan Sharp, *The Versailles Settlement: Peacemaking in Paris, 1919* (New York: St. Martin's, 1991), 169.

[46] Brian K. Digre, *Imperialism's New Clothes: The Reparation of Tropical Africa, 1914–1919* (New York: P. Lang, 1990); David Fromkin, *A Peace to End All Peace: The Fall of the Ottoman Empire and the Creation of the Modern Middle East, 1914–1922* (New York: Avon, 1990).

[47] Herron denounced the Versailles Treaty as a parody of the Millennium that Wilson initially seemed to herald. Calling the Treaty "greedy and savage and lawless," Herron declared that "These are not peace,—these treaties of Paris: they are rather a pitiless provision for a military and predatory government of the world. They are pregnant with wars more destructive . . . than history has yet registered." *The Defeat in the Victory* (London: C. Palmer, 1921), 3–4. According to Mitchell Pirie Briggs, "no one condemned more unsparingly the Treaty that finally came out of Paris [than Herron]." *George D. Herron and the European Settlement* (Stanford: Stanford University Press, 1932), 163.

George and browbeaten by the tough old tiger Clemenceau."[48] On this reading, the illiberal and totalizing aspects of the liberal internationalist project flowed not so much from Wilson's cultural presuppositions as from the cunning of Allied European leaders, who gutted the Treaty of Versailles and politicized it into an instrument of exclusion and imperialism all on their own.

This interpretation has some merit but eventually does not withstand critical scrutiny. On the one hand, Wilson did, for example, express serious antiannexationist sentiments when dealing with the issue of how to dispose of the former German and Ottoman colonies in Africa, Asia, and the Middle East. Instead of a traditional colonial readjustment based on the principle of victors collecting the spoils of war, he sought a system of impartial League trusteeship; anything less would discredit the League from the beginning.[49] In addition, when the mandates were being distributed among the Allies, Wilson claimed none for the United States. Yet on the other hand, he ultimately expressed satisfaction with the results of the Peace Conference. When the dismayed Herron asked him to evaluate the final settlement, the president responded clearly: "I am sorry that you are so deeply discouraged. . . . I think that on the whole we have been able to keep tolerably close to the lines laid down at the outset."[50] What reveals Wilson's very own illiberal leanings even more explicitly is the negative attitude with which he confronted the issue of rights and liberties of Native Americans, the colored community, and other disenfranchised groups within the United States—groups that glimpsed in his international program a potential pathway toward domestic reform. Prominent black leaders such as W. E. B. DuBois reminded Wilson repeatedly that his agenda of world democracy had not yet been accomplished at home, asking him to institute racial desegregation, universal suffrage, and equal rights; without these steps a large portion Americans had no stake in government, meaning that Wilson, the high priest of self-determination on

---

[48] Keylor, ed., *Legacy of Great War*, 3. This characterization of Wilson stands at the heart of both John Maynard Keynes' and Ray Stannard Baker's accounts of the Peace Conference, the only difference being that Keynes regarded Wilson as hopelessly naïve whereas Baker, a friend of the president, considered his liberal internationalist proposals essentially sound. See Keynes, *The Economic Consequences of the Peace* (New York: Harcourt, Brace & Howe, 1920); and Baker, *Woodrow Wilson and World Settlement*, 3 vols. (Garden City, N.Y.: Doubleday, 1922).

[49] Ambrosius, *Wilson and American Diplomatic Tradition*, 68; Sharp, *Versailles Settlement*, 169–70; MacMillan, *Peacemakers*, 107.

[50] Wilson to Herron (April 28, 1919), *PWW* 58:204–5.

the international stage, did not observe it in his own country.[51] Yet Wilson systematically ignored such calls and indeed expanded racial segregation to new areas, notably federal employment. His condoning of the colonial land grab orchestrated at Versailles, if not necessarily prompted by his domestic racial attitudes, was certainly not inconsistent with them. When shortly after the Armistice DuBois urged him to endorse self-determination in Africa and meet with black leaders to discuss the subject, Wilson did not even bother to respond.[52]

Therefore, Wilson was not simply "hoodwinked" or "browbeaten" into imperialism and other illiberal and totalizing tendencies by his European peers. Rather, these tendencies emanated directly from the cultural biases and prejudices underneath his liberal internationalist program and its core ideal: "the principle of justice to all peoples and nationalities, and their right to live on equal terms of liberty and safety with one another, whether they be strong or weak."[53] His selective and paternalistic understanding and application of this principle reflected his eschatological presupposition that white Protestant Americans of European ancestry, and he as their leader, possessed special knowledge of the providential path of liberty in the world. As such, the illiberal effects flowing from this presupposition fall within the scope of Wilson's responsibility.

Since this presupposition was far from unique to him, however, it simultaneously exonerates him. Already the first New England Puritans considered themselves divinely enlightened "Saints" building a model Christian community for the purpose of guiding humanity toward redemption, and already in their case the project entailed totalizing, repressive, and exclusionary practices. Wilson merely inherited and further perpetuated this self-comprehension and its implications. Neither he nor the Puritans paid any heed to what St. Augustine regarded as a matter of cardinal importance: that perfection is not to be expected in this *sæculum*, that history cannot be foreclosed through human efforts alone, and

---

[51] See, e.g., "Memorial to the President" (April 20, 1917), *PWW* 42:113–15; and DuBois to Wilson (October 10, 1916), *PWW* 42:459–60, in which DuBois, writing on behalf of the National Association for the Advancement of Colored People (NAACP), stated frankly that "A republic must be based upon universal suffrage or it is not a republic."

[52] Keylor, ed., *Legacy of Great War*, 14; MacMillan, *Peacemakers*, 113–14. For DuBois' "Memoranda on the Future of Africa," see DuBois to Joseph P. Tumulty (Nov. 27, 1918), *PWW* 53:236–38.

[53] Wilson, "Address to a Joint Session of Congress" (January 8, 1918), *PWW* 45:539.

that any ideologies claiming otherwise merely express the human desire to dominate others.

Final Thoughts
Wilson, Secularization Theory, and Contemporary U.S. Foreign Policy

The contemporary significance of revising the definition of Wilson's liberal internationalism to account for his neglected eschatological inspirations and their illiberal manifestations stems from the recognition that his political principles have survived the twentieth century largely intact and remained in force down to the present day. This is true not only on the domestic level, where his legacy includes such key and commonly accepted government institutions as the Federal Reserve System, established by Wilson to curb the pernicious effects of freewheeling market capitalism on the fabric of American society—a mandate made especially urgent by the recent financial crisis. Wilson's impact has been even more pronounced in American foreign relations.

This impact could not always manifest itself fully: the Cold War put dampers on the universal aspirations of American liberal internationalism by pitting the country against a rival superpower pursuing its own competing vision of world utopia. As the philosophical basis for America's engagement with the Soviet adversary, Wilsonian universalism consequently yielded to realist particularism: the idea that the United States should acknowledge international diversity, tolerate a plural world order composed of multiple independent military-industrial centers (America being one of them), and let them balance each other. In this perspective, propounded especially by George F. Kennan, the key to protecting American national interests lay not in trying to transform and homogenize the international order according to America's democratic image, but in allowing the independent power centers to combine and recombine at will, thereby preventing any one of them from achieving hegemony and empire over the others.[54] With respect to the Soviet Union, as Kennan famously recommended, "the main element of any United States policy . . . must be that of a long-term, patient but firm and vigilant containment

---

[54] John Lewis Gaddis, *Strategies of Containment: A Critical Appraisal of American National Security Policy during the Cold War*, rev. ed. (Oxford: Oxford University Press, 2005), 28.

of Russian expansive tendencies."[55] Attempting to convert the Soviet Union or any country in its sphere of influence to democracy was too risky: it could escalate the Cold War to a nuclear confrontation.

Yet not even Kennan, in the very document prescribing containment as the foundation for America's Cold War statecraft, avoided making distinctly eschatological and "destinarian" pronouncements about the country's role in the world. In the final analysis, he proclaimed, "Kremlin's challenge to American society" was "no cause for complaint," but rather a reason to "experience certain gratitude to Providence which, by providing the American people with this implacable challenge, has made their entire security as a nation dependent on their pulling themselves together and accepting the responsibilities of moral and political leadership that history plainly intended them to bear."[56] As devout and patriotic a Presbyterian as Wilson, even if, unlike the president, resolutely skeptical about the possibility of any lasting human progress, Kennan had no doubts that the United States was an exceptional country predestined to serve as a model for others to follow.[57] In due course, the superiority of American democracy to the Soviet project would be confirmed, and the United States would emerge from the Cold War victorious. Americans merely had to remain true to their core national principles such as liberty and rule of law, avoid succumbing to complacent consumerism, and stay in the fight against the Soviets long enough.

When the Soviet Union and the Eastern Bloc did disintegrate in 1989–1991, Wilsonianism reemerged in full force. The fall of the Berlin Wall set off bold celebrations of liberal principles and market capitalism, and predictions of their impending global expansion abounded: "When the Wall came down, the future seemed to stretch out before us like a broad highway leading to a modern world united by commerce, the free exchange of ideas, and the proliferation of liberal government. This was to be the age of globalization . . . conceived as the spread of Western values and institutions to the rest of the world."[58] This vision

[55] George F. Kennan [X, pseud.], "The Sources of Soviet Conduct," *Foreign Affairs* 25, no. 4 (1947): 575.

[56] Kennan, "Sources of Soviet Conduct," 582.

[57] For Kennan's religious views including his tendency to regard reality as fundamentally evil, a belief heavily influenced by his experience of Russian Orthodox Christianity, see John Lewis Gaddis, *George F. Kennan: An American Life* (New York: Penguin, 2011), 440.

[58] Michael Allen Gillespie, *The Theological Origins of Modernity* (Chicago: University of Chicago Press, 2008), ix.

was exemplified by Francis Fukuyama, who famously alleged that the passing of the Cold War marked the endpoint of humankind's ideological progress, with American-style liberal democracy as the final form of government; whatever history remained would merely translate the victory of liberal principles from the realm of consciousness to material reality.[59]

Coming against the backdrop of this triumphalism, the al-Qaeda attacks against the World Trade Center and the Pentagon caused shock and surprise: it suddenly became crystal clear that certain parts of the globe, notably the Islamic world, were far less receptive to American liberal principles than was widely assumed. Clear signs that the end of the Cold War did not, contrary to expectations, initiate a universal turn to liberalism appeared already in the 1990s: in Yugoslavia, the demise of communism led to violent nationalism, ethnic cleansing, and genocide. Tucked away in the Balkans, this particular challenge to the Wilsonian idea of worldwide progress to liberalism could still be ignored, but the challenge issued on September 11, 2001, could not. It took place on American soil and showcased the opposition to American values in an exceptionally graphic way.

This act of open hostility should have been sufficient to induce a thorough reexamination of the foundations of American statecraft, but sadly and distressingly no such self-reflection took place. Instead of pausing to take seriously the complex cultural, political, and economic grievances motivating Islamic terrorism, the American foreign policy community under President George W. Bush and Vice President Richard B. Cheney simply reasserted the fundamental validity of the Wilsonian agenda of spreading liberal democracy and market capitalism around the world. Frequently using the same kind of Manichean-apocalyptic imagery that permeated Wilson's 1876 essay "Christ's Army," the White House repeatedly portrayed the United States as the nation of God engaged in a righteous struggle against the "Axis of Evil": countries populated by fanatics driven to violent extremism by their religious beliefs. The claim that in combating them America is the first empire in history that is benevolent and accidental (in the sense of having its mission providentially dictated rather than self-selected) was propounded especially by neoconservative voices such as Charles Krauthammer, Robert Kagan, and David Frum.[60]

---

[59] See Fukuyama, "The End of History?" *National Interest* 16 (1989): 3–18; and idem, *The End of History and the Last Man* (London: Hamish Hamilton, 1992).

[60] For a highly critical survey of assertions to this effect, see David Ray Griffin et al., *The American Empire and the Commonwealth of God: A Political, Economic, Religious Statement* (Louisville, Ky.: Westminster John Knox, 2006), 3–11.

This "Myth of the Reluctant Superpower"[61] implied that neither the military foray into Afghanistan nor the subsequent invasion of Iraq was an aggressive war of choice, but rather an inevitable act of self-defense.

Nonetheless, a critical reconsideration of the Wilsonian idea of universal progress toward liberty, democracy, and market capitalism is unavoidable. To make sense of Islamic terrorism, it is necessary to stop dismissing its perpetrators as mere zealots and probe the sources of their fanaticism, initiating an inquiry that is bound eventually to become self-reflexive: turn the lens on the mission to spread American-style values and institutions worldwide. "The problem is not merely in our [Americans'] failure to understand these others [the terrorists] but in our failure to understand ourselves. . . . In order to begin to come to terms with the current challenge to modernity [exemplified by the attacks on the World Trade Center], we . . . must return to the question of the origin of the modern project."[62] Secularization theory helps to answer this question. It functions precisely as a tool of critical hermeneutics whose chief purpose is to reveal "that the present is and means far more than it knows of itself."[63]

Applied to Wilsonianism in contemporary American statecraft, secularization analysis reveals that it is far more culturally loaded than its universal self-portrayal lets on: the idea of worldwide progress to liberty carries heavy baggage in the form of patriotic Protestant eschatology. This means, among other things, that the conception of foreign policy as a religious mission is not specific to Islamic governments and militant groups. Narrating the current "war on terror" as a clash of American reason and secular values against Islamic unreason and religious fanaticism misses the point that religious presuppositions do not motivate only the Islamic side. In subtler and less conspicuous forms, they also remain at the heart of America's engagement with the world.

This finding, of course, is no news; already Alexis de Tocqueville had noticed and recorded the powerful nexus between politics and religion in America. Today this nexus is visible especially (but not only) in the close ties of the Republican Party to the Christian fundamentalist movement, whose influential ministers often preach sermons every bit as

---

[61] Andrew J. Bacevich, *American Empire: The Realities and Consequences of U.S. Diplomacy* (Cambridge, Mass.: Harvard University Press, 2002), 7.

[62] Gillespie, *Theological Origins*, x.

[63] Hans-Georg Gadamer, review of *Die Legitimität der Neuzeit*, by Hans Blumenberg, *Philosophische Rundschau* 15 (1968): 201.

fiery as radical Islamic clerics. Therefore, the significance of secularization analysis for contemporary American foreign policy lies not so much in exposing its religious foundations; these are obvious enough. Rather, it lies in serving as a constant reminder that defining the Kingdom of God in terms of a worldly empire perverts the meaning of the biblical story of salvation, turning spiritual eschatology into political narratives legitimating exclusion, oppression, expansionism, and war. It is as idolatrous in the case of contemporary *Pax Americana* as it was in the case of *Pax Romana* in the days of Emperor Constantine the Great and Bishop Eusebius of Cæsarea.

To this extent, as the United States continues to grapple with Islamic radicalism and growing resentment across the globe, including in Europe, the much-needed critical reexamination of American foreign policy should commence with a clear call for dissociating God and the Bible from the nation's global pretensions. This call might take its cue from, for example, the confessional situation created by Karl Barth, Dietrich Bonhoeffer, and Martin Niemöller in Germany in the early 1940s, who similarly denied the divine mandate of the Third Reich—proclaimed by many top Nazis as the "Holy Reich": the spiritual promise of authentic Protestant Christianity come to fruition in secular reality in the form of a thousand-year empire of the German *Volk*.[64] The Bible offers no more evidence that the United States is God's appointed redeemer than that the Lord placed the burden of saving the world from Satan on the shoulders of Hitler's Germany; both claims are equally preposterous. Espousing the eschatology of America's providential mission and the sense of moral preeminence flowing from it precludes recognizing and respecting the fundamental plurality of the world beyond America's borders. Insofar as this eschatology constituted an essential element of Wilson's statecraft and cannot be divorced from it, as a future guide for American foreign policy Wilsonian liberal internationalism is a dead-end street.

---

[64] For the latter point, see Richard Steigmann-Gall, *The Holy Reich: Nazi Conceptions of Christianity, 1919–1945* (Cambridge: Cambridge University Press, 2003).

BIBLIOGRAPHY

Agamben, Giorgio. *The Kingdom and the Glory: For a Theological Genealogy of Economy and Government*. Translated by Lorenzo Chiesa and Matteo Mandarini. Stanford: Stanford University Press, 2011.

Ambrosius, Lloyd E. *Wilsonian Statecraft: Theory and Practice of Liberal Internationalism during World War I*. Wilmington, Del.: SR Books, 1991.

———. *Wilsonianism: Woodrow Wilson and His Legacy in American Foreign Relations*. New York: Palgrave Macmillan, 2002.

———. *Woodrow Wilson and the American Diplomatic Tradition: The Treaty Fight in Perspective*. Cambridge: Cambridge University Press, 1987.

Anderson, Benedict. *Imagined Communities: Reflections on the Origin and Spread of Nationalism*. 2nd ed. London: Verso, 1991.

Andresen, C., ed. *Zum Augustin-Gespräch der Gegenwart*. Vol. 1. Darmstadt: Wissenschaftliche Buchgesellschaft, 1975.

Angell, Norman. *The Great Illusion*. 3rd ed. New York: G. P. Putnam's Sons, 1911.

Annin, Robert Edwards. *Woodrow Wilson: A Character Study*. New York: Dodd, Mead, 1924.

Annual Report of the President of Iowa College, 1898. Grinnell, Iowa, 1898.

Antonio, Robert J. "The Origins, Development, and Contemporary Status of Critical Theory." *The Sociological Quarterly* 24, no. 3 (1983): 325–51.

Applegate, Debby. *The Most Famous Man in America: The Biography of Henry Ward Beecher*. New York: Doubleday, 2006.

Arendt, Hannah. *The Human Condition*. Chicago: University of Chicago Press, 1958.

———. "Ideology and Terror: A Novel Form of Government." *Review of Politics* 15, no. 4 (1953): 303–27.

———. *Men in Dark Times*. New York: Harcourt, Brace & World, 1968.

———. *The Origins of Totalitarianism*. New York: Harcourt, Brace & World, 1966 [1951].

———. *On Revolution.* New York: Viking, 1965.

Aron, Raymond. *Democracy and Totalitarianism*. London: Weidenfeld & Nicolson, 1968.

———. *Une histoire du vingtième siècle*. Edited by Christian Bachelier. N.p.: Plon, 1996.

———. *The Opium of the Intellectuals*. Translated by Terence Kilmartin. Garden City, N.Y.: Doubleday, 1957.

Augustine, Saint. *Concerning the City of God against the Pagans*. Translated by Henry Bettenson. London: Penguin, 2003.

Babík, Milan. "Beyond Totalitarianism: (Re)Introducing Secularization Theory to Liberal Narratives of Progress." *Politics, Religion & Ideology* 13, no. 3 (2012): 289–309.

———. "George D. Herron and the Eschatological Foundations of Woodrow Wilson's Foreign Policy, 1917–1919." *Diplomatic History* 35, no. 5 (2011): 837–57.

———. "Nazism as a Secular Religion," *History and Theory* 45, no. 3 (2006): 375–96.

———. Review of *The Crisis of American Foreign Policy*, by G. John Ikenberry et al. *Millennium: Journal of International Studies* 38, no. 2 (2009): 470–73.

Bacevich, Andrew J. *American Empire: The Realities and Consequences of U.S. Diplomacy*. Cambridge, Mass.: Harvard University Press, 2002.

Bacon, Francis. *The Advancement of Learning*. Oxford: Clarendon, 1974.

Baehr, Peter. *Hannah Arendt, Totalitarianism, and the Social Sciences*. Stanford: Stanford University Press, 2010.

Bailyn, Bernard. *The Ideological Origins of the American Revolution*. Cambridge, Mass.: Harvard University Press, 1967.

Baker, Ray Stannard. *Woodrow Wilson: Life and Letters*. 8 vols. Garden City, N.Y.: Doubleday, Page, 1927–39.

———. *Woodrow Wilson and World Settlement*. 3 vols. Garden City, N.Y.: Doubleday, 1922.

Bärsch, Claus-Ekkehard. *Die politische Religion des Nationalsozialismus: Die religiöse Dimension der NS-Ideologie in den Schriften von Dietrich Eckart, Joseph Goebbels, Alfred Rosenberg und Adolf Hitler*. Munich: Fink, 1998.

Bartov, Omer. "Progress and Catastrophe." *Tikkun* 14, no. 6 (1999): 41–48.

Bateman, Bradley W., and Ethan B. Kapstein. "Between God and the Market: The Religious Roots of the American Economic Association." *Journal of Economic Perspectives* 13, no. 4 (1999): 249–57.

Becker, Carl L. "Everyman His Own Historian." *American Historical Review* 37, no. 2 (1932): 221–36.

———. *The Heavenly City of the Eighteenth-Century Philosophers.* New Haven, Conn.: Yale University Press, 1932.

Beecher, Henry Ward. *The Original Plymouth Pulpit.* Vol. 5. Boston: Pilgrim Press, 1871.

———. *Patriotic Addresses.* Edited by J. R. Howard. New York: Fords, Howard & Hulbert, 1889.

———. *Plymouth Pulpit.* Vol. 9. New York, 1873.

Beecher, Lyman. *A Plea for the West.* 2nd ed. Cincinnati: Truman & Smith, 1835.

Beer, Francis A., and Robert Hariman, eds. *Post-Realism: The Rhetorical Turn in International Relations.* East Lansing: Michigan State University Press, 1997.

Bellah, Robert N. *The Broken Covenant: American Civil Religion in Time of Trial.* 2nd ed. Chicago: University of Chicago Press, 1992.

Benbow, Mark. *Leading Them to the Promised Land: Woodrow Wilson, Covenant Theology, and the Mexican Revolution, 1913–1915.* Kent, Ohio: Kent State University Press, 2010.

———. Review of "George D. Herron and the Eschatological Foundations of Woodrow Wilson's Foreign Policy, 1917–1919," by Milan Babík. *H-Diplo Article Reviews*, no. 342 (2012): 1–4. Available at http://www.h-net .org/~diplo/reviews/PDF/AR342.pdf.

Berdyaev, Nicolas. *The Meaning of History.* Translated by George Reavey. London: Geoffrey Bles, 1936.

———. *The Origin of Russian Communism.* Ann Arbor: University of Michigan Press, 1969 [1937].

Berger, Peter L., and Thomas Luckmann. *The Social Construction of Reality: A Treatise in the Sociology of Knowledge.* Garden City, N.Y.: Doubleday, 1966.

Besançon, Alain. *The Rise of the Gulag: Intellectual Origins of Leninism.* Translated by Sarah Matthews. New York: Continuum, 1977.

Beveridge, Albert J. *The Meaning of the Times and Other Speeches.* Indianapolis: Bobbs-Merrill, 1908.

Bloch, Ruth H. *Visionary Republic: Millennial Themes in American Thought, 1756–1800.* Cambridge: Cambridge University Press, 1985.

Blumenberg, Hans. *The Legitimacy of the Modern Age.* Translated by Robert M. Wallace. Cambridge, Mass.: MIT Press, 1983.

———. *Die Legitimität der Neuzeit.* Frankfurt am Main: Suhrkamp, 1966.

———. "On a Lineage of the Idea of Progress." *Social Research* 41, no. 1 (1974): 5–27.

Bonomi, Patricia U. *Under the Cope of Heaven: Religion, Society, and Politics in Colonial America.* Updated ed. Oxford: Oxford University Press, 2003.

Bonomi, Patricia U., and Peter R. Eisenstadt. "Church Adherence in the Eighteenth-Century British American Colonies." *William and Mary Quarterly* 39, no. 2 (1982): 245–86.

Bormuth, Matthias. "Meaning in History—A Comparison between the Works of Karl Löwith and Erich Auerbach." *Religions* 3, no. 2 (2012): 151–62.

Bradford, William. *Of Plymouth Plantation, 1620–1647*. Edited by Samuel E. Morison. New York: Knopf, 1952.

Braun, Hermann, and Manfred Riedel, eds. *Natur und Geschichte: Karl Löwith zum 70. Geburtstag*. Stuttgart: Kohlhammer, 1967.

Brient, Elizabeth. "Hans Blumenberg and Hannah Arendt on the 'Unworldly Worldliness' of the Modern Age." *Journal of the History of Ideas* 61, no. 3 (2000): 513–30.

Briggs, Mitchell Pirie. *George D. Herron and the European Settlement*. Stanford: Stanford University Press, 1932.

Brown, Charles C., ed. *A Reinhold Niebuhr Reader: Selected Essays, Articles, and Book Reviews*. Philadelphia: Trinity Press International, 1992.

Brown, Chris. *Sovereignty, Rights, and Justice: International Political Theory Today*. Cambridge: Polity, 2002.

———. *Understanding International Relations*. 2nd ed. Basingstoke: Palgrave, 2001.

Bull, Hedley. "*The Twenty Years' Crisis* Thirty Years On." *International Journal* 24, no. 4 (1969): 625–38.

Bull, Malcolm, ed. *Apocalypse Theory and the Ends of the World*. Oxford: Blackwell, 1995.

Bultmann, Rudolf. *History and Eschatology*. Edinburgh: Edinburgh University Press, 1957.

Burke, Martin J. *The Conundrum of Class: Public Discourse on the Social Order in America*. Chicago: University of Chicago Press, 1995.

Burleigh, Michael. *Earthly Powers: The Clash of Religion and Politics in Europe from the French Revolution to the Great War*. New York: HarperCollins, 2005.

———. "National Socialism as a Political Religion." *Totalitarian Movements and Political Religions* 1, no. 2 (2000): 1–26.

———. "Political Religion and Social Evil." *Totalitarian Movements and Political Religions* 3, no. 2 (2002): 1–60.

———. *Sacred Causes: The Clash of Religion and Politics from the Great War to the War on Terror*. New York: HarperCollins, 2007.

———. *The Third Reich: A New History*. New York: Hill & Wang, 2000.

Burrin, Philippe. "Political Religion: The Relevance of a Concept." *History and Memory* 9, no. 1 (1997): 321–49.

Bury, J. B. *The Idea of Progress: An Inquiry into Its Origin and Growth*. New York: Macmillan, 1932.

Bushnell, Horace. *Building Eras in Religion*. New York: Charles Scribner's Sons, 1881.

Butler, Gregory S. "Visions of a Nation Transformed: Modernity and Ideology in Wilson's Political Thought." *Journal of Church and State* 39, no. 1 (1997): 37–51.

Butler, Jon. *Becoming America: The Revolution before 1776*. Cambridge, Mass.: Harvard University Press, 2000.

Buzan, Barry, and Richard Little. "Why International Relations Has Failed as an Intellectual Project and What to Do about It." *Millennium: Journal of International Studies* 30, no. 1 (2001): 19–39.

Calder, Isabel M. "John Cotton and the New Haven Colony." *New England Quarterly* 3, no. 1 (1930): 82–94.

———. *The New Haven Colony*. New Haven, Conn.: Yale University Press, 1934.

The Cambridge Modern History. Vol. 7. New York: Macmillan, 1902.

Carnegie, Andrew. "Wealth." *North American Review* 148, no. 391 (1889): 653–64.

Carr, E. H. *From Napoleon to Stalin, and Other Essays*. Basingstoke: Macmillan, 1980.

———. *The Twenty Years' Crisis, 1919–1939: An Introduction to the Study of International Relations*. 2nd ed. New York: Harper & Row, 1964 [1949].

———. *What Is History?* New York: Knopf, 1962.

[Cass, Lewis.] "Removal of the Indians." *North American Review* 30, no. 66 (1830): 62–121.

Cherry, Conrad, ed. *God's New Israel: Religious Interpretations of American Destiny*. Rev. and updated ed. Chapel Hill: University of North Carolina Press, 1998.

Churchill, Ward. *A Little Matter of Genocide: Holocaust and Denial in the Americas, 1492–Present*. San Francisco: City Lights Books, 1997.

Clark, Ian. "World Order Reform and Utopian Thought: A Contemporary Watershed?" *The Review of Politics* 41, no. 1 (1979): 96–120.

Cochrane, Charles Norris. *Christianity and Classical Culture: A Study of Thought and Action from Augustus to Augustine*. London: Oxford University Press, 1944.

Cogswell, James. *God, the Pious Soldier's Strength and Instructor*. Boston, 1757.

Cohn, Norman. *The Pursuit of the Millennium: Revolutionary Millenarians and Mystical Anarchists of the Middle Ages*. London: Paladin, 1970.

Coker, Christopher. *War and the Illiberal Conscience*. Oxford: Westview, 1998.

Coletta, Paolo E. *William Jennings Bryan*. Vol. 2. Lincoln: University of Nebraska Press, 1964–1969.

Conyers, A. J. "The Revival of Joachite Apocalyptic Speculation in Contemporary Theology." *Perspectives in Religious Studies* 12, no. 3 (1985): 197–211.

Cooper, John Milton, Jr. *Woodrow Wilson: A Biography*. New York: Knopf, 2009.

Corbin, Henry, ed. *Man and Time*. New York: Routledge & Kegan Paul, 1957.

Cotton, John. *An Abstract of the Lawes of New-England.* London, 1641.

————. *The Churches Resurrection, or the Opening of the Fifth and Sixth Verses of the 20th Chap. of the Revelation.* London, 1642.

————. *A Discourse about Civil Government in a New Plantation Whose Design Is Religion.* Cambridge, Mass., 1663.

Cox, Michael, ed. *E. H. Carr: A Critical Appraisal.* New York: Palgrave, 2004.

Cox, Robert W. "Social Forces, States and World Orders: Beyond International Relations Theory." *Millennium: Journal of International Studies* 10, no. 2 (1982): 126–55.

Crunden, Robert M. *Ministers of Reform: The Progressives' Achievement in American Civilization, 1889–1920.* New York: Basic Books, 1982.

Cullmann, Oscar. *Heil als Geschichte.* Translated by Sidney G. Sowers. New York: Harper & Row, 1967.

Daly, Robert. "William Bradford's Vision of History." *American Literature* 44, no. 4 (1973): 557–69.

Davies, Samuel. *The Curse of Cowardice.* Woodbridge, N.J., 1759.

Dickey, Laurence. "Blumenberg and Secularization: 'Self-Assertion' and the Problem of Self-Realizing Teleology in History." *New German Critique* 41 (1987): 151–65.

Digre, Brian K. *Imperialism's New Clothes: The Reparation of Tropical Africa, 1914–1919.* New York: P. Lang, 1990.

Dinkler, Erich. "Augustins Geschichtsauffassung." *Schweizer Monatshefte* 34 (1954/55): 514–26.

Domarus, Max, ed. *Hitler: Speeches and Proclamations, 1932–1945.* Vol. 1. Translated by Chris Wilcox and Mary Fran Gilbert. London: I. B. Tauris, 1992.

Donaggio, Enrico. "Zwischen Nietzsche und Heidegger: Karl Löwiths anthropologische Philosophie des faktischen Lebens." *Deutsche Zeitschrift für Philosophie* 48, no. 1 (2000): 37–48.

Dougherty, James E., and Robert L. Pfaltzgraff, Jr. *Contending Theories of International Relations: A Comprehensive Survey.* 5th ed. New York: Addison Wesley Longman, 2001.

"Dr. George D. Herron Expelled from Church." *New York Times,* June 5, 1901.

Elbe, Stefan. *Europe: A Nietzschean Perspective.* London: Routledge, 2003.

————. "European Nihilism and Annihilation in the Twentieth Century." *Totalitarian Movements and Political Religions* 1, no. 3 (2000): 43–72.

Eliade, Mircea. *The Myth of the Eternal Return, Or, Cosmos and History.* Translated by Willard R. Trask. Princeton, N.J.: Princeton University Press, 1991 [1949].

————. *The Quest: History and Meaning in Religion.* Chicago: University of Chicago Press, 1969.

Eliot, John. *The Christian Commonwealth.* London, 1651.

————. *The Glorious Progress of the Gospel amongst the Indians in New England.* London, 1649.

Emmerich, W. "Heilsgeschehen und Geschichte—nach Karl Löwith." *Sinn und Form* 46, no. 6 (1994): 894–915.

Endy, Melvin B., Jr. "Just War, Holy War, and Millennialism in the American Revolution." *William and Mary Quarterly* 42, no. 1 (1985): 3–25.

Evans, Richard J. "Nazism, Christianity, and Political Religion: A Debate." *Journal of Contemporary History* 42, no. 1 (2007): 5–7.

Faragher, John Mack, ed. *Rereading Frederick Jackson Turner: "The Significance of the Frontier in American History" and Other Essays*. New York: Holt, 1994.

Frei, Christoph. *Hans J. Morgenthau: An Intellectual Biography*. Baton Rouge: Louisiana State University Press, 2001.

Freud, Sigmund, and William C. Bullitt. *Thomas Woodrow Wilson, Twenty-Eighth President of the United States*. London: Weidenfeld & Nicolson, 1967.

Friedberg, Lilian. "Dare to Compare: Americanizing the Holocaust." *American Indian Quarterly* 24, no. 3 (2000): 353–80.

Friedrich, Carl J. "Religion and History." *Confluence: An International Forum* 4, no. 1 (1955): 105–15.

———, ed. *Totalitarianism*. Cambridge, Mass.: Harvard University Press, 1954.

Friedrich, Carl J., and Zbigniew K. Brzezinski. *Totalitarian Dictatorship and Autocracy*. Cambridge, Mass.: Harvard University Press, 1956.

Frisch, Morton J., and Richard G. Stevens, eds. *American Political Thought: The Philosophic Dimensions of American Statesmanship*. New York: Scribner, 1971.

Fromkin, David. *A Peace to End All Peace: The Fall of the Ottoman Empire and the Creation of the Modern Middle East, 1914–1922*. New York: Avon, 1990.

Fukuyama, Francis. "The End of History?" *National Interest* 16 (1989): 3–18.

———. *The End of History and the Last Man*. London: Hamish Hamilton, 1992.

Funkenstein, Amos. *Theology and Scientific Imagination from the Middle Ages to the Seventeenth Century*. Princeton, N.J.: Princeton University Press, 1986.

Gabriel, Ralph Henry. *The Course of American Democratic Thought*. New York: Ronald Press, 1940.

Gadamer, Hans-Georg. Review of *Die Legitimität der Neuzeit*, by Hans Blumenberg. *Philosophische Rundschau* 15 (1968): 201–9.

Gaddis, John Lewis. *George F. Kennan: An American Life*. New York: Penguin, 2011.

———. *Strategies of Containment: A Critical Appraisal of American National Security Policy during the Cold War*. Rev. ed. Oxford: Oxford University Press, 2005.

Garraty, John A. *Woodrow Wilson: A Great Life in Brief*. New York: Knopf, 1956.

Gay, Peter. "Carl Becker's Heavenly City." *Political Science Quarterly* 72, no. 2 (1957): 182–99.

————. *The Party of Humanity: Essays in the French Enlightenment*. New York: Norton, 1959 [1954].

————. *The Science of Freedom*. Vol. 2 of *The Enlightenment: An Interpretation*. New York: Norton, 1996 [1969].

Gentile, Emilio. "Fascism as Political Religion." *Journal of Contemporary History* 25, no. 2/3 (1990): 229–51.

————. "Fascism, Totalitarianism and Political Religion: Definitions and Critical Reflections on Criticism of an Interpretation." Translated by Natalia Belozentseva. *Totalitarian Movements and Political Religions* 5, no. 3 (2004): 326–75.

————. "Political Religion: A Concept and Its Critics—A Critical Survey." *Totalitarian Movements and Political Religions* 6, no. 1 (2005): 19–32.

————. "The Sacralization of Politics: Definitions, Interpretations and Reflections on the Question of Secular Religion and Totalitarianism." Translated by Robert Mallett. *Totalitarian Movements and Political Religions* 1, no. 1 (2000): 18–55.

————. *The Sacralization of Politics in Fascist Italy*. Cambridge, Mass.: Harvard University Press, 1996.

Gillespie, Michael Allen. *The Theological Origins of Modernity*. Chicago: University of Chicago Press, 2008.

Glad, Paul W., ed. *William Jennings Bryan: A Profile*. New York: Hill & Wang, 1968.

Gouldner, Alvin W. *The Two Marxisms*. New York: Seabury, 1980.

Grayson, Cary T. *Woodrow Wilson: An Intimate Memoir*. New York: Holt, Rinehart & Winston, 1960.

Griffin, David Ray, et al. *The American Empire and the Commonwealth of God: A Political, Economic, Religious Statement*. Louisville, Ky.: Westminster John Knox, 2006.

Griffin, Roger. "Cloister or Cluster? The Implications of Emilio Gentile's Ecumenical Theory of Political Religion for the Study of Extremism." *Totalitarian Movements and Political Religions* 6, no. 1 (2005): 33–52.

————. "God's Counterfeiters? Investigating the Triad of Fascism, Totalitarianism and (Political) Religion." *Totalitarian Movements and Political Religions* 5, no. 3 (2004): 291–325.

————, ed. *International Fascism: Theories, Causes, and the New Consensus*. London: Oxford University Press, 1998.

————. *Modernism and Fascism: The Sense of a Beginning under Mussolini and Hitler*. Basingstoke: Palgrave Macmillan, 2007.

————. "The Palingenetic Political Community: Rethinking the Legitimation of Totalitarian Regimes in Inter-War Europe." *Totalitarian Movements and Political Religions* 3, no. 3 (2002): 24–43.

Gurian, Waldemar. *Der Bolschewismus: Einführung in Geschichte und Lehre*. Freiburg: Herder, 1931.

————. *Der Kampf um die Kirche im Dritten Reich.* Luzern: Vita Nova, 1936.

————. "Totalitarian Religions." *Review of Politics* 14, no. 1 (1952): 3–14.

Habermas, Jürgen. *Philosophical-Political Profile.* Cambridge, Mass.: MIT Press, 1983.

Hall, David D. *Worlds of Wonder, Days of Judgment: Popular Religious Belief in Early New England.* New York: Knopf, 1989.

Hall, David D., John M. Murrin, and Thad W. Tate, eds. *Saints and Revolutionaries: Essays on Early American History.* New York: Norton, 1984.

Handy, Robert T. "George D. Herron and the Kingdom Movement." *Church History* 19, no. 2 (1950): 97–115.

Hatch, Nathan O. *The Sacred Cause of Liberty: Republican Thought and the Millennium in Revolutionary New England.* New Haven, Conn.: Yale University Press, 1977.

Heckscher, August. *Woodrow Wilson.* New York: Scribner, 1991.

Hegel, Georg W. F. *The Philosophy of History.* Translated by J. Sibree. Amherst, N.Y.: Prometheus Books, 1991 [1900].

Heimert, Alan. *Religion and the American Mind from the Great Awakening to the Revolution.* Cambridge, Mass.: Harvard University Press, 1966.

Heimert, Alan, and Perry Miller, eds. *The Great Awakening: Documents Illustrating the Crisis and Its Consequences.* Indianapolis: Bobbs-Merrill, 1967.

Hendrick, Burton J. *The Life and Letters of Walter Hines Page.* 3 vols. Garden City, N.Y.: Doubleday Page, 1924–1926.

Herron, George D. *The Christian State: A Political Vision of Christ.* New York: Crowell, 1895.

————. *The Defeat in the Victory.* London: C. Palmer, 1921.

————. *Germanism and the American Crusade.* New York: Mitchell Kennerley, 1918.

————. *The Greater War.* New York: Mitchell Kennerley, 1919.

————. *The Menace of Peace.* London: Allen & Unwin, 1917.

————. *The Message of Jesus to Men of Wealth.* New York: Revell, 1891.

————. *The New Redemption: A Call to the Church to Reconstruct Society According to the Gospel of Christ.* New York: Crowell, 1893.

————. *Woodrow Wilson and the World's Peace.* New York: Mitchell Kennerley, 1917.

Hoffmann, Stanley. "An American Social Science: International Relations." *Daedalus* 106, no. 3 (1977): 41–60.

Hofstadter, Richard. *America at 1750: A Social Portrait.* New York: Knopf, 1971.

————. *The American Political Tradition and the Men Who Made It.* 2nd ed. New York: Random House, 1974.

Horkheimer, Max. *Critical Theory.* Translated by Matthew J. O'Connell et al. New York: Herder & Herder, 1972.

Horkheimer, Max, and Theodor W. Adorno. *Dialectics of Enlightenment.* Translated by John Cumming. New York: Herder & Herder, 1972.

Howe, Paul. "The Utopian Realism of E. H. Carr." *Review of International Studies* 20 (1994): 277–97.

Hudson, Winthrop S., ed. *Nationalism and Religion in America: Concepts of American Identity and Mission.* New York: Harper & Row, 1970.

———. *Religion in America: An Historical Account of the Development of American Religious Life.* 2nd ed. New York: Scribner, 1973.

Hutchings, Kimberly. *International Political Theory: Rethinking Ethics in a Global Era.* London: SAGE, 1999.

Ikenberry, G. John, et al. *The Crisis of American Foreign Policy: Wilsonianism in the Twenty-First Century.* Princeton, N.J.: Princeton University Press, 2008.

Inaugural Addresses of the Presidents of the United States. Washington, D.C.: Government Printing Office, 1965.

Iriye, Akira. *The Globalizing of America, 1913–1945.* Vol. 3 of *The Cambridge History of American Foreign Relations.* Cambridge: Cambridge University Press, 1993.

Jackson, Robert, and Georg Sørensen. *Introduction to International Relations: Theories and Approaches.* 2nd ed. Oxford: Oxford University Press, 2003.

Jaimes, M. Annette, ed. *The State of Native America.* Boston: South End, 1992.

Jay, Martin. *Fin-de-Siècle Socialism and Other Essays.* New York: Routledge, 1988.

———. Review of *The Legitimacy of the Modern Age*, by Hans Blumenberg. *History and Theory* 24, no. 2 (1985): 183–96.

Jefferson, Thomas. *The Writings of Thomas Jefferson.* Vol. 10. Edited by A. E. Bergh. Washington, D.C.: Thomas Jefferson Memorial Association, 1907.

Jonas, Hans. *The Gnostic Religion: The Message of the Alien God and the Beginnings of Christianity.* Boston: Beacon, 1958.

Jones, Charles. *E. H. Carr and International Relations: A Duty to Lie.* Cambridge: Cambridge University Press, 1998.

Kennan, George F. [X, pseud.] "The Sources of Soviet Conduct." *Foreign Affairs* 25, no. 4 (1947): 566–82.

Keylor, William R., ed. *The Legacy of the Great War: Peacemaking, 1919.* Boston: Houghton Mifflin, 1998.

Keynes, John Maynard. *The Economic Consequences of the Peace.* New York: Harcourt, Brace & Howe, 1920.

Kissinger, Henry. *Diplomacy.* New York: Simon & Schuster, 1994.

Knock, Thomas J. *To End All Wars: Woodrow Wilson and the Quest for a New World Order.* New York: Oxford University Press, 1992.

Koselleck, Reinhart. *Critique and Crisis: Enlightenment and the Pathogenesis of Modern Society.* Cambridge, Mass.: MIT Press, 1988 [1959].

Kurtz, Stephen G., and James H. Hutson, eds. *Essays on the American Revolution.* Chapel Hill: University of North Carolina Press, 1973.

Lauter, Paul, et al., eds. *The Heath Anthology of American Literature.* Vol. 1. 2nd ed. Toronto: Heath, 1994.

Levin, N. Gordon. *Woodrow Wilson and World Politics*. New York: Oxford University Press, 1968.

Link, Arthur S. *The Higher Realism of Woodrow Wilson, and Other Essays*. Nashville: Vanderbilt University Press, 1971.

———. *The New Freedom*. Vol. 2 of *Wilson*. Princeton, N.J.: Princeton University Press, 1956.

———. *Wilson: Campaigns for Progressivism and Peace, 1916–1917*. Princeton, N.J.: Princeton University Press, 1965.

———, ed. *Woodrow Wilson: A Profile*. New York: Hill & Wang, 1968.

———, ed. *Woodrow Wilson and a Revolutionary World, 1913–1921*. Chapel Hill: University of North Carolina Press, 1982.

———. *Woodrow Wilson: Revolution, War, and Peace*. Arlington Heights, Ill.: AHM, 1979.

Link, Arthur S., et al., eds. *The Papers of Woodrow Wilson*. 69 vols. Princeton, N.J.: Princeton University Press, 1966–1994.

Linklater, Andrew. "The Transformation of Political Community: E. H. Carr, Critical Theory and International Relations." *Review of International Studies* 23, no. 3 (1997): 321–38.

Little, Richard, and Michael Smith, eds. *Perspectives on World Politics*. 3rd ed. New York: Routledge, 2006.

Long, David, and Peter Wilson, eds. *Thinkers of the Twenty Years' Crisis: Inter-War Idealism Reassessed*. Oxford: Clarendon, 1995.

Löwith, Karl. "Auslegung von Nietzsches Selbst-Interpretation und von Nietzsches Interpretationen." D.Phil. diss., University of Munich, 1923.

———. "Christentum und Geschichte." *Numen* 2, no. 1 (1955): 147–55.

———. *Jacob Burckhardt: Der Mensch inmitten der Geschichte*. Stuttgart: Kohlhammer, 1966.

———. *Meaning in History: The Theological Implications of the Philosophy of History*. Chicago: University of Chicago Press, 1949.

———. *Nature, History, and Existentialism, and Other Essays in the Philosophy of History*. Edited by Arnold Levison. Evanston, Ill.: Northwestern University Press, 1966.

———. Review of *Faith and History*, by Reinhold Niebuhr. *Theology Today* 6 (1949): 422–25.

———. Review of *Die Legitimität der Neuzeit*, by Hans Blumenberg. *Philosophische Rundschau* 15 (1968): 195–201.

———. *Weltgeschichte und Heilsgeschehen: Die theologischen Voraussetzungen der Geschichtsphilosophie*. Stuttgart: Kohlhammer, 1953.

Lubac, Henri de. *The Drama of Atheist Humanism*. Translated by Edith M. Riley. New York: New American Library, 1950.

MacIntyre, Alasdair. Review of *The Legitimacy of the Modern Age*, by Hans Blumenberg. *American Journal of Sociology* 90, no. 4 (1985): 924–26.

Maclear, J. F. "New England and the Fifth Monarchy: The Quest for the

Millennium in Early American Puritanism." *William and Mary Quarterly* 32, no. 2 (1975): 223–60.

MacMillan, Margaret. *Peacemakers: The Paris Conference of 1919 and Its Attempt to End War.* London: John Murray, 2001.

Magee, Malcolm D. *What the World Should Be: Woodrow Wilson and the Crafting of a Faith-Based Foreign Policy.* Waco, Tex.: Baylor University Press, 2008.

Mahaffey, Jerome Dean. *Preaching Politics: The Religious Rhetoric of George Whitefield and the Founding of a New Nation.* Waco, Tex.: Baylor University Press, 2007.

Maier, Hans. "Political Religions and Their Images: Soviet Communism, Italian Fascism, and German National Socialism." *Totalitarian Movements and Political Religions* 7, no. 3 (2006): 267–81.

———. "'Totalitarismus' und 'politische Religionen': Konzepte des Diktaturvergleichs." *Vierteljahrshefte für Zeitgeschichte* 43, no. 3 (1995): 387–405.

Maier, Hans, and Michael Schäfer, eds. *Totalitarismus und Politische Religionen: Konzepte des Diktaturvergleichs.* 3 vols. Paderborn: Schöningh, 1996, 1997, 2003.

Mandelbaum, Michael. *The Ideas That Conquered the World: Peace, Democracy, and Free Markets in the Twenty-First Century.* New York: Public Affairs, 2002.

Marcuse, Herbert. *Negations: Essays in Critical Theory.* Translated by Jeremy J. Shapiro. Boston: Beacon, 1968.

Masaryk, Tomáš G. *Světová revoluce za války a ve válce, 1914–1918.* Prague: Orbis a Čin, 1925.

Mathewes, Charles, and Christopher McKnight Nichols, eds. *Prophesies of Godlessness: Predictions of America's Imminent Secularization from the Puritans to the Present Day.* Oxford: Oxford University Press, 2008.

May, Henry F. *Ideas, Faiths, and Feelings: Essays on American Intellectual and Religious History 1952–1982.* New York: Oxford University Press, 1983.

———. *Protestant Churches and Industrial America.* New York: Octagon Books, 1963.

Mead, Sidney E. *The Lively Experiment: The Shaping of Christianity in America.* New York: Harper & Row, 1963.

———. "Through and Beyond the Lines." *Journal of Religion* 48, no. 3 (1968): 274–88.

Mearsheimer, John. "E. H. Carr vs. Idealism: The Battle Rages On." *International Relations* 19, no. 2 (2005): 139–52.

Mehring, Reinhard. "Karl Löwith, Carl Schmitt, Jacob Taubes und das 'Ende der Geschichte.'" *Zeitschrift für Religions- und Geistesgeschichte* 48, no. 3 (1996): 231–48.

Middlekauff, Robert. *The Mathers: Three Generations of Puritan Intellectuals, 1596–1728.* New York: Oxford University Press, 1971.

Miller, Perry. *Errand into the Wilderness*. Cambridge, Mass.: Harvard University Press, 1956.

———. *The New England Mind: From Colony to Province*. Cambridge, Mass.: Harvard University Press, 1953.

———. *The New England Mind: The Seventeenth Century*. Cambridge, Mass.: Harvard University Press, 1983 [1939].

———. Review of *The New Haven Colony*, by Isabel M. Calder. *New England Quarterly* 8, no. 4 (1935): 582–84.

Molloy, Seán. "Dialectics and Transformation: Exploring the International Theory of E. H. Carr." *International Journal of Politics, Culture, and Society* 17, no. 2 (2003): 279–306.

———. *The Hidden History of Realism: A Genealogy of Power Politics*. New York: Palgrave Macmillan, 2006.

Moltmann, Jürgen. "Christian Hope: Messianic or Transcendent? A Theological Discussion with Joachim of Fiore and Thomas Aquinas." *Horizons* 12, no. 2 (1985): 30–47.

———. *The Trinity and the Kingdom: The Doctrine of God*. San Francisco: Harper and Row, 1981.

Mommsen, Theodor E. "St. Augustine and the Christian Idea of Progress: The Background of the City of God." *Journal of the History of Ideas* 12, no. 3 (1951): 346–74.

Monod, Jean-Claude. *La querelle de la secularization de Hegel à Blumenberg: Theologie politique et philosophies de l'historie*. N.p.: Vrin, 2002.

Moravcsik, Andrew. "Taking Preferences Seriously: A Liberal Theory of International Politics." *International Organization* 51, no. 4 (1997): 513–53.

Morgan, Edmund S. *The Gentle Puritan: A Life of Ezra Stiles, 1727–1795*. New Haven, Conn.: Yale University Press, 1962.

———. "The Puritan Ethic and the American Revolution." *William and Mary Quarterly* 24, no. 1 (1967): 3–43.

———. Review of *Religion and the American Mind from the Great Awakening to the Revolution*, by Alan Heimert. *William and Mary Quarterly* 24, no. 3 (1967): 454–59.

———. *Visible Saints: The History of the Puritan Idea*. Ithaca, N.Y.: Cornell University Press, 1963.

Morgenthau, Hans J. "The Political Science of E. H. Carr." *World Politics* 1 (1948): 127–34.

———. *Politics among Nations: The Struggle for Power and Peace*. 6th ed. New York: Knopf, 1985 [1948].

———. *Scientific Man versus Power Politics*. Chicago: University of Chicago Press, 1946.

Mosse, George L. *The Nationalization of the Masses*. New York: Fertig, 1975.

Mulder, John M. "Wilson the Preacher: The 1905 Baccalaureate Sermon." *Journal of Presbyterian History* 51, no. 3 (1973): 267–84.

————. *Woodrow Wilson: The Years of Preparation*. Princeton, N.J.: Princeton University Press, 1978.

Müller, Christof. *Geschichtsbewusstsein bei Augustinus: Ontologische, anthropologische und universalgeschichtlich/heilsgeschichtliche Elemente einer augustinischen "Geschichtstheorie."* Cassiciacum, Band 39/2. Würzburg: Augustinus-Verlag, 1993.

Newman, Simon P. "The Hegelian Roots of Woodrow Wilson's Progressivism." *American Presbyterians* 64, no. 3 (1986): 191–201.

Newton, Isaac. *Sir Isaac Newton's Daniel and the Apocalypse*. Edited by William Whitla. London: Murray, 1922.

Nicolson, Harold. *Peacemaking: 1919*. New York: Harcourt, Brace, 1939.

Niebuhr, H. Richard. *The Kingdom of God in America*. Chicago: Willet, Clark, 1937.

Niebuhr, Reinhold. *Faith and History: A Comparison of Christian and Modern Views of History*. London: Nisbet, 1949.

————. *The Irony of American History*. New York: Scribner, 1952.

————. "The Religion of Communism." *Atlantic Monthly* 147 (1931): 462–70.

————. "The Religious Assumptions of Adam Smith." *Journal of Theology for Southern Africa* 44, no. 1 (1983): 6–23.

————. "The Religious Assumptions of Karl Marx." *Journal of Theology for Southern Africa* 44, no. 1 (1983): 24–41.

————. Review of *Meaning in History*, by Karl Löwith. *Journal of Religion* 29 (1949): 302–3.

Nietzsche, Friedrich. *The Gay Science*. Edited by Walter Kaufmann. New York: Vintage, 1974.

————. *On the Genealogy of Morality*. Edited by Keith Ansell-Pearson. Translated by Carol Diethe. Cambridge: Cambridge University Press, 1994.

————. *Untimely Meditations*. Edited by Daniel Breazele. Translated by R. J. Hollingdale. Cambridge: Cambridge University Press, 2000.

————. *The Will to Power*. Translated by Walter Kaufmann and R. J. Hollingdale. New York: Random House, 1968.

Ninkovich, Frank. *The Wilsonian Century: U.S. Foreign Policy since 1900*. Chicago: University of Chicago Press, 1999.

Notter, Harley. *The Origins of the Foreign Policy of Woodrow Wilson*. Baltimore, Md.: Johns Hopkins Press, 1937.

[O'Sullivan, John L.] "Annexation." *Democratic Review* 17, nos. 85–86 (1845): 5–10.

————. "The Great Nation of Futurity." *Democratic Review* 6, no. 23 (1839): 426–30.

————. "The Texas Question." *Democratic Review* 14, no. 70 (1844): 423–30.

————. "The True Title." *New York Morning News*, December 27, 1845.

Osuský, Štefan. *George D. Herron, dôverník Wilsonov počas vojny*. Brno: Prúdy, 1925.

Parkinson, F. *The Philosophy of International Relations: A Study in the History of Thought*. London: SAGE, 1977.

Parrington, Vernon Louis. *Main Currents in American Thought: An Interpretation of American Literature from the Beginnings to 1920*. 3 vols. New York: Harcourt Brace: 1927, 1930.

Patočka, Jan. *Kacířské eseje o filosofii dějin*. Prague: Academia, 1990 [1975].

———. *Péče o duši I*. Vol. 1 of *Sebrané spisy Jana Patočky*. Prague: Oikoymenh, 1996.

Pecora, Vincent L. *Secularization and Cultural Criticism: Religion, Nation, and Modernity*. Chicago: University of Chicago Press, 2006.

Pelikan, Jaroslav. *The Mystery of Continuity: Time and History, Memory and Eternity in the Thought of Saint Augustine*. Charlottesville: University Press of Virginia, 1986.

Perry, Bliss. *And Gladly Teach*. Boston: Houghton Mifflin, 1935.

Pick, Daniel. *War Machine: The Rationalization of Slaughter in the Modern Age*. London: Yale University Press, 1993.

Pippin, Robert B. "Blumenberg and the Modernity Problem." *Review of Metaphysics* 40 (1987): 535–57.

Plato. *Timaeus*. Translated by Benjamin Jowett. Indianapolis: Bobbs-Merrill, 1949.

Pocock, J. G. A. *The Machiavellian Moment: Florentine Political Thought and the Atlantic Republican Tradition*. Princeton, N.J.: Princeton University Press, 1975.

Porter, Brian, ed. *The Aberystwyth Papers: International Politics, 1919–1969*. London: Oxford University Press, 1972.

Pratt, Julius W. "John L. O'Sullivan and Manifest Destiny." *New York History* 14 (1933): 213–34.

———. "The Origin of 'Manifest Destiny.'" *American Historical Review* 32, no. 4 (1927): 795–98.

Preston, Andrew. "Bridging the Gap between the Sacred and the Secular in the History of American Foreign Relations." *Diplomatic History* 30, no. 5 (2006): 783–812.

Quirk, Robert E. *An Affair of Honor: Woodrow Wilson and the Occupation of Veracruz*. Lexington: University of Kentucky Press, 1962.

Rommen, Hans. "Realism and Utopianism in World Affairs." *Review of Politics* 6, no. 2 (1944): 193–215.

Royster, Charles. *A Revolutionary People at War: The Continental Army and American Character, 1775–1783*. Chapel Hill: University of North Carolina Press, 1979.

Ruether, Rosemary Radford. "Augustine and Christian Political Theology." *Interpretation* 29, no. 3 (1975): 252–65.

Ruggie, John Gerrard. *Winning the Peace: America and World Order in the New Era*. New York: Columbia University Press, 1995.

Sanford, Charles L. *The Quest for Paradise: Europe and the American Moral Imagination*. Urbana: University of Illinois Press, 1961.

Schaff, Philip. *America: A Sketch of Its Political, Social, and Religious Character*. Edited by Perry Miller. Cambridge, Mass.: Belknap, 1961.

Schmidt, Brian C. *The Political Discourse of Anarchy: A Disciplinary History of International Relations*. Albany: State University of New York Press, 1998.

Schmidt, Ernst A. *Zeit und Geschichte bei Augustin*. Sitzungsberichte der Heidelberger Akademie der Wissenschaften, Philosophisch-historiche Klasse, Jahrgang 1985, Bericht 3. Heidelberg: Carl Winter Universitätsverlag, 1985.

Schmitt, Carl. *Politische Theologie: Vier Kapitel zur Lehre von der Souveränität*. 2nd ed. Munich: Duncker & Humboldt, 1934 [1922].

Schulte Nordholt, Jan Willem. *Woodrow Wilson: A Life for World Peace*. Translated by Herbert H. Rowen. Berkeley: University of California Press, 1991.

Schurz, Carl. "Manifest Destiny." *Harper's New Monthly Magazine* 87, no. 521 (1893): 737–46.

Sharp, Alan. *The Versailles Settlement: Peacemaking in Paris, 1919*. New York: St. Martin's, 1991.

Silver, James W. *Confederate Morale and Church Propaganda*. New York: W. W. Norton, 1967.

Skinner, Quentin. "Meaning and Understanding in the History of Ideas." *History and Theory* 8, no. 1 (1969): 3–53.

Smith, James W., and A. Leland Jamison, eds. *The Shaping of American Religion*. Princeton, N.J.: Princeton University Press, 1961.

Smith, Michael Joseph. *Realist Thought from Weber to Kissinger*. Baton Rouge: Louisiana State University Press, 1986.

Sparn, Walter. "Hans Blumenbergs Herausforderung der Theologie." *Theologische Rundschau* 49, no. 2 (1984): 170–207.

Steigmann-Gall, Richard. "Christianity and the Nazi Movement: A Response." *Journal of Contemporary History* 42, no. 2 (2007): 185–211.

———. *The Holy Reich: Nazi Conceptions of Christianity, 1919–1945*. Cambridge: Cambridge University Press, 2003.

———. "Nazism and the Revival of Political Religion Theory." *Totalitarian Movements and Political Religions* 5, no. 3 (2004): 376–96.

———. "Rethinking Nazism and Religion: How Anti-Christian Were the 'Pagans'?" *Central European History* 36, no. 1 (2003): 75–105.

Stephanson, Anders. *Manifest Destiny: American Expansionism and the Empire of Right*. New York: Hill & Wang, 1995.

Stern, Fritz. *The Politics of Cultural Despair: A Study in the Rise of the Germanic Ideology*. Berkeley: University of California Press, 1974.

Strauss, Leo, and Eric Voegelin. *Faith and Political Philosophy: The Correspondence between Leo Strauss and Eric Voegelin, 1934–1964*. Translated and edited by Peter Emberley and Barry Cooper. Columbia: University of Missouri Press, 2004.

Strong, Josiah. *The New Era; or The Coming Kingdom.* New York: Baker & Taylor, 1893.

———. *Our Country: Its Possible Future and Its Present Crisis.* Edited by Jurgen Herbst. Cambridge, Mass.: Harvard University Press, 1963.

Sweet, Leonard I., ed. *Communication and Change in American Religious History.* Grand Rapids, Mich.: Eerdmans, 1993.

Taubes, Jacob. *Abendländische Eschatologie.* Würzburg: Königshausen & Neumann, 2001 [1947].

Taylor, Charles. *A Secular Age.* Cambridge, Mass.: Belknap, 2007.

Thornton, Russell. *American Indian Holocaust and Survival.* Norman: University of Oklahoma Press, 1987.

———. "Cherokee Population Losses During the Trail of Tears: A New Perspective and a New Estimate." *Ethnohistory* 31 (1984): 289–300.

Tocqueville, Alexis de. *Democracy in America.* Edited and translated by Harvey C. Mansfield and Delba Winthrop. Chicago: University of Chicago Press, 2000.

Todorov, Tzvetan. *The Conquest of America.* New York: Harper & Row, 1984.

———. "Totalitarianism: Between Religion and Science." Translated by Brady Brower and Max Likin. *Totalitarian Movements and Political Religions* 2, no. 1 (2001): 28–42.

Toulmin, Stephen. *Cosmopolis: The Hidden Agenda of Modernity.* Chicago: University of Chicago Press, 1990.

Tumulty, Joseph P. *Woodrow Wilson as I Know Him.* Garden City, N.Y.: Doubleday, 1921.

Turner, Frederick Jackson. *The Frontier in American History.* New York: Holt, Rinehart & Winston, 1920.

Tuveson, Ernest Lee. *Millennium and Utopia: A Study in the Background of the Idea of Progress.* Berkeley: University of California Press, 1949.

———. *Redeemer Nation: The Idea of America's Millennial Role.* Chicago: University of Chicago Press, 1968.

Tyler, Moses Coit. *A History of American Literature, 1607–1765.* Ithaca, N.Y.: Cornell University Press, 1975 [1949].

Van Dusen, Henry P., ed. *The Christian Answer.* New York: Scribner's Sons, 1945.

Voegelin, Eric. *The New Science of Politics.* Chicago: University of Chicago Press, 1952.

———. *Die politischen Religionen.* Vienna: Bermann-Fischer, 1938.

———. *Science, Politics and Gnosticism: Two Essays.* Chicago: Henry Regnery, 1968.

Vries, Hent de, and Lawrence E. Sullivan, eds. *Political Theologies: Public Religions in a Post-Secular World.* New York: Fordham University Press, 2006.

Wallace, Robert M. "Introduction to Blumenberg." *New German Critique* 32 (1984): 93–108.

———. "Progress, Secularization and Modernity: The Löwith-Blumenberg Debate." *New German Critique* 22 (1981): 63–79.

Walworth, Arthur. *Woodrow Wilson*. 2nd ed. Boston: Houghton Mifflin, 1965.

Wayland, Francis. *The Elements of Political Economy*. New York: Leavitt, Lord, 1837.

Weinberg, Albert K. *Manifest Destiny: A Study of Nationalist Expansionism in American History*. Baltimore, Md.: Johns Hopkins University Press, 1935.

Wenska, Walter P. "Bradford's Two Histories: Pattern and Paradigm in *Of Plymouth Plantation*." *Early American Literature* 13, no. 2 (1978): 151–64.

White, Hayden. *Tropics of Discourse: Essays in Cultural Criticism*. Baltimore, Md.: Johns Hopkins University Press, 1978.

Wigglesworth, Michael. *The Day of Doom: Or, a Poetical Description of the Great and Last Judgment*. Cambridge, Mass., 1666 [1662].

———. *The Poems of Michael Wigglesworth*. Edited by Ronald A. Bosco. Lanham, Md.: University Press of America, 1989.

Williams, Raymond. *Problems in Materialism and Culture: Selected Essays*. London: NLB, 1989.

Wilson, Peter. "Radicalism for a Conservative Purpose: The Peculiar Realism of E. H. Carr." *Millennium: Journal of International Studies* 30, no. 1 (2001): 123–37.

Wilson, Woodrow. *America's Greatness*. New York: Wise, 1931.

———. *The New Freedom: A Call for the Emancipation of the Generous Energies of a People*. New York: Doubleday, 1913.

———. *On Being Human*. New York: Harper, 1916.

———. *The State: Elements of Historical and Practical Politics*. Boston: D. C. Heath, 1889.

Wood, Gordon S. *The Creation of the American Republic, 1776–1789*. Chapel Hill: University of North Carolina Press, 1969.

Yack, Bernard. "Myth and Modernity: Hans Blumenberg's Reconstruction of Modern Theory." *Political Theory* 15, no. 2 (1987): 244–61.

Young, Brigham. *Discourses of Brigham Young*. Edited by John A. Widstoe. Salt Lake City, Utah: Deseret Book, 1954.

Zweig, Stefan. *Die Welt von gestern: Erinnerungen eines Europäers*. Hamburg: Fischer Verlag, 1982.

INDEX

Titles of works are in *italic*. Initial articles (A, An, The) are ignored in sorting titles. Footnotes are indicated by n following the page number.

CPSIA information can be obtained
at www.ICGtesting.com
Printed in the USA
LVHW110812140121
676407LV00003B/94